Women's Employment

and Pay in Latin America

Overview and Methodology

WORLD BANK

REGIONAL AND

SECTORAL STUDIES

Women's Employment

and Pay in Latin America

Overview and Methodology

GEORGE PSACHAROPOULOS

AND

ZAFIRIS TZANNATOS

The World Bank
Washington, D.C.

© 1992 The International Bank for Reconstruction
and Development / The World Bank
1818 H Street, N.W., Washington, D.C. 20433

The World Bank Regional and Sectoral Studies series provides an outlet for work that is relatively limited in its subject matter or geographical coverage but that contributes to the intellectual foundations of development operations and policy formulation. These studies have not necessarily been edited with the same rigor as Bank publications that carry the imprint of a university press.

The findings, interpretations, and conclusions expressed in this publication are those of the authors and should not be attributed in any manner to the World Bank, to its affiliated organizations, or to the members of its Board of Executive Directors or the countries they represent.

The material in this publication is copyrighted. Requests for permission to reproduce portions of it should be sent to the Office of the Publisher at the address shown in the copyright notice above. The World Bank encourages dissemination of its work and will normally give permission promptly and, when the reproduction is for noncommercial purposes, without asking a fee. Permission to copy portions for classroom use is granted through the Copyright Clearance Center, 27 Congress Street, Salem, Massachusetts 01970, U.S.A.

The complete backlist of publications from the World Bank is shown in the annual *Index of Publications,* which contains an alphabetical title list and indexes of subjects, authors, and countries and regions. The latest edition is available free of charge from Distribution Unit, Office of the Publisher, The World Bank, 1818 H Street, N.W., Washington, D.C. 20433, U.S.A., or from Publications, The World Bank, 66, avenue d'Iéna, 75116 Paris, France.

George Psacharopoulos is the senior human resources adviser to the World Bank's Latin America and Caribbean Technical Department. He previously taught at the London School of Economics. Zafiris Tzannatos is a labor economist with the Population and Human Resources Department at the World Bank. He is an honorary research fellow at the Universities of Nottingham and St. Andrews in the United Kingdom.

Cover design by Sam Ferro

Library of Congress Cataloging-in-Publication Data

Psacharopoulos, George.
    Women's employment and pay in Latin America : overview and
methodology / George Psacharopoulos and Zafiris Tzannatos.
        p. cm.
    Includes bibliographical references.
    ISBN 0-8213-2270-2
    1. Women—Employment—Latin America. 2. Wages—Women—Latin
America. I. Tzannatos, Zafiris, 1953– . II. Title.
HD6100.5.P79   1992
331.4'098—dc20   92-35611
                                                              CIP

Contents

Acknowledgments   xiii

Foreword   xv

1   Introduction and Summary   1

2   Trends and Patterns in Female Labor Force Participation 1950-1985   37

3   The Industrial and Occupational Distribution of Female Employment   71

4   Potential Gains from the Elimination of Labor Market Differentials   135

5   Gender Differences in the Labor Market: Analytical Issues   151

6   Summary of Empirical Findings and Implications   183

Appendix A: Contents of Companion Volume   213

Appendix B: Authors of Companion Volume   217

References   219

Index   241

List of Tables

1.1   Female Participation Rate and Female-Relative-to-Male-Pay   5

1.2   Aggregate Statistics for Selected Latin American Countries   8

2.1   Total Labor Force in Latin America (selected years)   39

2.2   Relative (F/M) Labor Force in Latin America and the Caribbean   42

2.3   Participation Rates for Prime Age Groups   45

2.4   Female Participation Rate by Age Group and Country's per Capita Income Early 1980s   54

2.5   Female Labor Force Participation Rate and Religion Early 1980s   54

2.6   Ratio of Employees in the Female Labor Force by World Region   58

A2.1   Age-Specific Female Labor Participation by Region and by Country (early 1980s)   63

3.1   Female Overrepresentation by Employment Status (1950s and 1980s)   80

3.2   Female Overrepresentation by Industry (1950s and 1980s)   83

3.3   Female Overrepresented Industrial Sectors in the 1950s and 1980s by Employment Status   84

3.4   Occupational Dissimilarity (Duncan index)   86

3.5   Structure and Sex Ratio Effects on Occupational Dissimilarity Over Time   92

3.6   Workers Who Would Have to Change Occupation to Reach Equality in the Employment Distribution of Women and Men, as a Percentage of the Total Labor Force   98

3.7   Dissimilarity Between Female and Male Occupational
        Employment in Selected Industrialized Countries (1970-
        1982)   103

3.8   Dissimilarity Between Female and Male Industrial
        Employment   105

A3-1a   Occupational Distribution of the Labor Force by Employment
        Status - Argentina   112

A3-1b   Occupational Distribution of the Labor Force by Employment
        Status - Bolivia   113

A3-1c   Occupational Distribution of the Labor Force by Employment
        Status - Chile   114

A3-1d   Occupational Distribution of the Labor Force by Employment
        Status - Colombia   115

A3-1e   Occupational Distribution of the Labor Force by Employment
        Status - Costa Rica   116

A3-1f   Occupational Distribution of the Labor Force by Employment
        Status - Ecuador   117

A3-1g   Occupational Distribution of the Labor Force by Employment
        Status - Guatemala   118

A3-1h   Occupational Distribution of the Labor Force by Employment
        Status - Honduras   119

A3-1i   Occupational Distribution of the Labor Force by Employment
        Status - Jamaica   120

A3-1j   Occupational Distribution of the Labor Force by Employment
        Status - Mexico   121

A3-1k   Occupational Distribution of the Labor Force by Employment
        Status - Panama   122

A3-1l   Occupational Distribution of the Labor Force by Employment
        Status - Peru   123

A3-1m   Occupational Distribution of the Labor Force by Employment
        Status - Uruguay   124

A3-1n   Occupational Distribution of the Labor Force by Employment
        Status - Venezuela   125

A3-2a   Industrial Distribution of the Labor Force by Employment
        Status - Argentina   126

A3-2b   Industrial Distribution of the Labor Force by Employment
        Status - Bolivia   127

A3-2c   Industrial Distribution of the Labor Force by Employment
        Status - Brazil   128

A3-2d   Industrial Distribution of the Labor Force by Employment
        Status - Colombia   129

A3-2e   Industrial Distribution of the Labor Force by Employment
        Status - Ecuador   130

A3-2f   Industrial Distribution of the Labor Force by Employment
        Status - Jamaica   131

A3-2g   Industrial Distribution of the Labor Force by Employment
        Status - Mexico   132

A3-2h   Industrial Distribution of the Labor Force by Employment
        Status - Peru   133

A3-2i   Industrial Distribution of the Labor Force by Employment
        Status - Venezuela   134

4.1   Results of the Within Industry Elimination of Occupational
        Differentials   142

4.2   Percentage Change in Female Wages   144

A4.1   Results of the Within Industry Elimination of Occupational
        Differentials   148

6.1   Female Participation by Selected Sample Characteristics   185

6.2   Decomposition of the Male Pay Advantage in the Region   185

6.3   Contribution (in log percentage points) of Selected Variables
        to the Male Pay Advantage in the Region   191

6.4   Female Wages (in local currency) and Female Relative to
        Male Wage in the Private and Public Sectors (selected
        countries)   201

A6.1   Percentage of Male Pay Advantage Attributed to Differences
        in Endowments (E) and Rewards (R)   203

A6.2a   Average Hours per Week and Coefficients on Log (hours) by
        Sex   204

A6.2b   Contribution of Differences in Hours to the Male Pay
        Advantage   205

A6.3a   Average Years of Schooling and Estimated Coefficients on
        Schooling by Sex   206

A6.3b   Contribution of Differences in Schooling to the Male Pay
        Advantage   207

A6.4a   Average Years of Potential Experience and Coefficients on
        Potential Experience by Sex   208

A6.4b   Contribution of Differences in Potential Experience to the
        Male Pay Advantage   209

A6.5   Contribution of Differences in the Constant Terms to the
        Male Pay Advantage   210

A6.6   The Value and Significance of the Coefficient on the Sample
        Selection Variable (Lambda) in the Earnings Functions   211

List of Figures

1.1   Female Labor Force Participation Rate in Latin American and the Caribbean Countries 1950s and 1980s   16

1.2   Female Age-Participation Profile in Latin American and Caribbean Countries 1950s and 1980s (Stylized)   17

1.3   Female Participation Rate in Industrialized and Latin American and Caribbean Countries (Stylized)   19

1.4   Female Labor Force Participation Rate by Selected Characteristics, Costa Rica 1989   25

1.5   Decomposition of the Male-Female Wage Gap (Stylized)   26

1.6   Female Labor Force Participation Rate in Latin American and the Caribbean Countries 1950s and 1980s   30

1.7   Female Monthly Earnings by Educational Level, Costa Rica 1989   31

2.1   Female/Male Labor Force in Latin American and Caribbean Countries   43

2.2   Female Labor Participation Rate by Age   46

2.3   Female/Male Labor Force Participation Rate by Age   50

2.4   Female Participation Rate by World Region and Age Groups   52

3.1   Percentage of the Labor Force in Agriculture in Nine Latin American and Caribbean Countries 1980s   75

3.2   Percentage of the Labor Force in Industry in Nine Latin American and Caribbean Countries 1980s   77

3.3   Percentage of the Labor Force in Services in Nine Latin American and Caribbean Countries 1980s   78

3.4   Distribution of the Labor Force in Nine Latin American and
        Caribbean Countries 1980s   79

3.5   Percentage of Change in Labor Force in Latin American and
        Caribbean Countries by Broad Industrial Sector 1950-1980   80

4.1   Effects of Sex-Differentials in the Labor Market   140-

5.1   Decomposition of the Gender Wage Gap   157

5.2   Costs and Benefits of Investment in Education   160

5.3   A Truncated Distribution   171

Acknowledgments

We have benefited from comments and encouragement from many people who read earlier versions of this volume and participated in seminars given at the World Bank, the University of St. Andrews, and conferences organized by the Comparative and International Education Society, the International Union for the Scientific Study of Population, and the European Society for Population Economics. In particular we would like to thank Ana-María Arriagada, Alessandro Cigno, Deborah DeGraff, Barbara Herz, David Huggart, Emmanuel Jimenez, Philip Musgrove, and Michelle Riboud for their helpful comments, Professor William Greene for providing purpose built routines for LIMDEP which facilitated the estimation procedures used in the country studies; Diane Steele and Carolyn Winter for their reviews of the book; Hongyu Yang for preparing the graphics; and Donna Hannah for typing and preparing the earlier versions of this book and Marta Ospina for taking these tasks over and eventually putting the book into its present form. The completion of the present study would have not been possible without the generous support of the Norwegian Trust Fund.

Foreword

Women's role in economic development can be examined from many different angles, including feminist, anthropological, sociological, economic, and legislative perspectives. This study employs an economic perspective and focuses on how women behave and are treated in the work force in a number of Latin American economies. It specifically considers the determinants of women's labor force participation and male-to-female earnings differentials. Understanding the reasons for "low" labor market participation rates among women, or "high" wage discrimination against women, can lead to policies that will improve the efficiency and equity with which human resources are utilized in a particular country.

The study is in two volumes. This volume presents aggregate data on the evolution of female labor force participation in Latin America over time, showing that in some countries twice as many women (of comparable age groups) work in the market relative to twenty years ago. The companion volume uses household survey data to analyze labor force participation rates and wages earned by men and women in similar positions, paying special attention to the role of education as a factor influencing women's decision to work. The results show that, overall, the more years of schooling a woman has, the more likely she is to participate in the labor force. In addition, more educated women earn significantly more than less educated women. The book also attempts analyses of the common factors which determine salaries paid to men and women in an effort to identify what part of the male/female earnings differential can be attributed to different human capital endowments between the sexes, and what part is due to unexplained factors such as discrimination. Differences in human capital endowments explain only a small proportion of the wage differential in most of the country studies. The remaining proportion thus represents the upper bound to discrimination.

It is our hope that this work will be followed up by a more careful look at labor legislation and the role it plays in preventing women from reaching their full productive potential.

S. Shahid Husain
Vice President
Latin America and the Caribbean Region

1

Introduction and Summary

1. Objective

This is a fact finding, policy oriented study about working women in 15 Latin American and Caribbean countries.[1] The aims are:

1.   To establish patterns and trends in women's characteristics in the labor market;

2.   To identify factors affecting women's decision to work for pay and to quantify their impact on female participation;

3.   To examine what part of the gap between women's and men's labor earnings cannot be explained by differences in their respective productive characteristics; and

4.   In view of these findings, to explore policy options that can enhance the functioning of the labor market and contribute towards the alleviation of poverty.

The evidence comes from country household surveys undertaken during the late-1980s and published data (primarily population censuses) covering the period between 1950 and 1980.

---

[1]   The countries are: Argentina, Bolivia, Brazil, Chile, Colombia, Costa Rica, Ecuador, Guatemala, Honduras, Jamaica, Mexico, Panama, Peru, Uruguay, and Venezuela. These countries accounted for approximately 90 percent of the total labor force in the region both in the 1950s and the 1980s. (See *Yearbook of Labour Statistics 1945-1989: Retrospective Edition on Population Censuses*, Geneva: ILO, 1990).

Though certain individual country peculiarities have been accommodated, this volume does not attempt to provide a complete analysis of specific country issues. Rather, a comparative methodology is applied in order to examine whether there are common factors operating in labor markets in the Latin American[2] region which can be used to set a policy framework and an agenda for research. In this respect, the general directions for the design of policy and management of services are established with a view towards facilitating behavioral and economic change. "Behavioral" does not mean changing people's culture and resulting choices; rather, it means the removal of constraints imposed by market failure which prevent women from exercising their choices.

There are two volumes to the present study. This volume provides an overview of women's characteristics in the labor market, summarizes the findings and outlines possible policy options. A companion volume deals with the situation in individual countries.

2.   The Problem

Research on women's role in development has been increasing rapidly in recent years.[3] Three factors have spurred this interest.

First, developing countries have been moving from a traditional mode of economic activity towards systems followed by the industrialized countries over the past 40 years or so. Today, the functional roles of women and men in developing countries are characterized less by breadwinning men in the labor market and "bread-processing" women at home. Women's welfare depends now more than ever before on the labor market where women earn less than men and are more likely to be unemployed than men. This change has earned women the title of a "vulnerable" group.[4] In many developing countries this vulnerability can, for practical purposes, be regarded as a synonym of, if not a euphemism for, poverty.

---

[2]   For brevity "Latin America" will be used to mean "Latin America and the Caribbean."

[3]   See the collection of papers in *World Development*, July 1989 (special issue on women in development) and references therein.

[4]   A consistent finding in recent developmental work has been that women and children bear disproportionately the burden of adjustment (Cornia, Jolly and Stewart 1987; UNICEF 1987; ECLAC 1990, 1991).

Second, the belief which was widely held in the post-war era of high growth -- that moving the locus of employment from the traditional rural sectors to the modern urban sectors would more or less automatically solve the problem of regional disparities -- began to be seriously questioned in the 1970s and was largely repudiated following the adverse economic developments of the 1980s.[5] Efficiency considerations have become more important than ever before. The omission of half a country's human capital from the development strategy clearly leads to inefficiency.

Third, the policy implications of the changing national economic environment and social fabric are complex and worth examining in situ. Simply copying lessons from elsewhere is not likely to be effective. With respect to the labor market, women's employment and economic status are typically inferior to those of men. This is more so in developing economies than industrialized ones.[6] Also, the economic and cultural characteristics of developing countries are more diverse than the characteristics of advanced economies and women's behavior is known to be more dependent upon these characteristics than men.[7] Therefore, women's labor market status and welfare are greatly affected by the prevailing conditions in the macro-economy. The study of women's issues would be incomplete if country specific socio-economic constraints are ignored.

Poverty, inefficiency and underdevelopment are interrelated issues which depend to a great extent on the functioning of the labor market. The greatest part of national income, and individual/family income, is generated from the buying and selling of labor in the market. Therefore, the way labor is priced and allocated in the market is of prime importance to economic development and social

---

[5]   See *World Labour Report*, ILO, 1987.

[6]   Anker, Buvinic and Youssef (1982); Buvinic, Lycette and McGreevey (1983); Bardhan (1984); Birdsall and Sabot (1991).

[7]   The view that women's reactions to changing socio-economic conditions are greater (more "elastic") than those of men is shared by all schools of thought and is also strongly confirmed by empirical evidence. For example, in the realm of conventional economic analysis women are categorized as "secondary" workers whose fate depends crucially on the stage of economic development in general and, within a particular developmental stage, on the cyclical fluctuation of the economy. At the other end of analysis, women are seen as a "reserve army" whose utilization depends on the productive forces and productive relations operating at a particular point in time. All theories assume or predict that most men will be permanently attached to the labor force, even if only as unemployed workers.

welfare. This observation leads to the following line of reasoning in the case of women in development:

> If *more* women worked for pay and if women were paid *more* for their work, then the value of output would increase and poverty would be reduced.

The evidence provided in Table 1.1 suggests that indeed more women could work for pay and female pay could be higher than it is at present.[8] The figures relate to female participation rates and relative (female to male) pay. Though the figures are subject to a number of qualifications (which are discussed in more detail in chapters that follow), they show that only one-third of women are currently in the labor market (column 2), and women's labor earnings are around 70 percent of the earnings of men (column 4). The former finding relates to extensive growth, that is, that more output can be produced if more persons are employed. The latter finding relates to intensive growth (that is, to a more efficient use of women workers) and, as a significant byproduct, to poverty and, especially, the feminization of poverty.[9]

It is clear, therefore, that the status of women in the labor market is a crucial determinant of economic development and social welfare. It is also a timely issue for Latin America where recent economic performance has been poor.

---

[8]   This proposition does not necessarily imply that more women should work or that women should be paid more. In fact, it is possible that the observed low rates of female participation and low levels of female pay are efficient. Also, one has to take into account the labor demand side. However, it is also possible and, given the experience of industrialized countries, more probable that the utilization of female labor in the region is less than optimal. Our concern is about the removal of constraints which lead to "unjustified" gender differentials in the labor market. Some of these constraints are discussed below.

[9]   Tokman (1989).

Table 1.1
Female Participation Rate and Female-Relative-to-Male-Pay

Country (age group)	Year	Female Participation Rate (percent)	Year	Relative F/M pay (percent)
	(1)	(2)	(3)	(4)
Argentina (20-60)	1980	33.1	1985	64.5
Bolivia (20-64)	1976	23.1	1989	62.3
Brazil (20-60)	1980	33.0	1980	61.2
Chile (20-60)	1982	28.9	1987	65.4
Colombia (25-60)	1985	39.4	1988	84.6
Costa Rica (20-60)	1984	26.4	1989	80.8
Ecuador (20-60)	1982	22.6	1987	63.7
Guatemala (20-60)	1981	14.7	1989	76.8
Honduras (20-60)	1974	18.0	1989	81.3
Jamaica (20-64)	1982	48.2	1989	57.7
Mexico (20-60)	1980	32.7	1984	85.6
Panama (20-60)	1980	35.7	1989	79.6
Peru (20-60)	1981	29.0	1990	65.7
Uruguay (20-60)	1985	46.0	1989	57.4
Venezuela (20-60)	1981	35.0	1989	70.6
Average		31.1		70.5

Note: Participation of prime-age women (aged 20 to 60 years).
Weekly earnings in Venezuela, Mexico, Colombia, Jamaica, Honduras, Chile and Bolivia, and monthly earnings in all other countries.

Source: Participation: constructed from ILO (1990), Table 1.
Relative pay: based on information provided in the companion volume.

3.   The Latin American Case

In Latin America, the study of women's earnings in the labor market and labor force participation is characterized by significant analytical, practical and statistical problems.

From an analytical point of view, one difficulty arises from the fact that the region is more diversified and complex than other developing areas.   Latin America as a group is second only to industrialized countries in terms of development, being far ahead of most African and mainland Asian countries.[10] Hence, the region is quite diverse both in terms of composition of the final output (primary, industrial and service sectors) and also in terms of social structure.   Table 1.2 presents some economic and social indicators which show this diversity.   Column 1 shows the level of 1988 per capita income (in US$) in the 15 countries under consideration which contain the bulk of the region's population (almost 90 percent).   In column 2, per capita income is expressed as a percentage of the corresponding figure for the United States in the same year. At the lower end is Bolivia and Honduras and at the higher end Argentina and Venezuela.   Social indicators are equally diverse; only six countries have a life expectancy of more than 70 years. In Bolivia life expectancy is 53 years.   In Guatemala and Peru the corresponding figure is 62 years (column 3).   The across country diversity in women's family characteristics may be inferred from the variation in the total fertility rate (column 4): in some countries (such as Uruguay, Argentina, Chile and Jamaica) the total fertility rate is lower than three children per woman while in other countries (Guatemala, Honduras and Bolivia) it is more than five children per woman.[11]   The diversity of women's status within countries can be assessed from the adult female and male literacy rates, which can be taken as a measure of women's absolute and relative position in terms of socio-economic welfare (columns 4 and 5).   Women's illiteracy rates are typically higher than men's and, in some cases, reach 35 percent -- in fact 53 percent in Guatemala.   Finally, a commonly noted fact,

---

[10]   For example, the weighted average for Latin America's per capita income is $1,840 (US$ in 1988) compared to $3,470 for high income countries, $320 for South Asia, $330 for Sub-Saharan Africa, $540 for East Asia, and $1,380 for the lower middle income economies taken as a group (World Bank, 1990: Table 1, p. 178).   The figures for income are closely related to health, nutritional, educational and demographic data and to women's conditions (*Ibid.*, Tables 27, 28, 29 and 31).

[11]   Total fertility rate (TFR) is the number of children that would be born to a woman if she were to live to the end of her childbearing years and bear children at each age in accordance with prevailing age specific fertility rates.

confirmed in this study, is that low aggregate female labor force participation rates for the region mask women's high participation rates in urban areas. This contrasts with other developing regions such as South East Asia, which has high-urban/high-rural female labor force participation, and the Middle East countries with low-urban/low-rural participation.[12] Data for Chile, Colombia, Puerto Rico, Costa Rica, El Salvador, Peru and Venezuela suggest that the female labor force participation in rural areas is only about 50 percent of the female urban participation rate.[13] These remarks suggest that it may not be as easy to make broad generalizations about the region as elsewhere in the developing world.

The study of Latin American women in the labor market *today* is beset with an additional practical problem: the data may reflect transitory characteristics of the labor force. More specifically, the region experienced considerable economic and social growth in the 1950s, 1960s and during some part of the 1970s. The main sources for economic growth have been, first, an expanding export sector dependent on primary commodities; and, second, an industrialization drive fuelled primarily by domestic demand and a sustained growth in investment (especially public investment). However, in the last 10 to 15 years the region experienced significant economic slowdown and macro-economic imbalances. The changing role of the public sector (in terms of capital formation and employment, the latter especially from the point of view of women) may have affected the present data. In addition, the importance of the growth and structure of the private/formal sector may be underplayed. The severity of the recession is shown in column 7 of Table 1.2. The annual percentage change of per capita GDP suggests that one-third of the countries under consideration (Venezuela, Argentina, Peru, Jamaica and Bolivia) have had negative growth in the last quarter century.[14] Three countries (Chile, Guatemala and Honduras) have had growth rates lower than one percent per annum. In another three countries (Uruguay, Panama and Costa Rica) the growth rate was between 1.2 percent and 1.6 percent. In the remaining four countries (Brazil, Mexico, Colombia and Ecuador), the 2.3 percent to 3.5 percent annual growth rates during the 1965-1989 period mask the fact that recent growth has been slower than in the earlier period, as low as 0.7 percent per annum in the case of

---

[12]   Standing (1981. p. 15).

[13]   *Ibid.*, Table 1, p. 17.

[14]   The annual rate of per capita GDP growth is based on World Bank's estimates calculated from constant price series using the least squares method. See World Bank, *World Development Report 1991: The Challenge of Development*, 1991 (chapter on technical notes).

Table 1.2
Aggregate Statistics for Selected Latin American Countries

Country	Per Capita GDP (US$ 1988)	% of US	Life Expectancy (years)	Total Fertility Rate (children per woman)	Adult Illiteracy Rate (percent) Female	Male	Annual rate of per capita GDP Growth 1965-89 (percent)
	(1)	(2)	(3)	(4)	(5)	(6)	(7)
Venezuela	3250	16.4	70	3.7	15	11	-1.0
Argentina	2520	12.7	71	2.9	5	5	-0.1
Uruguay	2470	12.4	72	2.4	4	6	1.2
Brazil	2160	10.9	65	3.4	24	20	3.5
Panama	2120	10.7	72	3.1	12	12	1.6
Mexico	1760	8.9	69	3.5	12	8	3.0
Costa Rica	1690	8.5	75	3.2	7	5	1.4
Chile	1510	7.6	72	2.7	--	--	0.3
Peru	1300	6.6	62	4.0	22	8	-0.2
Colombia	1180	5.9	68	3.1	13	11	2.3
Ecuador	1120	5.6	66	4.2	20	6	3.0
Jamaica	1070	5.4	73	2.6	--	--	-1.3
Guatemala	900	4.5	62	5.7	53	37	0.9
Honduras	860	4.3	64	5.5	40	40	0.6
Bolivia	570	2.9	53	6.0	35	17	-0.8

-- not available.

Source: *World Bank Development Report 1990,* Tables 1, 2, 27, 29 and 32; and *World Bank Development Report 1991,* Table 1.

Mexico in the 1980s.[15]   Consequently, though some economic recovery has already taken place in the region, surveys undertaken in the late 1980s (like those utilized in the present study) may be still affected by the recession/adjustment that has been under way for some time.   Disentangling cyclical variation from longer term trends is thus a complicated task.

Finally, an additional difficulty arises from the paucity of historical data on women's employment and pay in the region.   Published data cover a few broad employment aggregates but do not pursue the distinction between women and men in more detailed and meaningful presentations.   The case of pay is indeed

---

[15]   World Bank, *World Development Report 1990,* Table 1.

telling: nowhere in the most authoritative publication of world labor statistics can one find substantial information on women's wages in Latin America.[16]

The diversity in the characteristics and differences in the underlying trends in the Latin American economies suggest that the study of economic performance in general, and labor market performance and poverty in particular, are a challenging task for applied research in the region. These analytical, practical and statistical considerations have shaped the present study. The papers in this study make a comprehensive effort to identify, collate and analyze data that were available at the time of writing, and use these data to establish the characteristics of and trends in women's work and pay in the region and to examine whether women are treated differently than men in the labor market.

4. Methodology

The present study does not attempt to advance our theoretical understanding of issues pertaining to women's time allocation between home and market work, the differentiation of gender roles within the family, household formation and dissolution, or other issues not directly related to women's employment and pay. Instead this study utilizes (with appropriate qualifications) existing analytical approaches to investigate women's status in the Latin American labor market in two particular ways.

First, we do not (and, perhaps, we will never find out) what the "appropriate" size of female labor supply or the "appropriate" level of female pay is. However, we know that *women compared to men* have *lower* rates of both labor force participation and pay. We also know (or, reasonably, assume) that there are no innate material differences between the sexes that necessarily justify the observed gender differentials in the context of modern production that is successively characterized by more capital intensive techniques. Hence, most of the analysis undertaken in this study is based on comparisons between female workers and male workers.

Second, the country case studies adhere to similar techniques and utilize comparable specifications in order to facilitate comparisons of results.

---

[16] See International Labour Office, *Statistical Yearbook*, any issue, old or recent. For many countries, wages are broken down by sex at the economy wide level and separately for the manufacturing (aggregate and by about 20 industries), agriculture, transport, and storage and communication industries. However, in Latin America, such information is available only in one country (El Salvador) while there are some sporadic aggregate estimates for female and male wages in the Netherlands Antilles and Chile.

Obviously, the immediate objective was not to provide a set of indepth country studies but to examine whether there are some common patterns and factors at work in the Latin America region.

Before discussing the findings, it is worth dwelling on some aspects of the methodological approach adopted in the present studies as well as their implications for the empirical specification of the models that were used. Basically a human capital framework is utilized, that is, it is assumed that education and acquired labor market experience are among the most important determinants of individual earnings. The merits and limitations of the human capital approach are well known.[17]   Chapter 5 provides a detailed exposition of the methodological and practical problems in the study of discrimination and below we highlight two aspects of the discussion with additional reference to another important issue in the case of women, that is *labor market selectivity*.

Type of education.   There was no information in our data sets about the type of human capital held by women and men. The data on education (in effect, schooling) are reported simply in years (or highest grade completed) with no reference to the type of education which the individual has acquired. This lack of information necessitates the adoption of the uncomfortable assumption that there are no differences in the type of education acquired by women and men. In this way, our results may overstate the extent of sex discrimination in the labor market. However, we hasten to add that this may not be as serious a problem in Latin America as in the case of industrialized countries. The reason is that relatively few women in the region have attended school beyond the second education level. Many women workers have not even completed lower secondary education and it is at the end of lower secondary education when studies become specialized. In fact, even as late as in 1980, about 11 percent of all females in the region aged 15 to 24 were illiterate, 17 percent in the 25-34 age group and as many as 26 percent in the 35-44 age group.[18]   In conclusion, only a few observations in our samples are affected by the failure to standardize for the type of education women and men acquire.

Actual versus potential experience.   There was no information in the data sets about *actual* labor market experience. This statistical defect does not usually present problems in the case of men. Men are typically found in the labor force during most of their lives. Hence, *potential experience* (that is, the difference

---

[17]   For recent evaluations of the human capital specification in the study of labor earnings see Siebert (1985), Willis (1986) and Dougherty and Jimenez (1991).

[18]   UNESCO, 1990.

between age, and years of schooling and conventional school entry age) should be a fair approximation of men's actual experience. However, many women have interrupted work careers. Hence, potential experience usually overestimates the actual labor market experience of women. In the present context, the implication of using inappropriately measured experience understates the significance of this variable for women's earning power and overstates the extent of discrimination. There is no way out of this difficulty until more detailed data become available.[19] In the meantime, it can be noted that studies that had access to more complete data sets have shown that a substantial part of the pay gap between women and men remains unexplained, even if data on actual experience for women are used.[20] This conclusion still holds when "imputed" (that is, estimated from family characteristics) experience is used in an attempt to decrease the bias arising from the use of potential experience in the case of women.[21] However, one can add that, as in the case of education mentioned in the previous paragraph, the use of potential experience in Latin American countries may not be as damaging as in the case of industrialized countries. The reason is that the average age of women workers in our samples was typically about 35 years and as low as 31-32 years in Bolivia, Mexico and Peru. Thus the average age of women in the region is lower than that in industrialized countries and the measurement error between actual and potential experience should be correspondingly lower. In addition, the typical female age participation profile in the region suggests that women do not usually reenter the labor market after an interruption in employment. As a result, it is possible that many of the working women in our samples may have been continuously in the

---

[19]   Of course, to the extent that women's labor force participation decisions are affected by discrimination in the first instance, then even the use of actual experience in the earnings functions will produce biased results. This issue is explained in detail in Chapter 5.

[20]   Wright and Ermisch (1991) report that in the case of Britain, the use of actual experience reduces the unexplained part of the pay difference between women and men by one-third compared to the results derived from potential experience. The reduction in the part of the sex wage gap attributed to discrimination is practically the same when uncorrected and selectivity corrected earnings functions are used.

[21]   Miller (1987), Wright and Ermisch (1991). In fact, the latter study attributes the "success of imputed experience" to the strong predictive power of childbearing patterns for women's actual work experience (*Ibid.* p. 519). Similarly, an earlier study on British women concluded that the use of actual experience versus potential experience increases the percentage of the sex pay gap attributed to differences in endowments by only 5 to 10 percentage points still leaving a substantial part (up to two-thirds) of the pay gap open to a number of alternative interpretations (Zabalza and Tzannatos, 1985, Chapter 1).

labor market since they first started work. This presumption may be valid for another reason. In general, self-employment and family work are more prevalent in developing countries than in industrialized ones. These two types of work are more compatible with work at home than dependent employment and do not necessitate an interruption of employment when family formation starts. Therefore, a higher percentage of women in the region may have had continuous work experience since they started working compared with women in industrialized countries. Finally, it is possible that many women in the region who work in the formal sector have continuous work history as women are heavily employed in the public sector. These women have access to institutionalized maternity provisions which safeguard their return to work, if they wish to do so. Hence, family formation may not have severe adverse effects upon the building of women's labor market experience in the region and the bias arising from the use of potential experience may not be significant.

Selectivity bias. The issue of selectivity refers to whether workers are a random or a "selected" sample of the population. If the former applies, statistical inferences from *working* women about *all* women should be valid (within a chosen margin of error). If, however, women workers are not a representative sample of all women, then there will be estimation bias. The bias arising from selectivity is not considered to be significant in the case of men as most men are usually in the labor force throughout most of their lives. In contrast, a relatively small number of women are in the labor force at any point in time. Are, then, those women working because they face high wages in the market or because they have low productivity at home? If either is correct, then working women are not representative of all women in the economy. Under these circumstances, one should correct for selectivity bias. However, one could equally argue that most women are working at some stage in their lives and not being observed as working at the time of the survey is a matter of chance, that is, it depends on what year the survey was conducted. In this case, the sample characteristics of working women can be taken to reflect the characteristics of all women. We cannot know *ex ante* which of these cases is relevant to a particular sample of female workers. Hence, the present studies attempted to identify selectivity and correct the estimated earnings functions for it. The correction amounts to an evaluation of *wage offers* for all, working and non-working, women in the sample (who can be taken to be representative of all women in the economy) rather than to concentrate on the *actual wages* of working women in the sample. Empirical estimates that have been corrected for selectivity bias provide a better insight for public policy: from a developmental point of view what is of interest is not simply what happens to female workers at present and whether they are treated in an efficient (that is, non-discriminatory) way compared to men. The more important issue is whether women overall are or can become as productive in the labor market as men. This is an important extension in the recent literature on discrimination and all our country studies report results which have been corrected for selectivity.

5. Main Findings

A. *Cross-country comparisons*

In this volume the characteristics and trends of women in the labor market *across countries* are firmly established, a task long overdue.[22] The female labor force is examined with respect to its size as well as its distribution by age, industrial and occupational composition, and employment status (employee, self-employed, family worker). Then, women's characteristics are juxtaposed against the corresponding data for men in an attempt to standardize for possible cross-country differences in the treatment of labor by national statistical conventions and also to account for the fact that different countries are at different stages of development. The characteristics of female employment are thus put in context and then used to establish some general patterns to the extent possible by the region's diversity.

Trend in participation. Considering the region as a whole, the labor force participation rate of women was initially low, averaging only 24 percent in the 1950s. However, by the 1980s it had risen to 33 percent -- an overall increase of more than one-third or about 1 percent per annum (Figure 1.1).[23] The increase was as high as 20 percentage points in Colombia and 10 to 15 percentage points in Brazil, Panama, and Mexico. In the other countries under consideration, the increase was a high single figure (five to nine percentage points) with the exception of Venezuela (three percentage points) and Chile (a

---

[22]   Schultz (1989a; 1990) provides a world perspective of women's employment but little that relates specifically to women in Latin America's labor markets.

[23]   Unweighted average of the participation rate of prime age women (aged 20 to 60 years) calculated for 13 of the countries under consideration. Bolivia was excluded because there was no reliable information for the 1950s: the data suggest that the female participation rate was practically the highest in the region in 1950 (75 percent) and among the lowest in the 1980s (only 29 percent). Perhaps this counterintuitive and dramatic change is the result of a change in the national definition of what constitutes work. However, no conclusions could be made without more specific information. Honduras is also excluded because the labor force participation rate in the early period refers to all women and is artificially low as it includes children and persons aged 65 and over. For the actual figures and sources see Table 2.3.

Figure 1.1
Female Labor Force Participation Rate in Latin American
and the Caribbean Countries
1950s and 1980s

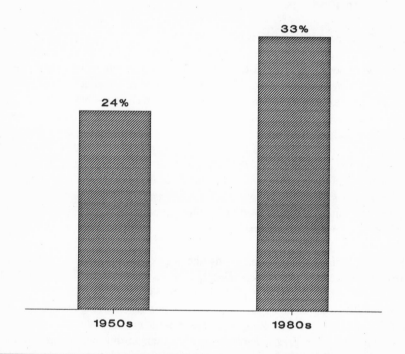

gain of one percentage point). The only country where the female participation rate declined over time was Jamaica where it dropped from 53 percent to 48 percent. However, Jamaica still has the highest female participation rate in the region.

It is difficult to attribute the rise in female participation in the region to any specific factor. For example, given the stagnant, and at times adverse, macro-economic conditions of the last 10 to 20 years, one could conclude that these changes for women were achieved *not via growth*, but by the removal of some of the inefficiencies that might have existed in the way women, as a factor of production, were treated in the 1950s and 1960s. If this were so, the economic crisis resulted in a more efficient use of female labor which has traditionally been underutilized in the region.   However, this may not be the only explanation. It is possible that the increased participation of women in the labor

Figure 1.2
Female Age-Participation Profile in Latin American
and Caribbean Countries
1950s and 1980s
(Stylized)

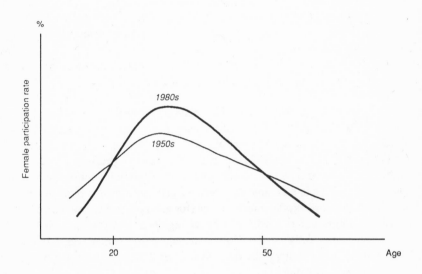

force has come primarily from the expanding employment opportunities for women in the public sector. It is a well established fact that the public sector is an increasingly important employer of female labor during development.[24] The expansion of the public sector could have caused, in turn, some of the stagnation in the macro-economic performance of these countries. If this has been the case, the distributional effects from the quantitatively greater and qualitatively better employment of women are suspect because the poor or poorest are less likely to end up with a job in the public sector. With the data in hand we cannot establish whether the increase in female participation has been the result of

---

[24]   One may note that our data have not allowed us to establish the relative importance of public and private sectors for female employment growth. However, the service sector, where most of the operations of the government are included, now accounts for more than 50 percent of the region's total GDP (*World Development Report 1990*, The World Bank, Table 3).

greater efficiency during the recession or greater role of the public sector. Perhaps the answer lies somewhere in between the "competitive" and "public sector" explanations, though it is harder to say whether it is closer to the former or the latter. A complicating factor is that women's labor force participation rates in the (predominantly Catholic) Latin America region were initially the lowest in the world -- save for Middle-East countries.[25] Hence, if there were ever to be a change in Latin America it was bound to be in the direction of greater representation of women in the labor force. In fact, this study shows that there has been considerable "regression towards the mean" in the change of female participation rates over time: countries with the lowest female participation rates in the 1950s have shown greater increases compared to countries whose female participation rates were initially high.

The age-profile of participation. The increase in female participation has come from an increase in the participation rates of women aged 20 to 50 years. Figure 1.2 presents a stylized profile of female participation in Latin America by age in the 1950s and 1980s (for detailed country profiles see Chapter 2). Naturally, younger and older women have lower participation rates than prime age women. This is a commonly observed pattern in many countries and there are straightforward explanations for this (for example, school enrollment for the younger groups and the existence of savings/pensions for the older groups). However, in the early period (1950s) female participation was relatively flat across all ages. By the 1980s, the two ends of the age distribution had dipped, but participation among prime age women had increased.

Figure 1.3 attempts, again in a stylized presentation, a comparison between the age participation profiles of women in industrialized countries and in Latin America. First, female participation in industrialized countries is higher than in Latin America. Second, the age profile of female participation in industrialized countries is characterized by a double peak: the first peak occurs just before childbearing starts while the second peak is reached after the last child goes to school. In contrast, there are no visible signs, at least in the

---

[25]   The underutilization of female labor in Latin America could be even more severe than that suggested by a comparison with the Middle East region since the officially low rates of female participation in the latter may be significantly affected by a "cultural reluctance" to admit that a woman is working, even when she does so (Boserup, 1970; Standing, 1981; Kozel and Alderman, 1988).

Figure 1.3
Female Participation Rate in Industrialized
and Latin American and Caribbean Countries
(Stylized)

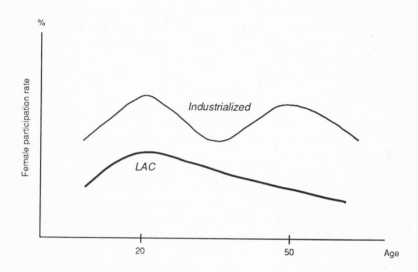

countries studied in this volume, that women reenter the labor market after an interruption in employment.[26]

Comparison between female and male participation rates. When changes in the male participation rate over time are taken into account, the change in female participation is even more impressive. The male labor force participation rate was lower in all our countries in the 1980s than it was in the 1950s. For example, in relative terms female participation rose even in Jamaica where the ratio of female to male participation was 55 percent in 1962 and 62 percent in 1982. In some countries the increase was dramatic. In Colombia, Brazil and

---

[26]   The current age profile of female labor force participation in Latin America is similar to the profile observed in advanced countries some time ago when women's participation "reflected a straightforward career pattern: work for pay (if you work at all) before marriage. Then stop." (Levy, 1987, p. 142: on women's participation in the early postwar United States.)

Mexico the female relative to male participation rate almost doubled. It is worth noting that the gains of women compared to men have been universal, across all countries and all age groups.[27]

Is the increase in female participation temporary or permanent? The increase in female participation in the region occurred somewhat contrary to expectations and textbook wisdom.   In particular, the low, or even negative in some countries, rates of output growth have not prevented the composition of the labor force from moving toward greater representation of women.   In this respect, Latin America has not followed the pattern of industrialized countries where women appear to have been "pulled" into paid employment during periods of consistently high economic growth and labor shortages.[28] Are Latin American women's higher participation rates in the more recent period the result of the "added worker" effect which can be contrasted with the "discouraged worker" effect?   The former effect suggests that more women enter the labor market during periods of economic recession in an attempt to preserve family income and level of consumption. The latter effect suggests that women drop out of the labor force during periods of recession because expected returns to search are not worth considering: wages are low and the probability of finding employment is small. We do not think that either effect has much to do with the rise in female participation in the region, even more so for the dominance of the added worker effect over the discouraged worker effect. There are three reasons for this belief. First, both the added and discouraged worker effects are operating at the margin and relate to cyclical, not long term, variation. Our observation period is sufficiently long for the task in hand (from the 1950s to the 1980s) so that any cyclical effect should not be sufficient to distort the overall picture. Second, empirical studies have consistently found that *in the case of women*, the discouraged worker effect is the dominant one. One of the reasons for this is that during an economic recession women leave employment and become economically inactive in contrast to men who move from employment to unemployment.[29]   Third, and finally, the drop in the participation rates of

---

[27]   See Chapter 2.

[28]   See Mincer (1962), Cain (1966), Oppenheimer (1974) for the American case; Nakamura, Nakamura and Cullen (1979a) for Canada; Joshi, Layard and Owen (1985) for Britain.   For a survey of the experience of the industrialized countries see Killingsworth and Heckman (1986).

[29]   For example, Joshi (1981) found no evidence that women in Great Britain have a different degree of cyclical change in employment than men though specific groups of women and men (such as the younger and pensioners) have different trends of cyclical instability.

younger women is not compatible with a dominant added worker effect. We, therefore, conclude that the rise in female participation that our data suggest for the 1980s compared to the 1950s is due to an underlying trend and cannot be attributed to the recession which has hit the region so hard in the eighties.

Employment dissimilarity between female workers and male workers. Another aspect of the labor force is the employment distribution of workers. We examined data by industries and occupations. The problems associated with the examination of qualitative characteristics of employment are well known.[30] Despite these limitations, the present evidence supports the view that women's employment distribution across occupations and industries is substantially different than the employment distribution of men. However there are signs that occupational and industrial dissimilarity in the region is decreasing over time. Dissimilarity among *all workers* decreased in seven of the countries studied in this volume while it rose in six countries.[31] In addition, the decrease in dissimilarity in the former countries was greater (in absolute terms) than the increase in dissimilarity in the latter countries. It is worth noting that when changes in dissimilarity are examined separately for the groups of self-employed workers, employees and family workers, the reductions in dissimilarity were greatest and more uniform among employees followed by self-employed workers. Therefore, workers in paid employment (rather than family workers) appear to have been the main beneficiaries from the increase in women's employment during the last 30 years. One should not, however, jump to the conclusion that dissimilarity is less of an issue today than it was in the 1950s. The reason is that, despite the reduction in employment dissimilarity between women and men over time, a higher percentage of the labor force today is in sex stereotyped employment because there are more female workers in the total labor force than ever before. This finding is important because it shows that the developmental effort of a country does not depend only on developments in the labor market but it also depends on the behavior of non-workers (this observation is of similar nature to the remarks made earlier with respect to selectivity bias). Two more observations can be made with reference to the decrease in dissimilarity over time. First, part of the reduction has been due to the decline in the agricultural sector and the concurrent decrease in the prevalence of unpaid family work. Obviously, this is a process that is bound to level off quickly -- in fact, it has done so in some of the more advanced

---

[30]   These problems are examined in detail in Chapter 3.

[31]   There was insufficient information for two countries, namely Bolivia and Brazil.

countries in the region.[32]   Second, the reduction in the employment dissimilarity was greater among employees than among the self-employed and family workers.   It is possible that the public sector "explanation" is relevant here as governments are often seen to be an equalizer of opportunities in employment matters.[33]

Formal and informal employment. The formal sector and in particular dependent employment ("employees") were found to be more important for women than men: the percentage of women workers in these sectors is higher than the corresponding percentage for men.   In addition, the percentage of employees in the total female labor force has increased over time in all but six of the countries in the region.[34]   These findings were somewhat unexpected: women are typically perceived to be working in the informal sector, most often within a family context, and dependent employment is usually affected more by adverse economic conditions than self-employment and family work. Again, it is possible that the increase in the share of employees in the female labor force and the greater reduction in dissimilarity among workers in the formal sector are due to the employment growth in the public sector. However, these findings may necessitate a reconsideration of the oft-quoted importance of the informal sector for women in developing countries. The experience of industrialized countries lends additional support to the importance of the formal sector in the long-run: historically the percentage of the labor force in dependent employment has increased in industrialized countries.

---

[32]   The contribution of agriculture to GDP decreased by almost 40 percent in Latin American and Caribbean countries between 1965 and 1988 and now accounts for only about 10 percent of all output. In other developing areas, such as East Asia and Sub-Saharan Africa, the reduction was less severe (about 20-30 percent), despite the fact that in both regions agriculture originally accounted for a much greater percentage of their GDP, around 45 percent (The World Bank, 1990: Table 3).

[33]   For example, among industrialized countries sex anti-discriminatory legislation was first introduced in the public sector and only later extended to the private sector (Gregory and Duncan, 1981; Tzannatos and Zabalza, 1984; Gunderson, 1989; Killingsworth, 1990). In fact, some empirical work in developing countries has shown that the unexplained wage difference among workers in the public sector are practically zero (see Birdsall and Fox, 1985, on the case of teachers' pay in Brazil).

[34]   The fact that women employees as a percentage of the labor force have increased over time in all but six countries in the region lends additional support to the view that the rise in female participation is not of cyclical nature.

Potential gains from gender equality in the labor market. The final issue examined in this volume is based on the observation that, if employment and pay differentials between women and men reflect some kind of inefficiency in the labor market (discrimination is only one such inefficiency), then the removal of this inefficiency should improve the competitive functioning of the labor market. The result will be, on the one hand, a reduction in labor market gender differentials and, on the other hand, an increase in the level of output and also an increase in real wages. In this context, we attempted to evaluate the following hypothetical question: what would happen to output and pay in the region, if pay and employment differentials were eliminated -- assuming that women and men are identical factors of production?[35] It is difficult to obtain a precise answer to this question. However, similar studies have been undertaken for advanced countries and we repeated this analysis for Latin America bearing in mind that the results are only "upper bound" estimates. Subject to a number of qualifications, our simulations suggest that the potential gains in output and rise in female wages could be substantial. Output may increase by about five percent and female wages by about 50 percent. Of course, such gains may not be easy to achieve even within the time span of a whole generation of workers. In addition, achieving complete gender equality in terms of labor market outcomes may be neither feasible (for example, due to physical differences between women and men) nor desirable (many people may be content with the present division of labor in the market and at home). However, the magnitude of the results in our simulations suggests that, even if a relatively small part of existing gender differentials in the labor market is due to some form of discrimination, its elimination is a policy issue worth exploring further.

B. Country studies

The companion volume focuses on the position of women in the labor market within each country. In particular, two issues are singled out as the most important for analysis within countries. First, the decision to participate in the labor market, the *sine qua non* for paid work, and, second, female labor "prices" (wages), the prime signal for economic efficiency and an important

---

[35]   This question was answered by assuming that women change occupations *within* the industries in which they are currently employed until occupational wage differentials are eliminated. This simulation assumes that women and men are perfect substitutes in production (on the labor demand side) and women are willing to work in all types of jobs currently undertaken by men and vice versa for men (on the labor supply side). In this respect, the results overestimate the gains that can be achieved but there are other factors which may mitigate this bias. These considerations are explored in more detail in Chapter 4.

individual's material welfare. Representative participation functions and earnings functions are estimated, and an attempt is made to answer the question as to whether women's productive characteristics in the labor market are rewarded in the same way as men's. If not, it may be possible to improve efficiency and alleviate poverty by introducing measures to make the functioning of the labor market more competitive (sex blind).

The determinants of female participation. The majority of studies confirm that women's decisions to work for pay and enter the labor market is greater (1) as they enter adulthood and up to the age of 40 to 45 years (after controlling for fertility); (2) if they reside in urban areas;[36] (3) the higher their education qualifications; (4) the more general (rather than technical/vocational) their education;[37] (5) the lower their family responsibilities (in terms of number of young children present in the household and whether they live in a male or female headed household); and (6) the lower other income and family wealth is (such as husband's earnings and house ownership). Figure 1.4 shows typical patterns of female participation in the region by some key factors with reference to Costa Rica. None of these findings is surprising but the effect of education on participation is particularly worth noting as education is potentially an important policy variable.

Wage differentials. On the question of what accounts for the pay differences between female and male workers, most country studies suggest that differences in human capital endowments between women and men explain only a small

---

[36] The exception to this is Kingston, Jamaica, where women have *ceteris paribus* a lower propensity to participate in the labor force than women in other areas of the country.

[37] This finding derives from the few studies in this volume which were able to pursue this distinction. However in Argentina the possession of a commercial or technical secondary qualification appears to have a greater impact on the decision to participate in the labor market. This finding is subject to two qualifications. First, Argentina is among the most developed countries in Latin America. Hence, there may be more demand for specialized skills. Second, the sample is drawn only from Buenos Aires, the most developed area of the country, and it is unlikely to reflect accurately the characteristics of the whole country (for example, almost 30 percent of working women in Buenos Aires are employed in the public sector while more than one in three women are involved in part-time employment and almost one in ten working women are foreign born; none of these characteristics is likely to hold outside the capital city). In any case, other research on the issue has typically found that returns to vocational education are not as high as those to general education (Grasso and Shea, 1979; Meyer and Wise, 1982; Psacharopoulos 1987).

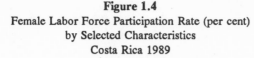

Figure 1.4
Female Labor Force Participation Rate (per cent)
by Selected Characteristics
Costa Rica 1989

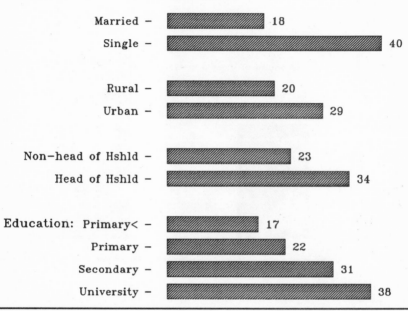

proportion of the wage differential. The way the labor market rewards productive characteristics appears to be dependent on whether the holder of these characteristics is a woman or a man. Detailed estimates are shown in the individual country studies that follow, but as a summary statement one can say that on average only 20 percent (or five percentage points) of the sex wage differential can be explained by differences in the stock of human capital that women and men have acquired. The remaining part of the sex wage gap can be seen as the upper bound of discrimination in *actual* wages. However, after correcting for women's self-selection in the labor market, the estimates suggest that an additional 20 percent (another five percentage points) of the unexplained gap that was previously attributed to discrimination is due to women's earning power (wage *offers*) being lower than that of men. Hence, the unexplained part is reduced to about 60 percent of the sex wage gap (or 20 percentage points) (Figure 1.5). One can mention here that the value of our estimates rests on the fact that studies for other countries (mostly advanced ones) have estimated lower "upper bounds" than those presented in this volume. We are not aware of any study, or collection of studies, which have addressed the issue from the point of view of a region (rather than individual country).

Figure 1.5
Decomposition of the Male-Female Wage Gap
(Stylized)

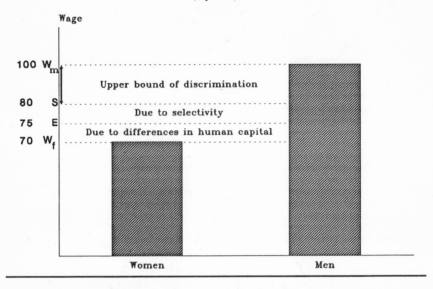

6.   Policy Issues

The direct and indirect effects of women's employment cannot be overstated.
The relationship between female participation in the labor force, fertility,
women's overall economic welfare and social status, and growth is well
established in the literature. What is less certain are the causes for the observed
differentials in employment and pay between women and men. The issue is a
complex one but our findings suggest that policies which enhance women's
productive characteristics (labor supply), eliminate differential treatment of
workers at the workplace on the grounds of sex (labor demand) and which
generally improve the competitive functioning of the labor market (institutional
framework) can be both growth enhancing and self-financing. In addition, their
distributional effects will be in the right direction as women are predominantly
employed in low pay, low status jobs.

Below, we highlight some key areas where (1) social policy can have rewarding
returns; (2) more analytical work can increase our understanding of the
functioning of the labor market; and (3) there is a need for better statistical
information.

Women, childbearing, and the decision to work for pay. A consistent finding in all studies in this volume is that, after controlling for other factors, women's propensity to work for pay is high even during the childbearing age. In this respect, women's behavior appears to be *ex ante* similar to that of men. However, the *actual* age profile of female participation dips during the reproductive age and all country studies confirm the negative effect of children upon women's decision to work for pay. The conflict between productive and reproductive decisions is obvious. In fact, it is this asymmetry, in part biological and in part stemming from societal norms, which largely destines women to the observed employment and pay characteristics in the labor market.

A number of options exist which can relieve women from some of the burden of family formation and increase women's contribution to production and women's welfare. One such measure is improving women's understanding, especially in rural or relatively poor areas, of how to avoid unwanted pregnancies. One may note here that education increases the level of contraceptive efficiency and lowers the expenditure on contraceptives necessary to reduce the risk of pregnancy at a given level.[38]

An additional increase in women's work effort can come through the encouragement of women's reentry into the labor market after an interruption in employment. This can be achieved by the provision of effective and cost-efficient pre-school and child-care facilities. Recall that the typical pattern for women in the region is to withdraw from the labor market upon childbearing with little tendency to reenter the labor market. The usual approach has been for governments either to provide such child-care facilities free heavily subsidized or not to provide them at all. Where free child-care facilities are offered, these have been largely urban based with a relatively limited number of places. As a consequence, the most needy groups have seldom been the beneficiaries of the subsidies. Offering pre-school care with selective cost recovery measures along social cost-benefit lines would enable more women to enter employment and, subsequently, to improve their income potential. It would also assist children from disadvantaged backgrounds by exposing them to organized pre-school education and by improving their socialization.[39] In addition, day-care can provide a medium through which children can be reached with targeted immunization, nutrition and other programs.

---

[38]   Michael (1974); Rosenweig and Wolpin (1982).

[39]   "New research indicates that our fears about average day-care programs are baseless: it shows that typical, not just ideal, day-care seems to have no ill effects..." (Nakamura, Nakamura and Cullen, 1979a, p. 135).

The family structure observed in industrialized countries is not that typical in the Latin American region. Internal and overseas migration ("women as urban domestic servants and men as industrial workers abroad") is quite significant while in some areas, especially in the Caribbean, visiting partnerships are not an uncommon form of arrangement. Also, given the longer life expectancy of women and the fact that in most marriages women are younger than their husbands, widowhood even during prime age is not uncommon.[40] In addition, societal norms may not encourage remarriage.[41] Finally, and in more general terms, the growth in the number of divorced and separated mothers is considered to be one of the primary reason for the continuing increase in single parent families.[42] These complex socio-demographic effects throw women into a vicious cycle of inability to work and poverty. In countries examined in this volume, female headed households accounted for between 10 and 15 percent of the sample in Argentina and Venezuela, and for as much as one-third in Jamaica (and around 50 percent in the Kingston area alone). Consequently, policies which directly (via the elimination of provisions in family law and taxation regulations which induce asymmetry in the treatment of women with respect to family/employment decisions)[43] or indirectly (via reducing the burden of child care) improve women's employment opportunities during the critical period of family formation are bound to have beneficial efficiency and distributional effects. The efficiency issue is self-obvious. In distributional terms, economic theory predicts[44] and empirical evidence suggests[45] an inverse relationship between income/class position and marital instability. Whether such policies should be adopted does of course depend on costs. This is an area of research with potentially significant returns.

Education and women's work and pay. Another systematic finding of the studies reported in the companion volume is the effect of education upon women's employment and pay. The participation functions show that, after

---

[40]   Mohan (1986).

[41]   Rosenhouse (1988).

[42]   Ermisch and Wright (1990).

[43]   A study of legal provisions which differentiate between women and men in the family and the labor market is already under way in the World Bank.

[44]   Becker, Landes and Michael (1977); Becker (1981).

[45]   Goode (1956, 1962); Bishop (1980); Kiernan (1986); Peters (1986).

for other factors, the probability of participation is greater the higher the woman's educational qualification. Similarly, women's earnings increase as formally acquired education increases. Although the issue of occupational choice has not been explicitly addressed in this study, the effect of education upon a woman's propensity to work and her level of pay is sufficiently clearcut to guide public policy.

Increasing opportunities for female education would enhance efficiency and alleviate poverty.[46] When women stay longer in the education system their natural (maximum) fertility rate is reduced. In addition it has been shown that there is a strong negative effect between female education and family size through a price substitution effect as well as birth control knowledge and contraceptive efficiency.[47] Finally, women are exposed to influences which typically alter their preferences away from the traditional view of the family toward fewer children.[48] These effects are implicit in Figure 1.6 which shows the relationship between education and fertility among women teenagers in four of the countries in the region. Apart from an effect via lower fertility, education increases women's propensity to work because the opportunity cost of staying at home (foregone income) also increases.[49] Women's greater attachment to the labor market can subsequently augment family income (in a conventional family context) and can help reduce the incidence of poverty among prospective female headed households.[50] The increase in female human capital also assures a more effective use of half of the country's potential work force and induces men to work in a more competitive environment. Finally education enhances family production as broadly defined. Children's well-being and educational attainment has been found to be highly correlated to mother's education. In addition, educated women are in a better position to prepare

---

[46]   Blau, Behrman and Wolfe (1988); Psacharopoulos and Tzannatos (1989).

[47]   Heer and Turner (1965); Westoff (1967); Harman (1969); Da Vanzo (1971); De Tray (1972, 1973); Cochrane (1979); Kelly and Da Silva (1980); Da Silva (1982); Mueller (1982).

[48]   Easterlin (1969); Tzannatos and Symons (1989).

[49]   Khandker (1987, 1988); Psacharopoulos and Tzannatos (1991).

[50]   Schultz (1969b).

Figure 1.6
Female Labor Force Participation Rate in Latin American
and the Caribbean Countries
1950s and 1980s

Annual number of live births per 1,000 women aged 15–19

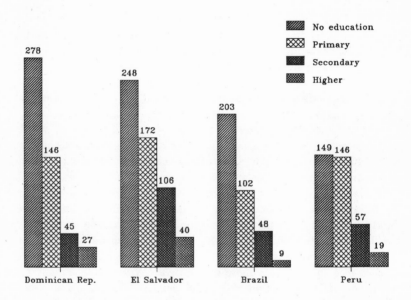

Source: The Allan Guttmacher Institute, *Today's Adolescents, Romorrow's Parents:*
A Portrait of the Americas, 1991.

meals in a more hygienic way and can look after ill members of the household
in a better way.[51]

Female earnings also increase with schooling, and do so faster than male
earnings. Thus, the distributional effects of more/better female education are
warranted and desirable from a social cost-benefit point of view; the same
marginal investment (one additional year of education) often yields higher
returns for women than men. Figure 1.7 shows another typical profile in the
region, this time with respect to education and earnings.

---

[51]   Chiswick (1974); Leibowitz (1974); Haveman and Wolfe (1984); Michael
(1984).

Figure 1.7
Female Monthly Earnings by Educational Level
Costa Rica 1989

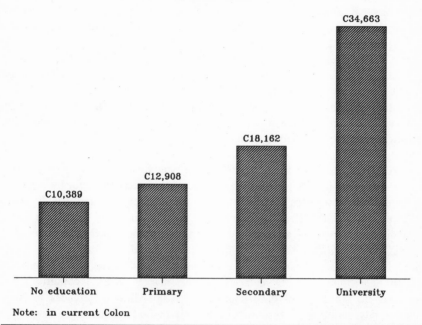

Note: in current Colon

Is a policy of expanding female education desirable given that the average length of schooling among female workers is already higher than that of men? The answer is "yes" because what is relevant is not the educational composition of the female labor force but that of the female population as a whole. The case even of the most advanced countries in this volume is telling indeed. In Venezuela, working women have, on average, 7.9 years of schooling while non-working women have only 5.5 years of schooling -- far behind the average attainment of men of 7.0 years. In Argentina, working women have 9.4 years of schooling compared to 8.8 years for men and only 7.8 years for non-working women (and the sample is drawn only from the capital city). The disparity between female and male length of schooling is even greater in the less advanced countries of the region and between urban and rural areas.

Providing more education to women appears to be a sound policy direction. In terms of simple arithmetic, average female education will increase more, and in a more cost-effective way, if many illiterate women attend primary school than if a few secondary school graduates attend a four year university course. In this respect, the high rates of return to female university education reported in this volume need to be qualified accordingly.[52]   First, the most qualified workers, especially females, find employment in the public sector, and the present estimates may simply reflect this.   Second, and more importantly, the earnings functions that are estimated in the conventional econometric form are based on the explicit assumption that the only cost of education is foregone earnings during the period of studies, which amounts to saying that education is a free good.   This is clearly unrealistic and the difference between the returns to primary and university education is not necessarily so great as to justify the public provision of more tertiary education at the expense of lower levels of education.[53]   Third, and finally, the pro-rich distributional effects of the emphasis on tertiary education, rather than basic education, in developing countries have been widely documented.[54]

The earnings gap.   The final objective of this study was to determine what part of the difference in female and male labor earnings is accounted for by workers' individual characteristics and effort.   Education, experience and weekly hours were singled out as appropriate variables.   All the studies in this report found that these three variables accounted for only about one-third of the observed earnings differential.   The rest of the difference is due to one of the "black boxes" of labor economics.   One may argue that, as the theoretical foundation of earnings functions rests on a competitive market clearing condition, this approach to the study of discrimination does not allow differences in labor supply between the sexes to show up separately in the final decomposition of the pay gap.   Alternatively, there may be genuine market imperfections, or government legislation, or societal conventions that are, at least in part, responsible for the unexplained difference.   The usual approach has been to label the differences in earnings unexplained by human capital characteristics as the "extent of our ignorance" and assign it the interpretation "upper bound of discrimination."   Though this may be correct in terms of semantics, it has little

---

[52]   This finding is quite common in developing countries (Haque, 1984; Khan and Irfan, 1985).

[53]   For estimates of the cost-efficiency of investment on different levels and types of education see Adelman (1975); Colclough (1982); Mingat and Tan (1988); Psacharopoulos (1977, 1985); Lockheed and Hamishek (1988).

[54]   The unintentional distributional effects of public expenditure on education have been shown by among others Ribich (1968); Selowsky (1979); Stromquist (1986); Lockheed and Hanushek (1991).

practical significance. The debate this unexplained difference has spurred in advanced industrialized countries indicates the complexity of the issue.[55]

Despite these limitations, the present study makes some valuable points. First, the estimated unexplained difference in the countries included in this volume is larger than that found in advanced countries where up to two-thirds of the differential has been attributed to differences in the productive characteristics between workers of different sex.[56] In this respect, there seem to be greater differences in the treatment of women in Latin America than in industrialized countries. Part of the explanation for this difference can be the fact that markets in developing countries have not matured sufficiently to take over from custom as an allocative mechanism. Powerful norms of female seclusion, which may still apply, restrict women from achieving a status comparable to men outside the family.[57] Second, it is likely that, in some countries, women's participation in certain types of employment and/or hours of work are still restricted by decree while women's pay may be determined (implicitly or explicitly) *pro rata* to male pay in the jobs in which they are employed. These overt restrictions continued to exist even in advanced countries (such as Australia, New Zealand, Britain and some other European countries) until they were repealed by equal pay/employment legislation enacted mostly in the 1970s.[58] Despite the fact that the present authors did not examine institutional factors governing collective pay and employment determination in the countries studied, some evidence was identified supporting the view that such discriminatory arrangements exist in Latin America.[59] There can be no economic justification for such employment or pay restrictions and, to the extent that such practices exist, concern for

---

[55]   For the detection of discrimination and applicability of policies designed to eliminate it see Zabalza and Tzannatos (1985); Dex and Sloane (1988); Gunderson (1989); Siebert (1990).

[56]   Cain (1986); Killingsworth (1990).

[57]   Cain, Khanam and Nahar (1979).

[58]   See, among others, Gregory and Duncan (1981); Tzannatos and Zabalza (1984); Tzannatos (1984, 1987b).

[59]   See chapters on Bolivia and Venezuela.

overall economic (allocative and distributional) efficiency calls for their elimination.[60]

Women's status and economic development. This is hardly measurable with the economists' tools. Most work in this area has come from other disciplines, especially sociology. However, if the general policy directions suggested in the present volume are followed and women's economic roles increase, it is clear that women's status will improve in social terms with subsequent beneficial effects on the macro-economy.[61]   For example, it has been argued that obtaining a job for wages outside the family enables women to control the returns to their own labor: the exercise of such a control has been found to augment women's relative power in the allocation of household resources.[62] The improvement in the economic status of women relative to men can, in turn, be associated with specific consumption patterns, investments in the health and nutrition of women and children, reduced child mortality, and eventual declines in fertility. This line of argument follows the observation that the reproductive function/power of women becomes less important for women the more they have other secure power (mostly economic) bases.[63]

Future research. The present research has shed light on some female issues in Latin America's labor markets but a number of issues remain unresolved. An agenda for future analysis can include the following issues:

1.   The existence of protective or other forms of legislation in the types of employment potentially accessible to women. If such provisions prohibit,

---

[60]   Something that should, perhaps, be stressed here is that, even if female and male productivity and wages rose at the same rate (that is, even if the gender wage gap persisted), this could be sufficient to increase women's participation in the labor market, reduce the onset of marriage and diminish lifetime fertility (Layard and Mincer 1985). However, the issue is not whether the economy will eventually get in an appropriate growth track in the long run (via the effect of real rather than relative wages upon female labor supply) but whether this process can be facilitated by a more competitive functioning of the market.

[61]   Deere et. al. (1982) note that there exists a complex interaction between various aspects/tiers of development (at international, national, regional, class and household levels) which result in a dynamic relationship between women's status and the macro-economy.

[62]   Boserup (1970).

[63]   Safilios-Rothschild (1982). See also Schultz (1969a).

in effect, women from certain activities, perpetuate sex stereotypes, and limit competition, their effects should be evaluated and corrected.

2. The nature of pay and employment determination -- especially public sector policies and collective labor market arrangements in the private sector. It is probable that wage setting is not geared to productivity and overall labor market conditions but it may reflect narrow interests of certain groups or societal norms no longer beneficial to modern production.

3. Labor market imperfections arising from different treatment of full-time vis-a-vis part-time, seasonal, and temporary work. The latter type of employment is undertaken primarily by women and can be discouraged by the existence of fringe benefit obligations on employers which are not fully prorationed compared to full-time employment.

4. The regional distribution of educational attainment and access to education, especially between metropolitan, other urban, and rural areas. The provision of public subsidies should be targeted to sectors where returns are highest.

5. The importance of the public sector in its capacity as an employer and as the main supplier of education. It is not uncommon for public policy to be dictated by short run political considerations rather than from the point of view of long term growth (dynamic efficiency).

6. The provisions included in public policy and their allocative and distributional effects, especially with respect to social policies associated with the labor market (such as unemployment benefits, income support measures, and pensions).

7. The distinction between, and relevance of, the formal and informal sectors and the implications for employment and overall developmental strategies adopted by the government.

8. The existence of statutes which provide for the differential treatment of women and men in the household (such as family law and taxation).

The need for better statistical information. One should emphasize that the scope of the analyses undertaken in the present research has been limited by the quality and coverage of data raised by household surveys in the region. In particular, in some (and, sometimes, in all) countries:

1. The surveys did not always provide information about the industrial sector of the worker and/or the occupational sector or the number of weekly hours worked.

2. One of the most important variables for the analysis of women in the labor market, namely *actual* labor market experience, was not found in any of the databases.

3. There was no useful information about the relationship between individuals in the same household: it would have made a lot of difference in the precision of female labor supply estimates if the researchers knew whether an extra adult in the household survey was a mother-in-law, sibling of either spouse, temporary visitor, or a domestic laborer.

4. Another useful piece of information typically missing from our databases was the number of days or weeks an individual was absent from work and the reasons for absence (for example, ill health, family reasons and so on).

5. On the issue of earnings, some surveys were undertaken in stages over a lengthy period and this has impaired the accuracy of earnings for estimates in countries with high inflation. Delays in data collection can also affect employment estimates, where employment is seasonal or cyclical.

6. Information on education/training needs to be more specific. Type of education needs to be included in the questionnaire (such as general academic, technical, vocational), as does quality, as proxied by the distinction between public/private school or location of school in rural/urban area. These questions should also be asked of training.

7. There is, finally, a need for improving the quality/stratification of the surveys. For example, in some databases the distinction between general and technical education was pursued but, since few women undertake the latter, the information that could be usefully utilized consisted of a handful of observations even at country level. Attempts to obtain more disaggregated information (for example, by region) proved of little value since in some cases there were hardly more than two or three observations left.

Unless the quality and scope of data improve, it will not be possible to take the analysis beyond some aggregate quantitative issues. Given the regional diversity that exists in developing countries with respect to their economies and societies, the need for broader and more accurate information is much greater than in industrialized countries.

2

Trends and Patterns in
Female Labor Force Participation
1950-1985

1. Introduction

This chapter examines the broad patterns and trends in the women's labor supply during the last 20 to 30 years. We look at the size of the female labor force and then at the female participation rate.[1] We also compare these two indicators of female labor supply with the respective figures for men. In this way we standardize for possible differences in the statistical treatment of labor at the national level, and also for the fact that countries are at different developmental stages. The female participation rate is also examined with respect to its age distribution and its distribution by employment status (dependent employment versus self-employment and family work). The main findings are, first, that female participation rates have increased as such and also in comparison to male participation rates. Second, the increase has come from prime age women. The participation rates of younger and older women has declined over time. Third, in all but six countries in the region there has been a shift in the locus of female employment from the informal to the formal sector.

2. The Size and Growth of the Labor Force

Table 2.1 shows the size of the total labor force by sex in 35 Latin American countries sometime in the 1950s and 1980s. The figures refer to all those

---

[1]   The labor force participation rate is the ratio of the economically active population ("labor force") to the population as a whole ("population at risk"). For a discussion on the theoretical and statistical shortcomings of the labor force and participation rate see Bowers (1975); Standing (1981); Psacharopoulos and Tzannatos (1989).

engaged in an economic activity broadly defined, that is, they include the self-employed/employers/own-account workers, the wage/salaried employees, and family workers as well as those classified as unemployed; and to all age groups. The data are drawn from national population censuses.

Subject to the many caveats which apply to the theoretical classification of an activity as an economic one and to national differences in the statistical treatment of work and unemployment, two points can be made even at this level of aggregation.[2] First, in the late 1950s the male total labor force was about 54 million while the female labor force was only 14 million. This implies that for every four male workers there was only one working woman. Therefore, the initial representation of women in the labor force was, by all standards, low. The only region with lower representation of women in the labor force was (and still is) the Middle East.[3]

Second, by the early 1980s the size of the male labor force had increased by about 33 million. The corresponding increase for the female labor force was 20 million. There were, therefore, 87 million male workers and 33 million female workers by the 1980s. This implies that the majority of new jobs during the last 25 years have been taken by men. However, the smaller initial size of the female labor force means that there has been an impressive rate of employment growth among women: it rose by 140 percent compared with half that figure for men (60 percent). As a result, the number of working women for every five working men has now increased to almost two. This compares more favorably with the rest of the world where the ratio of the male to female labor force is about 5:3.[4]

---

[2]   It has been shown that even within the same advanced country the long run measurement of female labor supply can vary considerably due to differences in either the census definition of work (Joshi and Owen, 1984, on "how elastic labor supply can be") or the particular year and stage of the economic cycle to which the census observations relate (Joshi and Owen, 1985, on whether "elastic retracts"). Part of the problem relates to women's flow, real or statistical, between work and inactivity rather than between work and unemployment (Lundberg, 1985).

[3]   One of the factors responsible for the low female participation rates in the Middle East (which is, however, less applicable to Latin America) is the cultural environment which does not encourage women to work in the open labor market (Boserup, 1970; Kozel and Alderman, 1988).

[4]   Sivard (1985).

Table 2.1
Total Labor Force in Latin America
(selected years)

Country	Year	Early Period Male	Early Period Female	Year	Late Period Male	Late Period Female
Bahamas	1953	31862	20086	1980	48275	38777
Barbados	1960	54478	36591	1980	57834	45199
Belize	1960	22123	4883	1980	36585	10742
Bermuda	1960	12700	6744	1980	17232	14204
Cayman Islands	1960	2229	930	1979	4711	3408
Cuba	1953	1706477	353182	1981	2434069	1106623
Dominica	1960	13328	10081	1981	16698	8635
Dominican Rep.	1960	732220	88490	1981	1361109	554279
El Salvador	1961	663273	143819	1971	914324	252155
Grenada	1960	16392	10922	1970	17482	11200
Guadaloupe	1961	70029	44238	1982	71220	52668
Guyana	1960	134828	39902	1980	180084	59247
Guyane Fr.	1961	8309	3672	1982	20786	11589
Haiti	1950	890756	856431	1982	1257416	872245
Martinique	1961	56952	35392	1982	72207	58293
Nicaragua	1963	379305	95655	1971	395003	110442
Paraguay	1962	453520	132895	1982	834308	204950
Puerto Rico	1960	449840	144260	1970	471369	212421
Suriname	1964	61196	19003	1980	58091	22730
Trinidad/Tobago	1960	203732	74415	1980	266592	108121
Total		5963549	2121591		8535395	3757928

Countries studied in this volume

Country	Year	Male	Female	Year	Male	Female
Argentina	1960	5879054	1645415	1980	7278034	2755764
Bolivia	1950	779691	581536	1976	1164619	336772
Chile	1952	1616152	539141	1982	2720822	959455
Brazil	1960	18597163	4054100	1980	31392986	11842726
Costa Rica	1963	330879	64394	1984	626633	177560
Colombia	1951	3054420	701189	1985	6419607	3138261
Ecuador	1962	1207235	235356	1982	1861652	484411
Guatemala	1964	1196745	166924	1981	1449058	247406
Honduras	1961	494717	73271	1974	643056	119739
Jamaica	1960	401191	253391	1982	433312	275130
Mexico	1960	9296723	2035293	1980	15924806	6141278
Panama	1950	212248	52371	1980	394012	152840
Peru	1961	2445427	679152	1981	3978410	1335481
Uruguay	1963	759987	262280	1985	785944	390864
Venezuela	1961	1929421	421870	1981	3387892	1305876
Total		48201053	11765683		78460843	29663563
Grand Total		**54164602**	**13887274**		**86996238**	**33421491**

Source: National Population Censuses. See ILO (1990), Table 1.

In conclusion, the size of the female labor force in the 1980s was about two and a half times bigger than in the 1950s. The annualized rate of growth of the female labor force (2.97 percent) was almost double the corresponding rate for men (1.59 percent) during the aforesaid period. Women's labor supply appears, therefore, to have increased considerably both in absolute and relative (to men) terms in a short period of time.

3.   The Relative (Female to Male) Labor Force

An examination of the female relative (to male) labor force can standardize in part for the across country differences in the statistical treatment of labor in a number of ways. It can also take into account the different conventions in the definitions of employment. For example, a country which appears to have a small female labor force may also have a small male labor force, if certain activities are not considered to be economic ones.[5] In addition, expressing the female labor force in terms of the male labor force should eliminate some of the differences stemming from the countries' different socio-economic and demographic characteristics. These differences may refer to variations across country in education enrollments (which affect the labor supply of younger cohorts); the existence and provision of pensions and other aspects of social policy (which affect older groups); and the different demographic profiles of the countries (such as rural/urban residence and average age/life expectancy). These factors are important because employment behavior typically varies with location and age.

Table 2.2 ranks the countries in the region from those which had the highest ratio of female to male labor force to those with the lowest ratio in the 1950s and early 1960s, and examines the change in the ratio over time.[6] Some countries have information from 1950 well into the 1980s while in others information exists only between 1960 and around 1980. Thus, it is better to concentrate on the *annual* percentage rates of growth rather than on the changes

---

[5]   The implicit assumption here is that the total population in a country is shared roughly equally between the two sexes and the age distribution of the sexes is similar.

[6]   Bolivia is excluded from Table 2.2 because it had one of the highest female to male ratios in the 1950s (75 percent) and one of the lowest in the 1980s (29 percent). This decrease corresponds to an annual rate of change of -3.6 percent. This dramatic decline and the initially high value of female relative labor force suggests some irregularity in the statistics for which no explanation can be offered.

themselves.[7] There is some clear evidence of regression towards the mean: gains have been greater in countries where the ratio of female to male labor force was initially low. Among the four countries where the ratio decreased, three countries had the highest ratios in the earlier period (Haiti, Dominica, and Grenada) and only Paraguay was somewhere in the middle. Of the countries which experienced a high annual rate of increase, most are found toward the lower end in terms of the initial ratio of the female to male labor force.

The effects of the differential growth in female labor force on the regional profile of the sex composition of the labor force are summarized in Figure 2.1. The countries are ranked in descending order of the female to male ratio around the 1950s/early 1960s (as they appear in the first column of Table 2.2).[8]

Compared with the 1950s, when the female participation rate was below 25 percent in as many as 13 countries, there are now only two countries below the 20 percent mark (Honduras and Guatemala -- 19 and 17 percent respectively). In all other countries the female/male labor force ratio is now equal to, or higher than, 25 percent. Almost one-third of the countries have a ratio of 35 to 50 percent. In another one-third of the countries the ratio is more than 50 percent. In conclusion, the female gains in the labor force appear to have been significant and have been achieved over a period of only 20 to 30 years. The region has become more homogeneous with respect to the sex composition of the labor force.

4. The Labor Force Participation Rate: Broad Trends

Having examined the behavior of the female labor force in both absolute and relative (to men) terms, we now turn to the participation rate (the ratio of the labor force to the total population). We concentrate on the countries studied in this volume, which represent about 90 percent of the total labor force in the region. Table 2.3 shows participation rates for prime age workers (20-60 years), by gender (columns 1 and 2) and then in relative terms (female to male,

---

[7] For present purposes, the annual rate of growth is calculated as the nth root of the ratio of the latest to the earliest figure minus 1, where n is the number years which elapsed between the earliest and latest observation. This is more appropriate than taking the difference between the later and earlier figures and simply dividing the result by the difference in the number of years, which amounts to a simple linear pattern of growth.

[8] Three-country moving averages are used for the both periods in order to smooth the variation.

Table 2.2
Relative (F/M) Labor Force in Latin America and the Caribbean
(percent)

Country[a]	Early period (1950s/early 1960s)	Late period (1980s)	Annual change (%)
Haiti	96.15	69.37	-1.0
Dominica	75.64	51.71	-1.8
Barbados	67.17	78.15	8.0
Grenada	66.63	64.07	-4.0
Guadaloupe	63.17	73.95	0.8
Jamaica	63.16	63.49	0.0
Bahamas	63.04	66.66	0.2
Martinique	62.14	80.73	1.3
Bermuda	53.10	82.43	2.2
Guyane Fr.	44.19	55.75	1.1
Cayman Islands	41.72	72.34	2.9
Trin. & Tob.	36.53	40.56	0.5
Uruguay	34.51	49.73	1.7
Chile	33.36	35.26	0.2
Puerto Rico	32.07	45.06	3.5
Suriname	31.05	39.13	1.5
Guyana	29.59	32.90	0.5
Paraguay	29.30	24.57	-0.9
Argentina	27.99	37.86	1.5
Peru	27.77	33.57	1.0
Nicaragua	25.22	27.96	1.3
Panama	24.67	38.79	1.5
Colombia	22.96	48.89	2.3
Belize	22.07	29.36	1.4
Mexico	21.89	38.56	2.9
Venezuela	21.87	38.55	2.9
Brazil	21.80	37.72	2.8
El Salvador	21.68	27.58	2.4
Cuba	20.70	45.46	2.9
Ecuador	19.50	26.02	1.5
Costa Rica	19.46	28.34	1.8
Honduras	14.81	18.62	1.9
Guatemala	13.95	17.07	1.2
Dominican Rep.	12.09	40.72	6.0

a.   Countries ranked in descending order of relative (F/M) labor force in early period.

Source: Table 2.1

Figure 2.1

F/M Labor Force in Latin American and Caribbean Countries

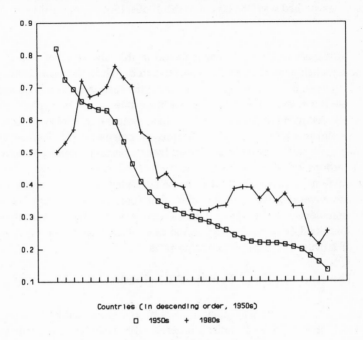

Countries (in descending order, 1950s)

□ 1950s   +   1980s

Source: Table 2.2

column 3). Column 4 shows the annualized rate of growth of the female relative participation rate. The data show that in the early period only two countries had a female participation rate greater than 30 percent (32 percent in Uruguay and 53 percent in Jamaica). In five other countries the female participation rate was between 20 and 30 percent, while in the remaining countries the rate was below 20 percent. In contrast, by the 1980s in only one country the female participation rate was below 25 percent (15 percent in Guatemala).[9] In the 1980s, the female labor force participation rate was 26 percent in Costa Rica, 29 percent in Peru and 30 percent in Chile. In most of the other countries the female participation rate had risen to between 30 and 35 percent. In Colombia, Uruguay, and Jamaica, however, it was 39, 46, and 48 percent respectively.

---

[9]   Excluding Honduras where the data refer to all ages (not prime age only); hence, the participation rates for both sexes are low and not comparable to the other countries.

Thus, the recent figures represent significant gains for the ratio of workers in the female population. The unweighted average of female participation rates in the countries studied was 24 percent in the 1950s/1960s compared to 33 percent in the 1980s.[10]

The improvement in women's participation in the labor market is even more convincing when compared to male participation. While the male participation rate has declined in all countries without exception between the two periods, the female rate has risen.[11] The decline in the male rate cannot be explained by the assumption that men remain in the educational system longer than women, since younger cohorts are excluded from the present comparison.[12] Neither can the decline in male participation be explained by arguments pertaining to retirement as only groups of workers below the age of 60 are examined. Thus, the increase in female participation rates can be attributed to factors that are separate from those governing the growth of the labor force as such during the process of economic development. The relative improvement in female participation is further discussed (and confirmed) in the next section with respect to the age profile of female and male participation rates.

5.   The Age Profile of Female Participation

Figure 2.2 shows female participation rates by age group and by country in the 1950s and 1980s (in alphabetical order). To facilitate comparisons, the participation (vertical) axis has been standardized and is measured from 0 percent to 60 percent. However, the age groups on the horizontal axis have been constructed *ad hoc* in order to enable *within* country comparisons between earlier and later periods. Consequently, some of the *between* country variations in age profiles may not necessarily reflect actual differences.

---

[10]   Excluding Honduras for both dates where the female participation rate refers to all ages, not prime age workers.

[11]   The only exception is Bolivia. ILO data suggest that the female labor force participation rate was 62 percent in 1950 -- the highest in the region, even higher than in Jamaica. By 1976 the same data indicate that the rate had dropped to 23 percent -- in effect the lowest in the region except Honduras where the participation rate for women aged 20 to 60 years was 18 percent. The levels of and magnitude of change in female participation rates in Bolivia suggest some irregularity.

[12]   In any case, the scholarity ratio of those aged 18 to 22 years is low and university enrollment accounts for a very small fraction of the total enrollment in education.

Table 2.3
Participation Rates for Prime Age Groups

| Country (Age Group) | Year | Participation rate (%) | | | Annual percentage change of F/M |
| | | Male | Female | F/M | |
		(1)	(2)	(3)	(4)
Argentina (20-60)	1960	92.8	24.4	26.3	
	1980	90.8	33.1	36.5	1.6
Bolivia (20-64)	1976	94.1	23.1	24.6	–
Brazil (20-60)	1960	95.0	18.2	19.1	
	1980	92.4	33.0	35.7	3.2
Chile (20-60)	1952	94.5	28.6	30.6	
	1982	87.2	28.9	33.8	0.3
Colombia (25-60)	1951	97.4	19.0	19.5	
	1985	85.4	39.4	46.1	2.6
Costa Rica (20-60)	1963	97.0	18.6	19.1	
	1984	89.7	26.4	29.4	2.1
Ecuador (20-60)	1962	97.8	17.7	18.0	
	1982	87.7	22.6	25.3	1.7
Jamaica (20-64)	1962	95.9	52.7	55.0	
	1982	78.4	48.2	61.5	0.6
Guatemala (20-60)	1964	96.2	13.1	13.5	
	1981	91.3	14.7	16.5	1.2
Honduras (all ages)	1961	52.7	7.7	14.7	
	1974	48.8	8.9	18.3	1.7
Mexico (20-60)	1960	96.5	19.1	19.8	
	1980	92.4	32.7	35.4	2.9
Panama (20-60)	1950	97.0	24.9	25.2	
	1980	87.3	35.7	40.9	1.6
Peru (20-60)	1961	96.8	22.7	23.3	
	1981	91.3	29.0	31.3	1.5
Uruguay (20-60)	1963	93.0	32.0	34.4	
	1985	92.4	46.0	49.8	1.7
Venezuela (20-60)	1961	96.4	22.1	23.0	
	1981	89.0	35.0	39.3	2.7

-- not available.
Source: Constructed from ILO (1990), Table 1.

Figure 2.2
Female Labor Participation Rate by Age

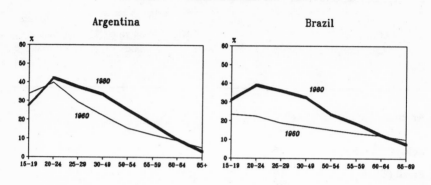

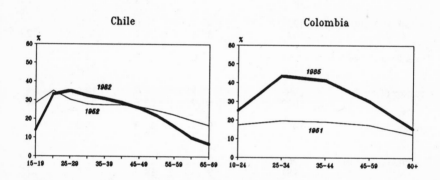

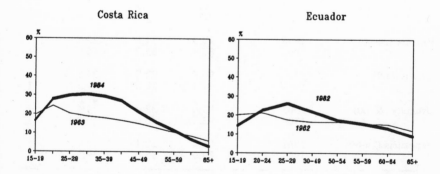

Figure 2.2 (cont)
Female Labor Force Participation Rate by Age

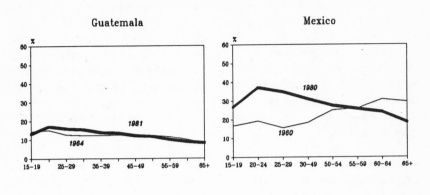

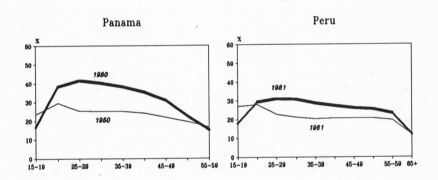

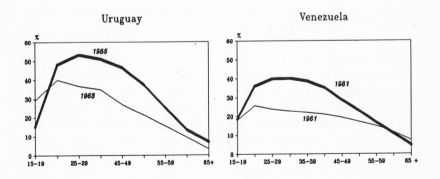

Source: ILO (1990), Table 1.

The age participation profile for prime age women in the second period is clearly above that for the first period.   However, in most countries the participation rates of younger women (below the age of 20) are lower in the second period than the first period.   The exceptions to this are Brazil, Colombia and Mexico.   The decrease in the participation rate of younger women may reflect the increase in female school enrollment.   The participation rates of older women (above the ages of 55 to 60 years) have also declined in all countries in the later period -- except in Colombia and Uruguay.   An explanation for the decline in the participation rates of older women can be sought in the provision of pensions and the presence of other income effects which are associated with economic growth.[13]

A second observation based on the age profile of female labor force participants is that an increasing percentage of women enter employment until their mid- and late-twenties but then drop out of the labor force (Mexico is an exception but only in the early period).   This pattern can be attributed to childbearing by women when they are relatively young.   The data are cross-sectional, rather than longitudinal and evidence from longitudinal data in industrialized countries suggests that the cohort profiles do not dip as sharply as the corresponding profiles derived from cross-section data.   The reason for the different pictures provided by cross-sectional and longitudinal data is that younger women are more work oriented than older women.   Nevertheless, one can still argue that the cross-sectional variation of the age profile of female participation suggests that reentry of women into the labor force after family formation takes place is not typical in Latin America.   In no country in our sample is there a "double peak" in the age participation profile. These observations hold for both the earlier and more recent periods under consideration.   It should also be mentioned that the dipping of the age participation profile after the mid-twenties or -thirties appears to be more severe in the later than earlier period. This decline is not confined to older age groups (such as those above the age of 50) who may have been affected by the increasing provision of social welfare or availability of pensions in the more recent period.

The decline in participation rates at the time of family formation has important welfare implications: past workers have already acquired human capital which is wasted if women do not reenter the labor market.   The effects become even greater when one takes into account the fact that the number of women in the labor market increases over time (hence, the percentage of the *total* labor force which is potentially underutilized/wasted is greater).   Finally, one should not

---

[13]   This argument is consistent with the experience of industrialized countries (see Mincer, 1962; Cain, 1966; Hornstein *et al.*, 1982).

forget that the empirical evidence conclusively suggests considerable downward occupational mobility for women rejoining the labor market after an absence for childbearing.[14]

An examination of the relative (female to male) age specific participation rate can shed some additional light on women's inroads into the labor force in recent years. What Figure 2.3 suggests is that, in practically all countries, the recent relative (female to male) age participation profiles are above the older ones. This finding suggests that the improvement of female participation relative to male participation has come from all age groups.

6. Comparisons With Other World Regions

In this section we focus on differences in the level and age distribution of the female participation rate between Latin America and other world regions. These differences can be assessed with reference to Figure 2.4. The data relate to the early-1980s.[15]

The rate of female labor force participation in Latin America is the second lowest among world regions. The region with the lowest female labor force participation rate is the Middle East. The regions with the highest female participation rates (in descending order) are the industrial market economies followed by the Southern European countries and the Sub-Saharan countries.[16]

---

[14] Martin and Roberts (1984). Of course, part of the downward occupational mobility may be due to supply factors such as women's willingness to combine family life with "some kind" of work. This complication is examined further in Chapter 5. The prevalent opinion is that women are usually overqualified compared to men in the same job (Frank, 1978) and that wage discrimination often takes the form of occupational segregation (Lloyd and Niemi, 1979; Reskin, 1984).

[15] For a more complete description of the data see Psacharopoulos and Tzannatos (1991).

[16] For the regional classification of countries see World Bank (1983) *World Tables, Volume II, Social Data,* 3rd edition, Johns Hopkins University Press, Baltimore, pp. xix-xx.

Figure 2.3
Female/Male Labor Force Participation Rate by Age

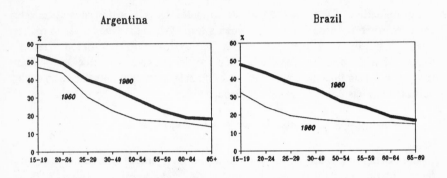

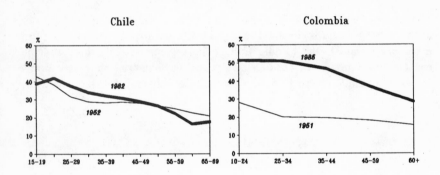

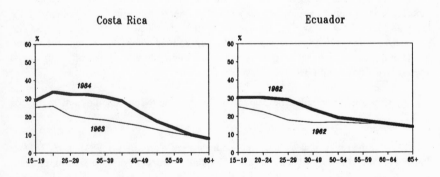

Figure 2.3 (cont.)
Female/Male Labor Force participation Rate by Age

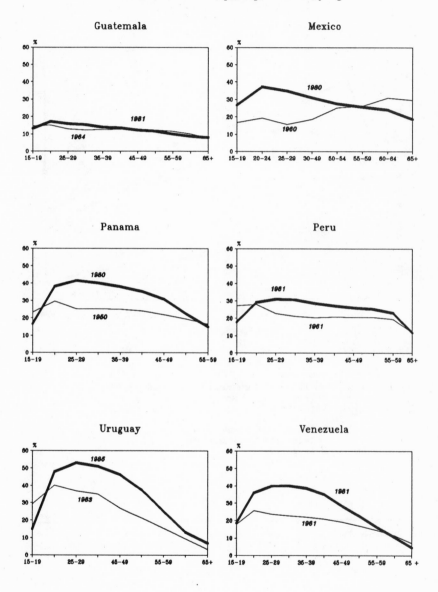

Figure 2.4
Female Participation Rate by World Region and Age Groups

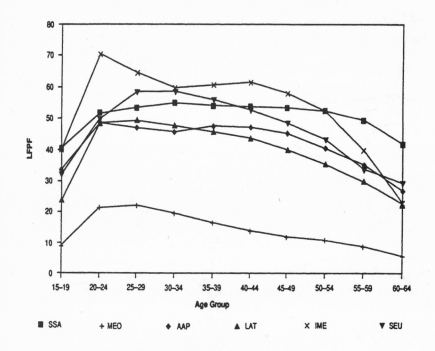

Mean Female Labor Force Participation by Age and Region, 1980s.
        SSA = Sub-Saharan Africa
        MEO = Middle East, North Africa and Oil Exporters
        AAP = Asia and Pacific
        LAT = Latin America and Caribbean
        IME = Industrial Market Economies
        SEU = Southern Europe

Source: Appendix Table A2-1.

The age profile of female participation rate suggests that in general female participation in most world regions dips after the age of early- to mid-twenties.[17] However, the decline in female participation after the family cycle has started is not uniform across regions. Industrial market economies, and Asian and Pacific countries experience only a mild decline in female participation at older ages. The age participation profile exhibits a noticeable decline at older ages in the remaining three regions (Southern Europe, Latin America, and the Middle East). With respect to Latin America the decline in female participation at successively older age groups is rather dramatic: the rate drops from approximately 50 percent at the age of 20 to approximately 30 percent at the age of mid-to-upper 50s.

The reasons for the regional differences in female labor force participation are many and complex. However, two explanations can be singled out. One explanation relates to changes in the sectoral pattern of production and employment during economic development. More specifically a subsistence economy makes heavy use of female labor as agricultural and related activities are mostly household based. During economic development the primary sector loses its importance and the structure of production moves at first toward manufacturing and then toward services. When industrialization is under way, it is usually the case that employment growth in the manufacturing sector is not fast enough to absorb the workers released from agriculture. The net result of the relatively fast contraction of agriculture and slow expansion of industry and services is a reduction in opportunities for female employment. In addition, the labor force status of a typical woman is either "employed" or "inactive" in contrast to men who are in most cases classified as either "employed" or "unemployed." This economic/statistical argument (called the U-hypothesis about the pattern of female participation during economic development) is consistent with the data presented in Table 2.4. The group of middle-income countries has lower female participation rates than the group of low-income countries and high-income countries. This observation is true for all age groups. As most Latin American countries can be classified as middle-income, the U-hypothesis may have some relevance to the observed patterns of female participation in the region.

Second, female participation is more dependent on non-economic factors than male participation. Male participation rates are rather uniform across countries and over time. The male labor force participation rate is around 90 percent in Latin America (see Table 2.3). Similar rates of male participation in the labor

---

[17]   The exception is Sub-Saharan Africa where the female participation rate is quite constant across most part of the age distribution.

Table 2.4
Female Participation Rate by Age Group and Country's per Capita Income
Early 1980s
(percent)

Country Type	15-19	20-24	25-29	30-34	35-39	40-44	45-49	50-54	55-59	60-64
Low Income	40	48	50	50	51	50	49	47	44	38
Middle Income	24	42	42	41	40	38	36	33	27	21
High Income	39	70	65	61	63	64	60	55	41	24

Source: Constructed from ILO *Yearbook of Labor Statistics*, 1985, Geneva, and World
Bank *World Tables: Volume II, Social Data*, 1983, Johns Hopkins University
Press, Baltimore.

Table 2.5
Female Labor Force Participation Rate and Religion
Early 1980s
(percent)

Country's Dominant Religion	Mean Female Participation
Islam	23
Roman Catholicism	33
Hinduism	42
Buddhism	48
Confucianism	48
Christianity (other than Roman Catholicism)	49
No major religion	58

Note: A country is classified under a given religion if 30 percent or more
of the population follows that religion.

Source: Based on Psacharopoulos and Tzannatos 1987, Table A-2.

force are observed in other world regions and countries.[18] Thus one can argue that male participation is relatively independent of demographic, social, cultural and other factors. In contrast, female participation appears to bear a rather clear relationship to some non-economic factors. Reference has already been made to the low female participation rates in the Middle East where the cultural environment is not conducive to women's work in the open labor market. Table 2.5 uses religion as a discriminating variable in the sense that many social norms derive directly from the religious basis of the country concerned. The data suggest that the link between custom and female work may be more real than apparent. Muslim and Roman Catholic countries have the lowest female participation rates while countries with no major religion (mostly socialist countries at the time when the data were drawn) have the highest female participation rates. Though there exist religious minority groups in some Latin American countries, the region can be safely classified as predominantly Roman Catholic. This may be another explanation for the observed low female participation rates in the region.

In conclusion, it seems that some common economic and non-economic explanations are relevant to the observed female labor force participation rates in Latin America.

7. The Employment Status of Working Women

We finally examine the changes in the employment status of women (dependent employment, self-employment, and family work) and compare it with the experience in other world regions. We differentiate principally between dependent employment (i.e. wage and salaried workers) and self-employment/ family work. This distinction is more important for women than men for three reasons. First, as will be shown later, the share of employees in the labor force is greater for women than men. Second, wage/salaried employment becomes increasingly more important for women during the process of economic development. And third, dependent employment is more directly influenced by public policy than self-employment and work within a family context.

In practically all world regions, the percentage of employees in the labor force is greater for women than men (though this statement is not necessarily correct for individual countries). The unweighted average of the share of employees in Latin America and the Caribbean was 57.9 percent for men and 68.5 percent for women in the 1980s. The share of employees in the male labor force exceeds

---

[18]   Standing (1981).

the share of employees in the female labor force in only three countries (El Salvador, Guyana and Peru) of the 21 countries for which data exist.

An interesting question is whether women in wage/salaried employment increased as a fraction of the female labor force in Latin America. It is possible that the large increase in female participation rates during the past three decades reflects increases in the number of self-employed and/or family workers as the importance of the informal sector might have increased because of the recession. In addition, it is possible that the growth of women's employment in the formal sector in Latin America might have been restricted more by labor market regulations than in other developing regions (such as Africa or South-East Asia). For example, the observation has been made that, although the fraction of wage earners has increased on average across the world since the 1950s, it fell in a number of countries "*many* of which are in Latin America" possibly as a result of "pervasive minimum wage legislation and general labor market regulations."[19] This is an important observation in terms of public policy formulation and can be examined against the available evidence. Table 2.6 presents the ratio of female wage earners in the labor force in 77 countries grouped in six world regions for two periods (typically sometime in the late 1950s and early 1980s).

Among the regional groups examined, only the countries in Eastern Europe and East Asia experienced a consistent increase in the share of wage/salaried workers in the female labor force. In the industrialized world and African countries there has been a decline in only one or two cases. In contrast, Latin America and South and West Asia each have six countries with negative growth. The six Latin American countries which experienced a decline in the share of female employees in the labor force are El Salvador, Mexico, Chile, Ecuador, Paraguay and Peru. However, a number of qualifications apply. First, Latin America is represented by 21 countries and the South and West Asia group by only 13. Even so, the latter group is artificially large as it includes Cyprus and Israel.[20] As the Latin American sample is more numerous than the South and West Asia group, the *number* of countries showing negative growth in the share of female wage/salaried workers in the labor force may not be as important as it originally appeared. In any case, among the 14 Latin America and Caribbean countries where the share of employees in the female labor force rose over time,

---

[19] Emphasis added; Schultz (1990).

[20] Israel has more in common with, and should be included in, the western group rather than with Nepal or Sri Lanka. Also, if Greece is included in the industrialized group, Cyprus should be. However, the original grouping is maintained to make the present analysis comparable with Schultz's (1990) study.

the increase exceeded five percentage points in more than half (Brazil, Bolivia, Panama, Nicaragua, Guatemala, Costa Rica, Puerto Rico and Haiti). As a result the share of employees in the female labor force has risen to 68.5 percent in the 1980s from 66.5 percent in the 1950s/1960s.

Second, what matters is not only the number of countries which experienced a decline in the share of employees in the labor force, but also the magnitude of the decline. The annualized percentage rate of decline has been less than 1 percent in two of the six Latin American countries, namely Ecuador and Chile. The rate of decline in the other four countries (El Salvador, Mexico, Paraguay and Peru) did not exceed 1.4 percent per annum. In contrast, the decline in countries in other regions was substantially higher. For example, among the South and West Asia countries the rate of decline was more than 1 percent per annum in practically all cases and was sometimes as high as 3.5 percent per annum.

Third, Latin America started from a "high" base compared to other countries which had initially low shares of female employees in the labor force. In the predominantly Muslim countries and South Korea the share was around 16 percent in the early 1950s while in Thailand it was as low as 2 percent. In terms of unweighted averages, the early figure for Latin America was almost 67 percent compared to 55 percent or less in the other developing regions (and as low as 38 percent in South and West Asia).

The decline observed in a few Latin American countries has been, in quantitative terms, relatively unimportant and could easily be due to cyclical effects. The continuing importance of wage/salaried employment for women in the Latin America and Caribbean region is substantiated further by the evidence examined in the next chapter. In addition, some recent research does not support the view that Latin American labor markets are more inflexible than elsewhere.

For example, some authors have argued that there is more flexibility in hours of employment and wages in the labor markets of Latin America than is the case for many other developing economies.[21]

In conclusion, from a female employment perspective there does not seem to have been a decrease in the importance of the wage/salaried sector in the region during the last three decades or so. The argument that labor market regulation has been responsible for the relative decline (or slow growth) of the share of employees in the female labor force needs to be further substantiated.

---

[21]   Behrman and Wolfe (1984, p. 264).

Table 2.6
Ratio of Employees in the Female Labor Force by World Region

Region/Country	Year	Ratio	Year	Ratio
Eastern Europe				
Bulgaria	1965	0.98	1975	1.00
Czechoslovakia	1961	0.94	1970	0.99
Hungary	1963	0.81	1980	0.94
Poland	1960	0.41	1970	0.56
West				
Japan	1955	0.33	1980	0.64
Australia	1954	0.89	1981	0.88
New Zealand	1951	0.91	1981	0.92
Canada	1951	0.92	1981	0.96
United States	1960	0.92	1980	0.96
Denmark	1960	0.86	1981	0.91
Finland	1960	0.65	1980	0.87
Iceland	1950	0.73	1960	0.85
Ireland	1951	0.71	1981	0.92
Norway	1960	0.91	1980	0.92
Sweden	1960	0.91	1980	0.95
United Kingdom	1966	0.94	1971	0.96
Greece	1951	0.49	1981	0.56
Italy	1961	0.69	1981	0.80
Malta	1957	0.60	1981	0.88
Portugal	1960	0.87	1981	0.79
Spain	1966	0.56	1970	0.79
Austria	1951	0.54	1981	0.85
Belgium	1961	0.71	1980	0.83
France	1954	0.59	1975	0.83
West Germany	1959	0.70	1980	0.85
Luxembourg	1966	0.65	1970	0.79
Netherlands	1960	0.84	1981	0.88
Switzerland	1950	0.87	1980	0.96
Africa				
Mauritius	1962	0.91	1972	0.89
Reunion	1961	0.82	1982	0.93
Cameroon	1976	0.03	1982	0.03
Algeria	1966	0.74	1977	0.96
Egypt	1960	0.59	1976	0.83
Libya	1960	0.36	1973	0.58
Tunisia	1956	0.06	1975	0.43
Botswana	1964	0.04	1981	0.35

Continued -

Table 2.6 (Cont.)
Ratio of Employees in the Female Labor Force by World Region

Region/Country	Year	Ratio	Year	Ratio
Latin America				
Cuba	1953	0.88	1970	0.99
Dominican Rep.	1960	0.72	1981	0.76
Haiti	1950	0.10	1982	0.20
Martinique	1961	0.82	1967	0.84
Puerto Rico	1961	0.83	1980	0.93
Costa Rica	1963	0.88	1973	0.93
El Salvador	1961	0.72	1980	0.55
Guatemala	1973	0.67	1981	0.72
Honduras	1974	0.64	1977	0.65
Mexico	1960	0.80	1977	0.66
Nicaragua	1963	0.61	1971	0.69
Panama	1960	0.78	1980	0.89
Chile	1960	0.78	1982	0.66
Uruguay	1963	0.77	1975	0.78
Bolivia	1950	0.16	1976	0.41
Brazil	1960	0.51	1980	0.76
Ecuador	1950	0.85	1982	0.64
Guyana	1946	0.66	1965	0.67
Paraguay	1972	0.52	1982	0.46
Peru	1961	0.51	1981	0.41
Venezuela	1961	0.75	1981	0.78
East Asia				
Hong Kong	1958	0.62	1981	0.93
South Korea	1960	0.16	1980	0.37
Indonesia	1965	0.29	1978	0.36
Philippines	1960	0.35	1978	0.41
Singapore	1957	0.74	1980	0.90
Thailand	1954	0.02	1980	0.17
South and West Asia				
Bangladesh	1961	0.30	1974	0.19
India	1961	0.26	1971	0.53
Iran	1956	0.58	1976	0.47
Nepal	1961	0.10	1976	0.07
Pakistan	1951	0.15	1981	0.38
Sri Lanka	1963	0.84	1981	0.79
Bahrain'	1971	0.96	1981	0.99
Kuwait	1965	0.97	1980	1.00
Syrian Arab Republic	1960	0.53	1970	0.40
United Arab Emirates	1975	0.97	1980	0.99
Cyprus	1976	0.59	1982	0.61
Israel	1972	0.84	1976	0.81
Turkey	1975	0.09	1980	0.14

Source: Schultz (1990).

8.   Discussion and Conclusions

The increase in female labor supply has been well documented in this chapter with the use of a variety of indicators (size of the female labor force and its relation to the male labor force, the female participation rate and its comparison to the male rate).   Official statistics in Latin America suggest that the contribution of women to employment in the past was, in general terms, low: only one in four prime age women was found in the labor force thirty years ago. However, the latest censuses indicate that this is no longer the case. By the 1980s almost one in three prime age women were in the labor force. Countries with lower female participation rates in the 1950s have experienced higher rates of growth and the region has become more homogeneous with respect to the gender composition of the labor force.

The improvement in female participation is even more convincing when examined in relative (to men) terms. The annual increase in the female relative (to male) participation rate has been approximately one to two percent with the exceptions of Jamaica, which had originally the highest female labor force participation rate, and Bolivia, for which a statistical irregularity is suspected. The increase in the relative size of female employment is impressive, given that most Latin American countries experienced economic difficulties during the period under consideration. In fact, in some of the countries, per capita income has been declining over the last 25 years. The rise in female participation appears to be at present a general trend determined more by the developmental stage of a country than the country's cyclical/transitory characteristics as such.

Equally noticeable is the fact that employees, as a group, have increased their share in the region's total labor force, although this increase has been neither universal nor uniform across countries. The importance of the formal sector for women's employment was somewhat unexpected given the (real or apparent) high level of government intervention in the labor markets of these countries, and the adverse economic conditions that have prevailed in the region since the mid-1970s.   Equally, one could argue that the rise in the importance of dependent employment for women has been the result of expansionary government policies. The government sector is typically more female dominated in terms of employment than the private sector -- if only in the areas of education, health, and social services, where jobs are predominantly filled by women as teachers, nurses and junior non-manual workers. If it were clear that the absolute and relative rise in women's employment was the outcome of uninhibited market forces, rather than the result of the potentially distortionary employment growth in the public sector and government regulation, these changes should be welcome from an efficiency point of view. However, what one observes can easily be the *net* effect of expansionary government policies with *contractionary* effects upon the private sector. The historical data used in this study do not allow us to establish whether the government sector has been responsible for the rise in female participation. One should also not forget that Latin America started with low levels of women's labor force participation in the late 1950s/early 1960s. Hence, future gains may be more difficult to achieve than in the past 20 to 30 years. Further country specific research needs be undertaken which can look, on the one hand, at the institutional framework within which labor is priced and allocated and, on the other hand, at the effects of employment growth in the government sector. The findings of such a study would definitely yield rewarding findings for guiding public policy formulation.

Given the present state of information, future policies can move in two directions. First, an attempt can be made to create an environment which could be conducive to further increases in women's participation, should the present female participation rates reflect some kind of inefficiency (such as employment and/or pay discrimination against women). It should be remembered that, despite recent gains, women's participation continues to be low. There would be two kinds of benefits associated with an increase in female participation. First, as the incidence of poverty falls disproportionately upon women (and children), an increase in female employment will mean additional monetary income for certain types of households as well as a more continuous employment record and increased labor market experience for women. The latter can in turn increase female earnings in the future. In terms of efficiency, women as a factor of production will be utilized more fully than at present. Consequently, economic growth can be faster.

Second, given the significant decline in female participation rates during childbearing and women's failure to reenter the labor market after this interruption, policies contributing to the current age participation profile can be reassessed. Candidate policies for abolition are those which place women on a different footing than men in either the family or the market. This includes overt or hidden arrangements governing the determination of female pay on the assumption that women are "supplementary" workers in a conventional family context (whereas female headed households are quite common in Latin America); and the unjustified exclusion or restriction of women from certain types of employment, in certain areas, or at certain times. Protective legislation in the labor market, if justified, should not revert to prohibiting norms. Neither should legislation induce an asymmetry in the treatment of individuals within the family, especially with respect to benefit and taxation matters.

Statistical Appendix to Chapter 2

The tables in this Appendix present "age-specific" labor force participation rates and the "all ages" labor force participation rates. Age-specific labor force participation rates are calculated as the ratio of the labor force in an age group to population in the same group. The all-ages labor force participation rates are calculated as the ratio of the total labor force to the total population.

Appendix Table A2.1

Age-Specific Female Labor Participation Rates by Region and by Country

(early 1980s)

Sub-Sahara Africa	Year	15-19	20-24	25-29	30-34	35-39	40-44	45-49	50-54	55-59	60-64	all ages
Botswana	85	42.0	74.7	76.9	76.9	73.5	73.5	69.5	69.5	60.5	60.5	36.0
Chad	80	22.0	28.1	28.0	28.0	28.0	28.0	25.2	25.6	25.6	13.1	16.4
Comoros	80	21.8	26.2	28.2	29.4	30.3	31.5	30.7	31.2	28.9	27.2	15.6
Ethiopia	84	57.9	61.0	63.7	65.5	62.9	60.8	56.8	50.1	41.2	33.8	34.3
Gambia	83	61.9	68.3	71.1	73.9	74.6	77.2	75.3	76.2	72.4	71.5	43.6
Guinea-Bissau	79	2.2	4.0	3.2	2.7	2.3	2.3	2.3	1.8	2.2	1.7	2.6
Madagascar	75	58.2	69.3	78.1	78.4	79.0	79.4	82.5	82.9	76.7	76.7	44.8
Malawi	83	78.0	85.6	90.1	88.3	91.6	90.0	90.5	89.4	89.8	84.3	51.7
Mauritius	84	24.3	38.7	32.3	32.3	32.9	32.9	29.7	29.7	16.1	16.1	19.4
Mozambique	80	68.9	87.6	91.4	91.4	91.4	92.7	92.7	92.7	92.7	82.0	—
Niger	77	6.3	6.5	6.5	7.1	8.0	9.1	10.2	10.1	10.4	8.0	4.4
Nigeria	83	13.6	24.6	37.2	40.3	47.8	49.3	55.4	57.1	78.3	43.6	20.6
Reunion	82	25.9	56.7	50.3	46.9	43.7	40.4	37.0	32.4	25.9	11.9	23.6
Rwanda	78	88.2	96.1	97.1	97.4	98.0	98.0	97.2	95.3	90.9	81.7	55.6
Sao Tome & Principe	81	23.2	46.4	48.9	48.9	48.6	48.7	44.0	42.7	30.8	24.1	20.4
Senegal	85	54.0	54.9	61.4	98.1	67.7	56.7	73.5	72.3	68.0	58.8	39.1
Seychelles	85	60.0	84.2	82.9	69.6	70.0	62.2	46.2	37.2	26.9	7.0	35.9
Sudan	73	16.1	18.5	20.3	21.4	24.1	27.0	28.1	28.8	27.4	26.4	11.9
Tanzania	78	53.4	86.0	90.3	93.1	94.2	94.9	94.9	93.0	90.8	84.0	45.2
Zambia	84	44.9	29.8	24.0	24.1	24.1	24.1	34.4	42.3	37.6	37.6	17.4
Zimbabwe	82	46.8	50.9	48.5	50.2	51.3	52.6	52.4	50.6	50.7	31.7	25.4
Mean		41.4	52.3	53.8	55.4	54.5	53.9	53.7	52.9	49.7	42.0	26.9
Variance		559.9	757.6	823.6	885.7	797.8	774.4	777.4	767.1	831.5	801.1	250.7
Standard Deviation		23.7	27.5	28.7	29.8	28.2	27.8	27.9	27.7	28.8	28.3	15.8

— not available.

Continued

Appendix Table A2.1 (cont.)

Age-Specific Female Labor Participation Rates by Region and by Country

(early 1980s)

Middle East & North Africa	Year	15-19	20-24	25-29	30-34	35-39	40-44	45-49	50-54	55-59	60-64	all ages
Algeria	82	1.4	9.7	9.7	4.6	4.6	4.6	4.6	4.6	4.6	1.8	2.9
Bahrain	85	7.3	35.0	30.0	27.0	16.0	8.0	5.0	4.0	3.0	2.0	10.0
Brunei	81	17.0	47.1	43.4	36.7	32.9	28.6	22.7	20.5	14.5	10.4	18.7
Egypt	83	12.6	21.9	20.6	19.9	19.9	13.7	13.7	13.7	13.7	5.9	12.5
Iran	82	8.8	19.6	18.8	14.8	10.9	7.5	4.9	4.0	3.5	3.0	7.2
Iraq	77	10.9	15.5	19.0	20.8	19.2	19.3	18.6	18.3	16.5	13.0	9.4
Jordan	79	3.4	15.7	13.5	8.7	5.2	3.3	2.4	2.0	1.8	1.1	3.3
Kuwait	80	5.0	21.4	29.9	27.4	23.9	24.1	21.8	18.9	13.2	7.6	10.9
Morocco	82	19.0	20.4	20.9	17.7	16.2	14.7	14.1	14.6	14.6	11.2	11.6
Syria	83	9.5	13.5	13.9	10.4	11.3	9.0	7.7	6.9	4.5	2.6	5.6
United Arab Emirates	80	4.5	14.6	21.9	24.7	19.4	18.3	13.2	9.5	5.9	3.4	8.8
Mean		9.0	21.3	22.0	19.3	16.3	13.7	11.7	10.6	8.7	5.6	9.2
Variance		28.1	105.7	81.4	80.9	61.7	60.7	47.9	42.2	29.5	16.5	18.4
Standard Deviation		5.3	10.3	9.0	9.0	7.9	7.8	6.9	6.5	5.4	4.1	4.3

Continued

Appendix Table A2.1 (cont.)
Age-Specific Female Labor Participation Rates by Region and by Country
(early 1980s)

Asia and Pacific	Year	15-19	20-24	25-29	30-34	35-39	40-44	45-49	50-54	55-59	60-64	all ages
American Samoa	80	8.6	40.1	46.0	48.8	50.0	50.0	40.4	40.4	23.7	20.2	21.0
Bangladesh	84	7.0	8.7	7.7	8.6	9.4	8.1	8.4	8.7	7.1	4.4	5.4
China	82	77.8	90.3	88.8	88.8	88.5	83.3	70.6	50.9	32.9	16.9	46.4
Fiji	82	22.8	22.8	22.9	22.9	22.9	22.9	17.0	17.0	17.0	17.0	13.3
Hong Kong	85	35.3	83.2	68.8	52.7	52.2	54.2	51.8	41.6	30.8	24.8	37.4
India	81	26.5	29.2	32.1	34.7	36.4	36.0	36.0	29.8	29.8	14.0	19.8
Indonesia	80	31.1	33.2	36.1	38.5	42.3	45.1	46.2	44.7	40.1	32.0	23.2
Korea, Republic of	85	18.6	49.1	35.9	43.2	55.8	60.0	61.8	55.9	50.7	38.0	29.3
Malaysia	80	33.9	52.6	43.9	40.7	43.0	44.1	42.2	37.6	32.5	26.7	25.3
Maldives	77	52.2	62.1	64.7	64.8	70.7	71.9	73.3	68.1	61.5	52.3	--
Nepal	81	51.3	47.6	44.9	43.3	44.1	44.7	44.9	44.7	43.3	39.9	--
Pakistan	85	10.9	11.6	13.2	12.3	12.5	14.0	12.3	10.4	9.2	7.2	7.2
Philippines	85	31.4	47.6	53.4	53.4	60.0	60.0	58.9	58.9	49.1	49.1	--
Singapore	85	33.8	78.9	66.5	48.8	44.7	39.6	36.3	25.9	18.4	11.9	34.3
Sri Lanka	81	19.0	36.8	36.5	33.9	32.1	28.7	25.6	19.8	13.3	7.6	--
Thailand	82	72.4	81.7	87.2	88.7	90.1	88.9	88.9	79.0	79.0	31.7	50.6
Vanuatu	79	64.9	80.1	79.8	81.3	84.3	83.3	85.7	85.8	86.1	82.4	42.5
Western Samoa	81	6.0	26.1	21.7	20.8	18.2	16.2	13.8	11.5	9.3	4.0	8.3
Mean		33.5	49.0	47.2	45.9	47.6	47.3	45.2	40.6	35.2	26.7	20.2
Variance		462.6	616.5	563.6	524.8	567.2	559.3	571.7	505.1	508.2	388.3	273.9
Standard Deviation		21.5	24.8	23.7	22.9	23.8	23.7	23.9	22.5	22.5	19.7	16.6

-- not available.

Continued

Appendix Table A2.1(cont.)
Age-Specific Female Labor Participation Rates by Region and by Country
(early 1980s)

Latin America & Caribbean	Year	15-19	20-24	25-29	30-34	35-39	40-44	45-49	50-54	55-59	60-64	all ages
Argentina	85	24.6	46.7	41.3	37.9	35.7	34.1	30.9	26.1	18.0	9.9	19.9
Bahamas	80	34.5	72.3	75.0	72.3	72.4	68.2	63.5	59.5	49.4	37.8	36.0
Barbados	83	34.7	79.5	83.0	77.5	76.5	72.2	73.1	58.2	45.1	29.2	39.7
Belize	80	42.1	34.4	28.7	26.9	22.9	23.1	20.6	17.3	17.5	15.7	15.0
Bermuda	80	32.7	85.2	83.9	79.8	76.3	79.4	66.5	66.5	66.5	66.5	51.3
Bolivia	85	21.5	26.8	27.7	26.3	24.7	24.3	23.3	21.3	19.0	16.8	14.4
Brazil	80	31.2	39.1	35.9	34.2	34.2	30.0	30.0	21.4	21.4	10.3	–
Chile	83	11.6	42.0	44.3	43.7	41.5	37.1	34.7	28.1	19.5	13.6	19.9
Costa Rica	84	20.8	33.7	33.7	35.4	35.4	27.2	27.2	16.3	16.3	8.7	17.5
Cuba	81	12.9	43.2	50.9	52.4	51.8	48.7	40.7	30.9	18.1	7.8	23.0
Dominica	81	33.2	54.9	52.6	48.5	45.2	45.3	41.4	35.9	33.5	25.0	23.3
Dominican Rep.	81	20.4	33.3	38.3	37.1	32.4	33.3	32.3	28.9	28.1	26.9	19.7
Ecuador	82	14.6	22.7	26.2	24.2	22.1	20.4	18.9	17.4	15.6	13.1	12.0
French Guiana	82	15.0	63.4	67.3	65.1	66.7	63.8	62.1	58.5	54.0	32.9	33.5
Guadeloupe	82	19.1	66.7	69.7	66.9	64.8	61.5	57.1	51.5	46.7	25.3	31.6
Guatemala	81	13.0	16.9	15.9	15.3	14.0	13.6	12.2	11.7	10.0	8.8	8.1
Guyana	80	21.3	36.3	33.2	30.2	27.4	27.0	26.9	25.4	21.8	15.1	15.5
Haiti	82	35.1	53.5	56.7	55.5	58.4	57.5	60.2	57.8	54.2	46.6	33.5
Honduras	84	16.1	23.5	22.5	21.0	19.5	17.1	15.7	14.3	13.2	10.9	–
Jamaica	82	38.9	83.3	88.1	88.1	86.9	86.9	82.7	82.7	67.8	67.8	43.2
Martinique	82	17.6	70.0	77.0	74.2	71.9	66.7	60.8	52.1	44.8	25.3	34.6
Mexico	80	26.8	37.3	34.9	32.5	31.3	30.2	29.1	27.5	25.8	24.1	18.2
Neth. Antilles	83	22.5	73.4	70.4	61.3	53.9	44.7	37.7	29.7	22.0	12.7	32.1
Panama	80	16.8	38.3	41.6	40.2	38.1	35.3	30.8	22.6	15.0	7.2	18.2

– not available.

Continued

Appendix Table A2.1 (cont.)
Age-Specific Female Labor Participation Rates by Region and by Country
(early 1980s)

Latin America & Caribbean (cont.)	Year	15-19	20-24	25-29	30-34	35-39	40-44	45-49	50-54	55-59	60-64	all ages
Paraguay	82	20.0	27.5	27.4	26.4	24.8	23.2	20.7	18.2	15.9	12.7	13.6
Peru	81	18.3	29.2	31.2	31.0	29.4	27.9	26.7	25.8	23.4	22.9	15.7
Puerto Rico	85	9.1	31.6	43.5	43.5	46.9	46.9	34.1	34.1	14.1	14.1	–
St Christopher & Nevis	80	43.2	76.5	71.9	66.7	61.9	54.1	49.9	44.5	39.1	29.0	31.3
Trinidad & Tobago	80	18.0	45.5	42.8	40.5	38.7	36.7	34.1	30.9	28.4	18.2	20.8
Uruguay	84	26.1	65.6	64.9	65.2	61.4	61.3	54.3	43.6	31.1	17.3	32.0
Venezuela	81	18.5	35.8	39.5	39.9	39.0	35.7	28.9	23.4	16.6	10.7	17.9
Mean		23.6	48.0	49.0	47.1	45.4	43.0	39.6	34.9	29.4	22.0	22.3
Variance		84.1	389.5	408.6	376.6	377.4	368.1	326.3	308.2	257.7	227.6	151.8
Standard Deviation		9.2	19.7	20.2	19.4	19.4	19.2	18.1	17.6	16.1	15.1	12.3

— not available.

Continued

Appendix Table A2.1 (cont.)
Age-Specific Female Labor Participation Rates by Region and by Country
(early 1980s)

Industrial Market Economies	Year	15-19	20-24	25-29	30-34	35-39	40-44	45-49	50-54	55-59	60-64	all ages
Australia	85	56.1	73.5	57.7	57.7	61.4	61.4	50.2	50.2	27.1	11.1	45.7
Austria	81	46.7	69.8	62.2	59.1	59.9	62.2	58.2	50.8	25.8	5.5	32.8
Canada	85	52.1	74.9	70.7	70.7	70.0	70.0	61.3	61.3	33.8	33.8	—
Denmark	85	61.0	82.1	86.9	88.8	86.4	84.7	80.3	71.1	57.3	25.6	48.6
Finland	85	37.2	71.4	83.2	85.5	89.7	90.8	89.2	83.3	66.5	38.9	49.3
France	84	13.7	66.0	72.8	67.8	67.3	64.9	61.0	54.1	41.4	18.0	34.8
Germany, Fed. Rep.	84	40.9	71.3	65.6	59.9	59.8	60.3	56.4	49.7	40.2	11.8	35.3
Ireland	84	33.7	75.2	52.2	30.9	24.2	25.8	25.3	25.8	21.1	15.3	21.9
Italy	85	25.9	59.6	58.6	56.9	51.6	46.0	40.4	32.7	20.8	10.2	28.2
Japan	85	16.6	71.9	54.1	50.6	60.0	67.9	68.1	61.0	51.0	38.5	38.6
Luxembourg	81	44.1	70.5	58.0	46.1	41.8	36.9	30.3	25.6	20.1	12.4	17.5
Netherlands	86	25.5	71.7	62.9	48.0	47.8	48.5	42.4	31.1	20.7	8.9	—
New Zealand	81	49.5	63.7	42.3	39.9	49.2	54.9	53.0	44.3	31.6	12.1	28.8
Norway	85	45.8	67.7	72.5	73.8	77.1	80.3	79.2	72.6	60.0	46.2	—
Spain	85	31.8	55.1	54.3	41.0	33.6	30.8	27.5	24.4	23.6	16.1	—
Sweden	85	48.3	81.3	87.3	88.4	89.2	92.1	90.5	85.6	74.4	46.4	—
Switzerland	80	51.1	76.2	58.6	48.9	50.3	52.3	50.8	46.9	41.1	24.4	34.4
United Kingdom	81	45.0	69.4	55.5	53.4	62.3	68.4	68.1	63.1	51.9	22.4	35.8
United States	85	41.4	70.9	70.4	69.7	70.9	72.6	67.5	60.5	50.2	33.0	41.8
Mean		40.3	70.6	64.5	59.8	60.7	61.6	57.9	52.3	39.9	22.7	26.0
Variance		158.6	40.6	141.2	261.3	301.9	333.9	355.3	332.3	273.4	163.2	300.5
Standard Deviation		12.6	6.4	11.9	16.2	17.4	18.3	18.8	18.2	16.5	12.8	17.3

— not available.

Continued

Appendix Table A2.1 (cont.)
Age-Specific Female Labor Participation Rates by Region and by Country
(early 1980s)

Southern Europe	Year	15-19	20-24	25-29	30-34	35-39	40-44	45-49	50-54	55-59	60-64	all ages
Greece	84	22.9	45.9	48.9	49.3	47.5	44.6	44.6	36.1	28.1	22.7	26.6
Israel	83	31.4	31.4	58.6	58.6	56.2	56.2	47.2	47.2	29.9	29.9	–
Portugal	85	46.1	66.5	72.8	73.3	67.9	59.7	52.6	46.7	37.2	25.8	37.0
Turkey	80	51.8	49.5	44.7	44.6	47.2	49.4	50.5	49.5	47.0	43.7	31.4
Yugoslavia	81	10.1	58.8	68.4	67.4	61.2	54.2	47.9	37.7	27.8	22.1	32.9
Mean		32.5	50.4	58.7	58.6	56.0	52.8	48.6	43.4	34.0	28.8	25.6
Variance		230.5	142.4	117.0	115.2	63.7	28.0	7.6	29.7	53.9	62.9	174.6
Standard Deviation		15.2	11.9	10.8	10.7	8.0	5.3	2.8	5.4	7.3	7.9	13.2

– not available.

Source: ILO Statistical Year Book (various issues).

3

The Industrial and Occupational Distribution of Female Employment

1.   Introduction

The previous chapter examined the size of the female labor force and found that women have improved their employment position both in absolute terms and relative to men. This chapter goes beyond the aggregate female participation rate and examines the employment distribution of women by status (self-employment, dependent employment and family work), industry and occupation. The first objective is to identify the important sectors for women's employment and changes -- if any -- in the importance of sectors over time. The second objective is to establish whether women are now employed in a more equitable way relative to men with respect to the jobs they undertake.

2.   Methodology

Of the three key aspects of labor supply -- participation, wages, and type of work -- the last is the most difficult to measure. Various approaches to quantifying occupational attainment have been proposed in order to make the issue susceptible to empirical investigation. However many of these measures range from arbitrary to, at best, ordinal rankings.[1] The difficulty increases when one asks the tempting question "... and in what industry?" At this point the demand for labor creeps into the analysis. Are women found in some occupations because of their own lifetime optimization decisions?   Or, are women absent from some industries because of overt exclusion or subtle discriminatory practices? If it is the former, then employment differentials are efficient in the sense that they reflect the choice of individual agents. If it is the

---

[1]   See, for example, Goldthorpe and Hall (1974).

latter, then one can argue that this is a prime example of a rather rare combination in economics: intervention and higher efficiency.[2]

The original difficulty has increased further: to what extent are employment differentials, whether occupational or industrial, justified? There is no easy answer to this.[3] Below a methodology is employed which helps, first, to establish the dissimilarity in employment between women and men and, second, to estimate the percentage of the labor force who would, in theory, have to change jobs so that the employment distributions of women and men eventually look alike. This is a promising exercise as welfare losses of any type are conventionally (and more meaningfully) expressed in percentage terms of the target variable to which they refer -- in this case, the size of the total labor force. In this respect the analysis is carried to the limit: how far away from sex equality are labor markets in Latin America? In the absence of relevant country institutional information and specific knowledge of factors governing household formation and employment decisions, this is a legitimate question. Though equality may still sound hypothetical in some developing countries, experience elsewhere has shown the obvious: in many cases there are no real differences in what women and men can do in the labor market which justify the acute sex differentials still observed in many countries.[4] Hence the present analysis and results stand if adjusted by a factor, the choice and magnitude of which are left to be decided by the reader.

---

[2]   In some countries women were (and still are) excluded from some types of employment by decree. Moreover, their wages were (are) set in an arbitrary way relative to male wages. The idea behind this preferential treatment of men is that men are usually expected to be the main breadwinners and supporters of the family while women's employment and pay is considered to be "secondary" or "supplementary" within a family context. As a result, the introduction of relevant legislation can unleash competitive forces and enhance the working of allocative mechanisms in the labor market and the economy.

[3]   The difference between measurable variables, such as wages, can be established and analyzed more easily. In fact, this is done in other sections of this volume. However, it is harder to measure the difference in the type of work between, say, a doctor and an economist, or an economist in the private sector and an economist in the public sector.

[4]   In some Scandinavian countries women's wages are almost equal to men's while sex differences between their respective employment levels and employment distributions have been drastically reduced over time. See the appropriate tables in the recent editions of the *Statistical Yearbook,* ILO.

Given the large number of countries to be studied, it would be tedious to proceed with a long list of tabulations[5] to show the obvious, that women are overrepresented in a couple of sectors and that the importance of these sectors has increased, as expected, during the process of development.[6] Instead, if one examined women relative to men, one could indirectly obtain this kind of information. What this study seeks to show is whether women, as a factor of production, exhibit different characteristics and are subject to different treatment than men. Consequently, this section examines, first, whether women, relative to men, are more likely to be found in the labor force as employers, self-employed and own-account workers, wage/salaried employees, or as family workers. Second, it examines which industrial sectors have higher proportions of women employees compared with the proportions of male employees found in the same sectors. After the scene is set, a dissimilarity index is presented in order to capture in a quantitative way the difference in the employment distributions of women and men in the labor force.[7] The properties of the index are evaluated and applied to broad occupational and industrial data.

Before detailed estimates are presented, it would be useful to get a bird's eye view of the employment distribution of women and men in the region. For brevity we concentrate on industries. Looking at broad industrial employment patterns could also provide a first feeling about the occupational and employment status of the labor force. For example, in terms of employment status "agriculture" means to a large extent family work for women while in terms of occupation "services" in many Latin American countries implies domestic work for women. Figures 3.1 to 3.3 illustrate the percentage of the labor force by country and sex during the early-1980s in the three main industrial groupings, namely agriculture, production industries, and services.[8] Countries have been

---

[5]   There are 7 occupations, 8 industries and 15 countries which can be examined by three separate employment groups (self-employed, employees and family workers) at two points in time and separately for women and men -- in all 10,080 information cells.

[6]   Women are typically found in non-manual occupations and service industries. It is precisely these two groups whose share in the labor force increases with time. This view was expressed early on by Clark (1940) and has subsequently been confirmed in a number of studies (Kuznets, 1955, 1957, 1971; Oberoi, 1978; Ahluwalia, Carter and Chenery, 1979).

[7]   The labor force includes the employed and unemployed.

[8]   Production industries in the present context are defined as mining, manufacturing and utilities. For the exact definition and dates see the Appendix to this chapter.

ranked in descending order of the percentage of the male labor force who are engaged in agricultural activities. In this way one can observe patterns of employment from the least to the most "modern" labor markets.

In the top panel of Figure 3.1 two of the countries shown, Colombia and Bolivia, have more than 50 percent of the male labor force in agriculture. The corresponding percentage in five other countries, Peru, Mexico, Ecuador, Jamaica and Brazil, is between 37 and 43 percent. In two of the nine countries shown, Argentina and Venezuela, the percentage of the male labor force in agriculture is approximately 20 percent. With respect to women, the importance of agriculture seems to be declining when the male ranking is maintained -- though Colombia and Brazil appear to defy this observation (lower panel in Figure 3.1). However, the most important finding is that the share of agricultural employment in the female labor force is only a fraction of the corresponding share for men. For example, the female share is, first, approximately half that of the male share in Bolivia (27.2 and 54.2 percent respectively), Peru (24.6 percent to 43.4 percent) and Mexico (19.2 to 42.6 percent) and, second, approximately one-third to one-fifth in the other countries -- and as low as one-tenth in Venezuela (1.7 percent to 17.5 percent). It is possible that this comparison is biased by some underreporting of women engaged in agricultural tasks given that the distinction between home production and work is not clear in agrarian environments. However, the census data used in the analysis (see Appendix to this chapter) include family workers and any statistical bias should not be sufficient to change the main conclusion that agriculture is not perhaps an important employer of women after some point in development.[9] We explore this proposition in more detail in the next section after we examine the regional pattern of female and male employment in production industries and services.

---

[9]   Of course, one is tempted to ask what the wives and daughters of the 50 percent of male workers who are in agriculture in, for example, Colombia or Bolivia are doing. Our point here is that in terms of contribution to broadly defined market production and women's independent labor power agriculture is not as important as the other two main industrial sectors. This may be an important observation in a dynamic developmental context because historical trends suggest that women move further away from subsistence activities during periods of economic growth. Hence, though agriculture may still be an important sector in the short run, women are expected to be utilized in industry and services in the future even more than they are today. If polices which correctly anticipate the future are considered appropriate, then due emphasis should be given to the modern sectors in the economy.

Figure 3.1
Percentage of the Labor Force in Agriculture
in Nine Latin American and Caribbean Countries
1980s

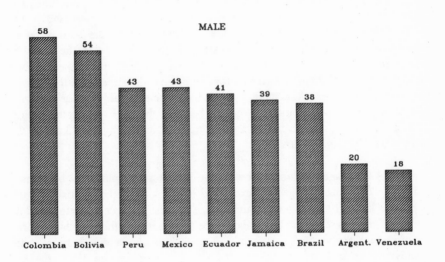

MALE

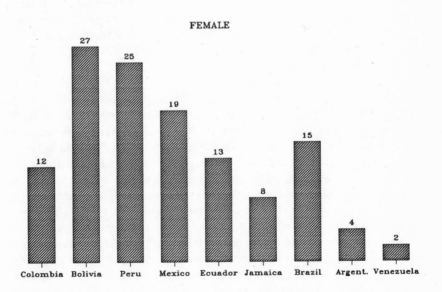

FEMALE

Source: Constructed from Appendix Tables A3.1 and A3.2.

The top panel in Figure 3.2 shows the share of industrial employment in the male labor force. In four countries about one-quarter of the male labor force is engaged in industry (Colombia, Bolivia, Peru and Ecuador) while it is about one-third in three other countries (Mexico, Jamaica and Brazil). In Argentina and Venezuela the share rises to 40-45 percent. The share of male industrial employment is increasing from left to right -- countries are presented in the same order as in Figure 3.1, from the most agrarian to the least agrarian economies. No clear increasing/decreasing pattern emerges in the cases of women (lower panel in Figure 3.2). The share of industrial employment among women workers is rather invariant across countries. If one argued that one in five female workers is occupied in industry this would be an accurate generalization. In addition the difference between the male and female shares is not as dramatic as in the case of agriculture. Similarly, Figure 3.3 shows the share of employment in services.

Figure 3.4 takes another look at the change in sectoral employment of women and men. This time changes are expressed in terms of the original size of the respective labor force of women and men. (That is, changes refer to absolute numbers -- not shares in the total labor force.) This is why the male labor force in agriculture shows an increase of 2.4 percent although the share of male employment in agriculture declined from 50.6 percent in the 1950s to 38.3 percent in the 1980s. What is interesting is that the size of the female labor force in agriculture actually decreased during this 30 year period. Two more observations are equally interesting. First, the increase in the number of women engaged in industry was greater than the increase for men (82 percent compared to 56 percent). And second, the increase in the labor force engaged in the services sector was practically the same for both sexes (90.2 percent for women and 89.5 percent for men).

These findings are summarized in Figure 3.5 when a comparison with the situation in the 1950s is also attempted. The pie-charts show that in the 1950s more than half of the male labor force was in agriculture while more than half of the female labor force was in services. In contrast, services used to be the least favorable sector for men and industry for women. By the 1980s the representation of men in the industrial and services sectors had increased -- in fact, industry was not far behind agriculture (34 percent versus 38 percent). In terms of female work, the share of agriculture was reduced by half (from 26.1 percent in the 1950s down to 13.8 percent in the 1980s) while the share of industrial employment increased by about 10 percent (from 21.0 percent to 23.7 percent). The share of women workers in services increased almost 20 percent (from 52.9 percent to 62.5 percent) and, given the initial size of the services sector, this change was sizeable.

Figure 3.2
Percentage of the Labor Force in Industry
in Nine Latin American and Caribbean Countries
1980s

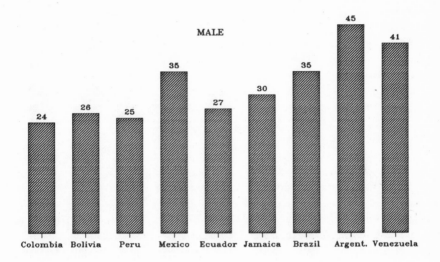

MALE

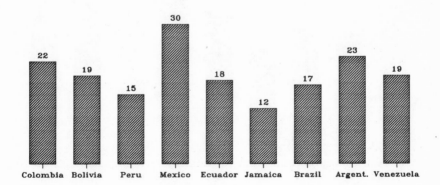

FEMALE

Source: Constructed from Appendix Tables A3.1 and A3.2.

Figure 3.3
Percentage of the Labor Force in Services
in Nine Latin American and Caribbean Countries
1980s

MALE

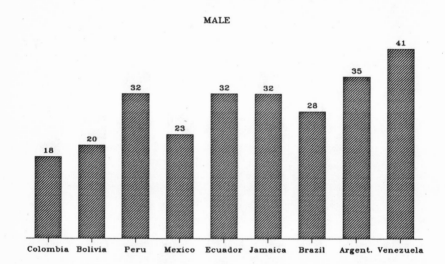

FEMALE

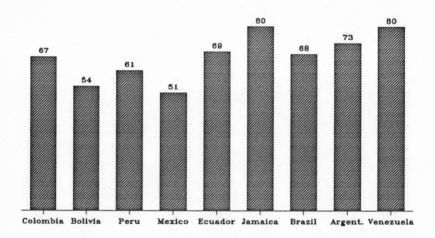

Source: Constructed from Appendix Tables A3.1 and A3.2.

Figure 3.4
Distribution of the Labor Force
in Nine Latin American and Caribbean Countries
1980s

MALE 1950s

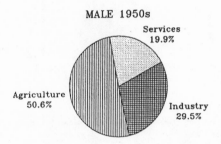

FEMALE 1950s

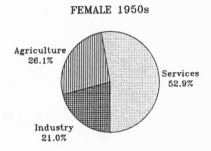

MALE 1980s

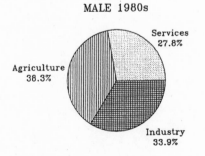

FEMALE 1980s

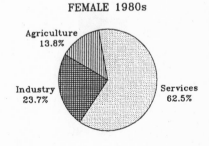

Note: Industry = Mining, Manufacturing, Construction, Transport, Utilities.
            Services = Commerce, Trade, Other Services.
Source: Constructed from Appendix Tables A3.1 and A3.2.

Figure 3.5
Percentage of Change in Labor Force in Latin American and
Caribbean Countries by Broad Industrial Sector
1950-1980

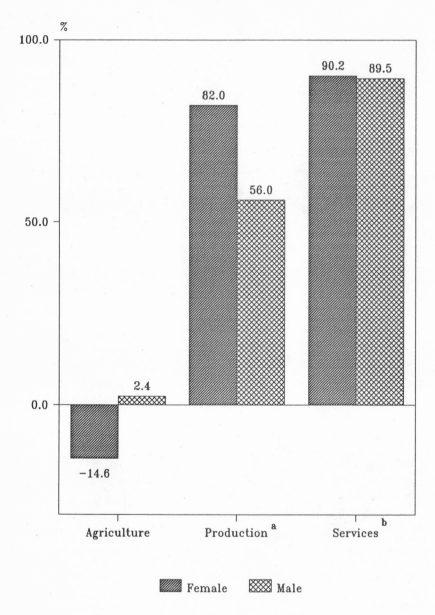

a.   Mining, Manufacturing, Construction, Transport, Utilities.
b.   Commerce, Trade, Other Services.
Source: Constructed from Appendix Tables A3.1. and A3.2.

This introductory examination of the sectoral composition of the labor force runs counter to traditional thinking. One popular belief is that females are predominantly family workers and that more women than men are found in the agricultural sector. Neither of these two expectations appears to hold true in Latin America. In the next section we undertake a more rigorous analysis of these issues by distinguishing between industrial, occupational and employment status characteristics of the female labor force and male labor force. A sector is defined as "female overrepresented" if the ratio of women workers in the sector relative to the female labor force exceeds the corresponding ratio for men.[10] For the moment the analysis is restricted to eight countries for reasons of data availability.[11]

3. The Pattern of Female Employment by Status and Industrial Sector

Table 3.1 shows whether the percentage of the female labor force in the three main groupings of employment status (self-employment, dependent employment, family work) exceeds the corresponding ones for men. An easy generalization is that more women than men were not found among the group of employers, self-employed and own-account workers either in the early or the late period in any country. The picture is less clear for family workers. In only three countries were women initially overrepresented among family workers (Bolivia, Brazil and Peru) although more countries joined this group (Argentina and Mexico) in the second period. Thus, the relative representation of women among family workers has increased but this may be a short lived phenomenon. One explanation for this increase can be the adverse economic conditions which have prevailed in many countries in the region during the last decade: in the absence of rising opportunities in other employment sectors women may have found refuge in family work. Surprisingly, the highest representation of women workers is found in dependent employment. The exception is Bolivia where family work prevailed but only in the earlier period. In all countries, women are now overrepresented in wage/salaried employment. Consequently, the conclusion noted in the previous chapter, that wage/salaried employment has been, and still is, an important employment sector for women during the process of development, is maintained.

---

[10]   That is, a sector is over-represented if $(F_i/F)-(M_i/M) > 0$, where F and M refer to the number of female and male workers respectively and i is the sector.

[11]   The eight countries are Argentina, Bolivia, Brazil, Colombia, Ecuador, Mexico, Peru, and Venezuela.

Table 3.1
Female Overrepresentation by Employment Status
(1950s and 1980s)

Country	Self-employed	Employees	Family Workers
Argentina	0	xx	x2
Bolivia	0	x2	xx
Brazil	0	xx	xx
Colombia	0	xx	0
Ecuador	0	xx	0
Mexico	0	xx	x2
Peru	0	xx	xx
Venezuela	0	xx	0

Notes: 0   No female overrepresentation in either period
         xx   Overrepresentation in both the 1950s and the 1980s
         x2   Overrepresentation in the 1980s only

Source: Calculated from ILO, 1990, Table 2.

Table 3.2 gives a summary picture of female overrepresentation by industry. The construction and transport industries are not included because female over-representation did not occur in any of the countries in either of the two time periods. Again, a surprising finding is that agriculture was important in only one country (Bolivia) and only in the earlier period. This holds true for mining and utilities respectively for Colombia and Brazil. The service industry, however, has been overrepresented in all countries in both periods. Women are now also overrepresented in commerce in all countries but one (Argentina). Women's position in the manufacturing sector is mixed as there has been over-representation in four of the eight countries in both periods but one country has dropped out of the group (Venezuela) and another has joined (Bolivia). In short, women's "favorite" place appears to be in the service and commercial sectors while the case for manufacturing is still to be proven. Women are less likely to be employed, in relative terms, in agriculture, mining and utilities. The transport and construction industries appear to have been, and still are, unimportant.

Table 3.3 combines the information presented in the previous two tables and gives a more detailed view of industrial employment by status. The prominence of the service sector noticed earlier can now be examined further: in all countries, and for all three types of employment status, women are over-

Table 3.2
Female Overrepresentation by Industry
(1950s and 1980s)

	Service	Commerce	Manufacturing	Utilities	Agriculture	Mining
Argentina	xx	0	0	0	0	0
Bolivia	xx	x2	x2	0	x1	0
Brazil	xx	x2	0	x1	0	0
Colombia	xx	xx	xx	0	0	x1
Ecuador	xx	x2	xx	0	0	0
Mexico	xx	xx	0	0	0	0
Peru	xx	xx	x	0	0	0
Venezuela	xx	x2	x1	0	0	0

0 No female overrepresentation in either period.
xx Overrepresentation in both the 1950s and the 1980s.
x1(x2) Overrepresentation in the 1950s (1980s) only.

Note: No female overrepresentation in the construction and transport industries in either period.

Source: Calculated from ILO, 1990, Table 2.

represented in services. However, in four cases the female self-employed and family workers seem to have lost their lead over men in the service sector but, perhaps, this was due to women moving sideways and enforcing the ranks of employees. The commerce industry is almost as important for women as services (except for the self-employed) and its importance has increased over time (seven new cases were added in the later period). The third important sector is manufacturing, although women are overrepresented there primarily as self-employed or as family workers.

The data, albeit aggregated, have somewhat shaken the conventional views on women's employment distribution. It is true that large *numbers* of women are engaged in family work (most often unpaid) and in agriculture. It is also true that the groups of self-employed and family workers are sizeable in *absolute* terms. However, when taking into account the structure of the male labor force, the evidence for manufacturing changes the view (at least in the countries studied) that the industrial worker is a man, and the evidence by employment status suggests that women's involvement in the open labor market as employees is, relative to men, more important than alternative forms of economic activity.

Table 3.3
Female Overrepresented Industrial Sectors in the 1950s and 1980s
by Employment Status

Industrial sector	Self-employed	Employees	Family workers
Agriculture		Ecuador(1)	Bolivia Brazil Peru
Mining	Colombia Mexico(2)	Mexico(2)	Bolivia(1) Colombia Mexico(2)
Manufacturing	Argentina Bolivia Brazil(1)[a] Colombia Ecuador(2) Mexico Peru Venezuela	Colombia Ecuador Mexico(2)	Argentina Bolivia Brazil[a] Colombia Ecuador Mexico Peru Venezuela
Utilities	Brazil(1)	Brazil(1)	Bolivia(1) Brazil(1)
Commerce	Bolivia(2) Ecuador(2) Mexico Peru	Argentina Bolivia(2) Colombia Ecuador Mexico Peru Venezuela(2)	Argentina Bolivia Brazil(2) Colombia Ecuador(2) Mexico Peru Venezuela(2)
Services	Argentina Bolivia(1) Brazil Colombia Ecuador(1) Mexico Peru(1) Venezuela	Argentina Bolivia Brazil Colombia Ecuador Mexico Peru Venezuela	Bolivia(1) Brazil Colombia Ecuador Mexico Peru Venezuela

a.   Mining, manufacturing, construction industries combined
(1)/(2)   Overrepresentation in the first (second) period only
Note: No female overrepresentation in the construction or transport industries in either period.

Source: Calculated from ILO, 1990, Table 2.

With respect to the former finding, women are perhaps not often seen as industrial workers because women are rarely engaged in heavy industries, especially in manual tasks requiring physical strength, and they are outnumbered by men in absolute terms. However, "industry" in less developed countries need not be synonymous with the conventional use of the term in advanced countries: industrial activities in developing countries evolve predominantly around the production of food, drink, tobacco, clothing, and similar goods. The production of these goods is similar to tasks undertaken by women at home and, in fact, the majority of workers in these industries tend to be women. In addition, the presence of a sizeable cottage and handicraft industry in the earlier stages of development offers another explanation for the prominence of women in manufacturing. What is more difficult to explain is the second finding, the prevalence of employee status among women compared to men. A promising direction of research would be to examine the importance of the public sector as an employer of female labor compared to the private sector.

Given this evidence, one is tempted to argue that the emphasis generally given to the informal sector as an employment generator and income guarantor for women is still to be proven.[12] However, one may suspect that the importance of wage employment for women, as evidenced in the previous analysis, is possibly the result of the way women's contribution to production, broadly defined, is statistically treated: the data are based on official statistics, and employment in the formal sector is more easily detected than other types of work. Hence, employees are disproportionately represented in the final estimates for women since about half of all women are reported to be economically inactive -- and this may not be a reliable estimate of the overall economic activity broadly defined.[13] This does not apply to men as practically all prime age men are counted as workers. Consequently, male employees appear to be

---

[12]   Of course, this discussion does not deny that during periods of economic crisis women's involvement in the informal sector may increase at least in the short run. Therefore, measures which facilitate women's adjustment efforts during periods of transition can be well justified. However, it should be clear that such measures may work against the longer term tendencies of the development process, if they persist after the economic crisis is over.

[13]   In many developing countries women are not reported to be economically active in the sense that men are: self-employment and family work by women may be easily classified as "housekeeping" (Standing, 1981; Kozel and Alderman, 1988).

a less important subgroup of the total male labor force.[14] This discussion can only advance if more detailed data become available but, given the findings of this section, it would be inadvisable to pay less attention to the importance of wage employment for women (compared with work in the informal sector) in the context of a dynamic development strategy.[15]

4.   Measuring Employment Dissimilarities Between Women and Men

The most commonly used summary statistic of dissimilarity in the employment distributions of any two groups of workers is the Duncan index.[16] In the case of sex differentials the index, D, takes the form

$$D = \frac{1}{2} \sum_{i=1}^{N} |f_i - m_i|$$

where i $(= 1,2,..., N)$ is the total number of sectors of interest (for example, industries or occupations), f_i and m_i are the sectoral employment ratios of women and men to their respective labor force, and the summation refers to the absolute differences between these two ratios within each sector.[17] The value of the index varies between 0, when women and men have identical employment distributions across sectors, and 1 when there is complete dissimilarity (no women and men work in the same sector).

---

[14]   While men's movements are usually confined to work and unemployment women's typical flows are between work and inactivity (Bowers, 1975; Jelin, 1982; Lundberg, 1985).

[15]   Even if salaried employment were not as important as work in the informal sectors, strategies which focus on the formal sector are bound to be more efficient in the longer run as this is the direction in which any developing economy is moving. In addition, public policies are usually considered to be responsible for the shift in the gains arising from technological changes toward male workers in the formal sector rather than (female) workers in the non-market sector (Blumberg, 1984; Ngwira, 1987).

[16]   Duncan and Duncan (1955).

[17]   Absolute differences are used because, by definition, the excess female and male labor in some sectors is exactly equal to their respective shortages in the other sectors. This also explains why the resulting sum is divided by two.

The popularity of the index is easily explained. On intuitive grounds, the sum of employment differences within sectors should give an idea of the extent of dissimilarity in the total labor force. On theoretical grounds, the index satisfies a number of criteria typically desired in similar exercises.[18] And on practical grounds, a change in the value of the index can be decomposed into two parts: that due to changes in the sex ratio within sectors and that due to changes in the size of the sectors.[19]

5. Interpreting the Index

The micro-foundations of the Duncan index are obvious. The index simply reflects relative employment both within and across occupations. If women's employment doubled but remained distributed as before and this were the only change, then there would be no change in the value of the index. Equally, if the rate of employment growth were the same across sectors, then *ceteris paribus* the index would return the same value. However, the weakness of the index is that, while it identifies that a symptom is present, it makes no reference to its importance: the size of the labor force does not enter into these calculations, nor does the overall ratio of women to men.

Despite the absence of any obvious macro-foundations, most authors have typically interpreted the value of the Duncan index as "the proportion of *either women or men* who would have to be transferred from one sector to another in order to obtain equal proportions across sectors" (emphasis added).[20] This is clearly not the case as the index has a single value although there are usually fewer women than men in the labor force. The index does not even refer to the percentage of the *total* labor force which would have to change sectors to reach equality in the female and male employment distributions across sectors. In fact, it has been shown that the index is simply the "standardized" ratio of *required* reallocations to *potential* reallocations, had the employment distributions of

---

[18]   Such criteria include unidimensionality, boundedness, and an increase in the value of the index when segregation increases. See Hall and Tideman (1967).

[19]   See Fuchs (1974); Blau and Hendricks (1979); or Humphries (1988).

[20]   Quoted from Brown *et al.* (1980b, p. 515). In fact identical phrases are found in Blau and Hendricks (1979, p. 199); Joseph (1983, p. 147); Beller (1984, p. 12); and Beller and Han (1984, p. 91).

women and men been as dissimilar "as possible."[21] "As possible" means that, even if the intention were to allocate women to certain sectors and men to the rest, it is almost certain that there would be some workers of either sex who cannot be accommodated in the sector of their respective sex and would *have* to work in the sector(s) originally reserved for the other sex. This could happen if the female labor force exceeds total employment in the sectors originally assigned to women. In conclusion, the index fails to say anything about how far from equality the employment distributions are, unless the overall sex mix *and* size of the labor force are explicitly taken into account in tandem with the size of the sectors.[22]

6.   Results

The Duncan index was estimated separately for seven occupational and eight industrial sectors in the 15 countries studied in this volume.[23]   In general terms, the occupational data suggested a higher value of the index (an unweighted average of about 0.49 in both periods compared with about 0.40 for industrial data).[24] The slight dominance of the occupational dissimilarity over the industrial one at aggregate levels is maintained for the group of employees, though the reverse is true in the case of self-employed workers. Family workers appear to be a mixed case and the one kind of dissimilarity dominates over the other in as many cases as the latter over the former. In other respects the results derived from the industrial data and occupational data were quite comparable. Part of the explanation for the similarity of the results between occupational data and industrial data is the fact that at the aggregate level of data examined in this

---

[21]   The index is standardized for (insensitive to) the size and sex mix of the total labor force.

[22]   See Tzannatos (1990b).

[23]   The international conventions for occupational and industrial classifications of employment changed in 1968. In order to enable comparisons between the data for the 1950s and the data for the 1980s the following groupings for occupations and industries were constructed. The seven occupational sectors refer to professional, administrative, clerical, sales, service, farming, and manual tasks. The eight industrial sectors are agriculture, mining, manufacturing, construction, utilities, commerce, transport and services. For more information see the Appendix to this chapter.

[24]   At the country level, only Colombia appears to have higher industrial dissimilarity in both periods and Peru in the first period only. Bolivia has a higher value for industrial dissimilarity in the later period but there are no data for occupations in the earlier period.

report the groupings were quite similar. For example occupation "farmer" versus industry "agriculture," or "professional-administrative-commerce" versus "services," or "laborer" versus "manufacturing," or "sales" versus "commerce" and so on. Given the broad uniformity of the two sets of results, we concentrate below on occupational data only. A summary picture of industrial dissimilarity is presented later in this chapter when estimates for Latin America are compared with estimates from other countries.

The value of the Duncan index for occupational dissimilarity is presented in Table 3.4.[25] Estimates are presented for the total labor force and are then broken down by employment status (self-employed/own-account workers and employers, employees and family workers). The table shows that dissimilarity is generally higher among employees than among self-employed and family workers. Family workers were much less differentiated in the earlier period than the self-employed with the exception of Costa Rica and Mexico, though in the latter country the difference between the two groups was only one percentage point. In the 1980s, the picture became somewhat mixed as dissimilarity among family workers, albeit still low, increased in three countries. In contrast, the groups of self-employed workers and employees have had a more uniform experience that suggests a decrease in dissimilarity over time. This finding may imply that during the process of development there are different forces at work between those who work for pay and those who offer their services within a family context.[26]

It is worth noting that the changes in dissimilarity among employees have been considerably more uniform than those among the self-employed. On the one hand, the rates of decline in occupational dissimilarity among the employees varied between 0.2 and 1.7 percent per year. On the other hand, the rate of decline for the self-employed varied between 0.3 and 2.9 percent per year while in Argentina the rate of decline was as high as 4.9 percent and in Chile, Honduras and Peru (practically) there has been no change. The discrepancy in the rates of decline of dissimilarity among workers of different employment status can be attributed to the fact that salaried employment is subject to more consistent forces than employment in the informal market (as proxied here by the self-employed). Self-employment may be less standardized across countries

---

[25]   The value of the Duncan index will in general be lower the more aggregated the data (that is, the fewer the sectors examined). This point is pursued in England (1981).

[26]   In fact, it has been found that in some developing economies there exists high substitutability between self-employment and salaried employment, but not between these two and family work (Hill, 1983).

Table 3.4
Occupational Dissimilarity (Duncan index)

	Year	Index	Year	Index	Annual change (%)
All workers					
Argentina	1960	0.4270	1970	0.4486	0.5
Bolivia			1976	0.3670	
Brazil			1970	0.4913	
Chile	1952	0.4283	1982	0.5259	0.7
Colombia	1951	0.5543	1964	0.5177	-0.5
Costa Rica	1963	0.5894	1984	0.4981	-0.8
Ecuador	1962	0.4856	1982	0.4648	-0.2
Guatemala	1950	0.6220	1981	0.5732	-0.3
Honduras	1961	0.7515	1974	0.6584	-1.0
Jamaica	1960	0.4668	1982	0.5411	0.7
Mexico	1960	0.3891	1980	0.3182	-1.0
Panama	1950	0.5348	1980	0.5916	0.3
Peru	1961	0.3087	1981	0.3289	0.3
Uruguay	1963	0.4192	1985	0.4333	0.2
Venezuela	1961	0.5510	1981	0.4708	-0.8
Self-employed					
Argentina	1960	0.3584	1970	0.2174	-4.9
Bolivia			1976	0.4610	
Brazil			1970	--	
Chile	1952	0.3416	1982	0.3452	0.0
Colombia	1951	0.5009	1964	0.4572	-0.7
Costa Rica	1963	0.6155	1984	0.4792	-1.2
Ecuador	1962	0.4997	1982	0.3230	-2.2
Guatemala	1950	0.7341	1981	0.6783	-0.3
Honduras	1961	0.7943	1974	0.7892	0.0
Jamaica	1960	0.5246	1982	--	
Mexico	1970	0.3950	1980	0.2948	-2.9
Panama	1950	0.5930	1980	--	
Peru	1961	0.3314	1981	0.3397	0.1
Uruguay	1963	--	1985	0.3168	
Venezuela	1961	0.5057	1981	0.3953	-1.2

- Continued

Table 3.4 (Cont.)
Occupational Dissimilarity (Duncan index)

	Year	Index	Year	Index	Annual change (%)
Employees					
Argentina	1960	0.4675	1970	0.4880	0.4
Bolivia			1976	0.5882	
Brazil			1970	–	
Chile	1952	0.5407	1982	0.4877	-0.3
Colombia	1951	0.6497	1964	0.6296	-0.2
Costa Rica	1963	0.6079	1984	0.4718	-1.2
Ecuador	1962	0.6164	1982	0.5251	-0.8
Guatemala	1950	0.6450	1981	0.6084	-0.2
Honduras	1961	0.7404	1974	0.6005	-1.6
Jamaica	1960	0.5723	1982	–	
Mexico	1970	0.4457	1980	0.3742	-1.7
Panama	1950	0.5590	1980	–	
Peru	1961	0.4968	1981	0.3991	-1.1
Uruguay	1963	–	1985	0.4640	
Venezuela	1961	0.5946	1981	0.4467	-1.4
Family workers					
Argentina	1960	0.1877	1970	0.3534	6.5
Bolivia			1976	0.0969	
Brazil			1970	–	
Chile			1982	0.5275	
Colombia	1951	0.4898	1964	0.4766	-0.2
Costa Rica	1963	0.7370	1984	0.7342	0.0
Ecuador	1962	0.3797	1982	0.1320	-5.1
Guatemala	1950	0.4023	1981	0.4880	0.6
Honduras	1961	0.7262	1974	0.6924	-0.4
Jamaica	1960	0.1838	1982	–	
Mexico	1970	0.4093	1980	0.3155	-2.6
Panama	1950	0.1429	1980	–	
Peru	1961	0.0796	1981	0.0574	-1.6
Uruguay	1963	–	1985	0.2683	
Venezuela	1961	0.2827	1981	0.5952	3.8

– not available

Source: Calculated from ILO, 1990, Table 2.

as it is affected more by local conditions and less by employment legislation, trade unions and competitive practices. The higher variance that characterizes the estimates for family workers, whose employment is even more informal than that of self-employed workers, is consistent with this explanation.

With respect to all workers, dissimilarity decreased in seven countries while it increased in six countries. The average for the countries which experienced a decline comes to around -0.65 compared to an average of 0.45 for the countries which experienced an increase. One can, therefore, summarize the trend in dissimilarity as declining. The decline has come primarily from women working for pay, that is, on the one hand, employees and, on the other hand, the self-employed/own-account workers and employers. It was also found that the variance of the over time changes of the index within each subgroup varies indirectly with the level of the index of the group: the changes have been more uniform for employees who have the highest value of the index, while the changes have varied widely in the case of family workers who have the lowest value of the index. Consequently, it appears that there are more consistent forces operating in the formal sector during development than in the informal sector.

7.   The Decomposition of Changes in Dissimilarity

The Duncan index evaluates sex employment differentials *within* sectors and calculates their sum *across* these sectors. Thus the index is affected by changes in these two different aspects of employment, namely the prevailing sex ratios within occupations and the occupational structure of the total labor force. Since the index has generally declined during the period under examination, it would be interesting to examine the extent to which the change in dissimilarity was due to some equalization of the sex ratios within occupations as women have slowly made inroads into previously male dominated occupations (sex ratio effect). Alternatively, some of the decline in dissimilarity could be due to different growth rates in the size of occupations over time (structure effect). For example, if total employment in the female overrepresented sectors has increased faster than employment in the female underrepresented sectors, the Duncan index will also register an increase, even if the sectoral sex ratios have remained the same.

To examine these two effects the change (Δ) in the value of the Duncan index can be decomposed in the following (stylized) way:[27]

$$\Delta (D) = \sum \left[\Delta (\textit{sex ratio effect})_i + \Delta (\textit{total employment effect})_i + (\textit{cross effect})_i \right]$$

---

[27]   The full expression can be found in Humphries (1988).

Table 3.5 shows the sign of the structure and sex ratio effects on the change in the value of the Duncan index by employment status for the 13 countries for which this calculation was possible. The table reads as follows: a positive sign suggests that the value of the index increased over time. A positive sign with respect to a particular effect suggests that, had this been the only effect, dissimilarity would have increased over time. The interpretation of negative signs is the opposite. Bearing this in mind, the first column of the table shows that the structure effect is in the same direction as the change in the value of the Duncan index in all cases with the exception of Chile and Panama; the sex effect is also in-line with the structure effect in eight countries and also in line with the total change in 10 countries. Out of the five countries where structure effect and the sex ratio effect worked in different directions, the former dominated over the latter in three cases and the latter over the former in the other two cases.[28]

A similar inspection of dissimilarity among the self-employed (column 2) shows that the structure and sex ratio effects worked in the same direction in all but three countries: in two of these countries the structure effect dominated (Honduras and Peru) while in the other country the sex ratio effect was the dominant one (Colombia). With respect to employees and family workers (columns 3 to 4), the structure and sex ratio effects moved together in almost half of the cases,[29] while in the other half the structure effect dominated the sex ratio effect in almost as many cases as the latter dominated the former.

Given this evidence one could argue that there is a mild dominance of the structure effect at the aggregate level. One interpretation of this may be that *the growth of occupations* is a more important determinant of women's relative position in the labor market than the improvement of *women's occupational distribution*. This can be explained by the fact that where there exists an excess supply of labor, as is the case in Latin America (particularly among women who are characterized by low participation rates), women are utilized in the customary occupations unless (or, until) shortages arise which enable them to enter "male" sectors. However, the prominence of the structure effect is not that strong and a closer examination of the effects by detailed employment status (columns 2 to 4) may dilute to some extent the significance of this view. Therefore, one could also argue that the reduction in dissimilarity has come

---

[28]   The interaction term has been omitted as it relates directly to the other two effects and its interpretation is not readily obvious for policy matters.

[29]   Ecuador, Peru and Venezuela for employees, and Argentina, Mexico, and Venezuela for family workers.

Table 3.5
Structure and Sex Ratio Effects on Occupational Dissimilarity Over Time

	All groups	Self-employed	Employees	Family Workers
Argentina				
Change in the index	+	-	+	+
Structure effect	+	-	-	+
Sex ratio effect	+	-	+	+
Chile				
Change in the index	+	+	+	
Structure effect	-	+	-	
Sex ratio effect	+	+	+	
Colombia				
Change in the index	-	-	-	-
Structure effect	-	+	-	+
Sex ratio effect	-	-	+	-
Costa Rica				
Change in the index	-	-	-	-
Structure effect	-	-	-	+
Sex ratio effect	-	-	-	
Ecuador				
Change in the index	-	-	-	-
Structure effect	-	-	-	+
Sex ratio effect	-	-	-	-
Guatemala				
Change in the index	-	-	-	+
Structure effect	-	+	-	+
Sex ratio effect	-	+	+	+
Honduras				
Change in the index	-	-	-	-
Structure effect	-	-	-	+
Sex ratio effect	+	+	-	-

- Continued

Table 3.5 (Cont.)
Structure and Sex Ratio Effects on Occupational Dissimilarity Over Time

	All groups	Self-employed	Employees	Family workers
Jamaica				
Change in the index	+			
Structure effect	+			
Sex ratio effect	+			
Mexico				
Change in the index	-	-	-	-
Structure effect	-	-	-	-
Sex ratio effect	+	-	+	-
Panama				
Change in the index	+			
Structure effect	-			
Sex ratio effect	+			
Peru				
Change in the index	+	+	-	-
Structure effect	+	+	-	+
Sex ratio effect	+	-	-	+
Uruguay				
Change in the index	+			
Structure effect	+			
Sex ratio effect	+			
Venezuela				
Change in the index	-	-	-	+
Structure effect	-	-	-	+
Sex ratio effect	+	-	-	+

Note: " + " ("-") indicates an increase (decrease) in the value of the index.
Source: Calculated from ILO, 1990, Table 2.

from the simultaneous beneficial effect of the changing structure of the labor force and the improved distribution of female workers within occupations.

It should be noted again that the change in the gender composition and distribution of paid employment (self-employed and employees) has been more responsible for the improvement in the overall employment distribution of women workers than family work. This evidence lends additional support to the view that women's position in the labor market may improve more rapidly as more women enter employment in the formal sector of the labor market.[30]

8. Qualifications

A number of observations have emerged with respect to the occupational dissimilarity between women and men workers in Latin America, the changes in employment dissimilarity over time, and the separate experiences of workers by status (employees, self-employed and family workers). First, dissimilarity varies directly with the "formality" of employment: the occupational distribution of family workers is least diverse, followed by the self-employed. The occupational distribution of workers in these two groups is, in turn, considerably less differentiated than that of salaried/wage workers. Second, there has been a clear tendency, in aggregate, for dissimilarity to decrease over time. The decline has been more uniform among the salaried/wage workers compared to the self-employed.

These findings may create some optimism since women appear to be employed successively more like men during the process of development. However, this has to be qualified in two respects. First, the nature and availability of data have allowed us to examine only the incidence of horizontal dissimilarity -- and this was done at a very aggregate level. It is common knowledge that within each occupation the extent of vertical dissimilarity is severe and, perhaps, more important than horizontal dissimilarity. An example of vertical dissimilarity within the non-manual group could be that the chairman of an organization is male while his secretary is female or, within a more narrow context, an occupational group labelled "medical" may include a doctor as well as a nurse. In the absence of more informative data, little more can be said in this respect other than to state that in practice dissimilarity must be greater than what the present estimates suggest and to caution about the reliability of the results, in

---

[30] One must also take into account the effect of public sector growth and the implications for women's employment, something which could not be examined in the present analysis.

that the change in dissimilarity over time might look different had changes in vertical dissimilarity been taken into account.

Second, it should be remembered that the analysis was based on a comparison of the relative employment distributions of women and men. Though dissimilarity, if unjustified, is a *sine qua non* condition for misallocation, the extent of misallocation and resulting welfare loss cannot be estimated from such a comparison.[31] Therefore the decline suggested by the index might not have been accompanied by a reduction in the percentage of the labor force who are employed in the "wrong" occupation. This "paradox" is worth pursuing further as it has important implications for efficiency and public policy. This is done in the following section.

9. From Dissimilarity to Misallocation

While accepting that the value of knowing the extent of employment dissimilarity across occupations is important, it should be recognized that the inefficiency induced from the misallocation of the labor force cannot be assessed in relative terms (women to men). One should also identify the implications of dissimilarity for the whole economy (women and men). We propose a method which (1) enables the calculation of the number of workers who would have to change occupation for the employment distributions of women and men to become identical, and then (2) expresses it as a percentage of the total labor force. The Duncan index is explicitly incorporated. Hence, the proposed approach provides more insight to our understanding of employment dynamics as it encompasses both the type of information already provided by the Duncan index as well as the size and sex ratio of the *total* labor force.

In the previous section the value of the Duncan index was derived, first, by aggregating the absolute differences in the sectoral employment differentials and then by dividing the resulting sum by 2. In fact, one could derive the same

---

[31]   The term "misallocation" is used in a narrow sense. It denotes the gross difference between the actual female (male) employment in a sector and "expected" female (male) employment in that sector, had women and men been identical factors of production and been distributed equally across the sectors. It is hard to say which part of the difference between the employment distributions of women and men indicate misallocation (inefficiency, in the economist's sense) in the absence of information about the characteristics of workers and their respective wages. Some of these aspects are tackled in other sections of this book.

result by taking into account only the female overrepresented sectors.[32] For example, consider an economy where women are overrepresented in some sectors. Let the level of employment in all such sectors, k, be F_k and M_k respectively, and the total female and male labor force F and M respectively. Thus the actual value of the Duncan index, D, when calculated only from the female overrepresented sectors, is:

$$D = \left[\frac{F_k}{F}\right] - \left[\frac{M_k}{M}\right]$$

To reach equality a number, R_k, of female workers would have to move out of the k female overrepresented sectors while an equal number of male workers would have to move in, that is:

$$\frac{(F_k - R_k)}{F} - \frac{(M_k + R_k)}{M} = 0$$

From the last two equations one can obtain R_k, the number of female or male workers who should be reallocated

$$R_k = D\,M\,f$$

where f is the share of all female workers in the total labor force (F/(F+M)). This implies that reallocations depend on the extent of inequality within sectors (the Duncan index) but only in part as the size of the male labor force and the share of all women workers in the total labor force should be also be taken into account. To find out the percentage of the labor force which would have to change sector, one should multiply R by 2 and divide the resulting number by the size of the total labor force.

Table 3.6 presents the estimates for the percentage of the labor force which would have to change occupation in order to reach equality in the employment distribution of the sexes. With respect to the total labor force, the estimates typically vary from 10 to 20 percent. This figure is high and implies that up to half of all female workers may be "misallocated" -- if, of course, the initial

---

[32]   The only difference in the second case, that is when one examines only the female overrepresented sectors, is that there is no need to divide the resulting sum of employment differentials within sectors by 2.

dissimilarity in the occupational distributions of women and men were due to discrimination.[33]

The required reallocations among family workers are estimated to be relatively low (typically between 5 percent and 15 percent). Family workers appear to be more uniform across countries than workers in the other two employment groups. However, in all but two countries (Ecuador and Peru) the percentage of family workers who would have to change occupation has increased or remained the same. Initially the self-employed had slightly higher values than family workers but have experienced a decline in all countries except in Honduras and Mexico, though the increase has been a trivial one in the latter country. Self-employed workers have also become more homogeneous in the recent period: with the exception of Argentina, reallocations in this sector vary typically between 8 percent and 12 percent. Employees have had an experience similar to that of the self-employed. Though negative changes are observed in six countries compared to positive changes in four countries, the positive changes are hardly greater than one percentage point. However, the percentage of reallocations among employees still remains about double the figure for the other two groups.

Given the difference in the experience of the groups of self-employed, employees and family workers, the interesting question becomes whether overall reallocations, as a percentage of the labor force have been on the rise. The present estimates suggest that reallocations have increased over time in all but three countries which have, however, registered a negligible decline of less than half of one percentage point (Colombia, Guatemala, and Mexico).

Comparing the results for reallocations to the values of the Duncan index reported earlier, one can easily notice that high *levels* of dissimilarity are associated with high percentages of misallocated workers. However, the *changes* in the two measures over time are only loosely related to each other, suggesting opposite movements more often than not. This is because the Duncan index is equal to the ratio of *necessary* to *potential* reallocations, while the percentage of the labor force who would have to change sector is the ratio of the necessary reallocations divided by the *actual* size of the labor force.[34] This observation

---

[33]   This is so because women typically comprise only about one-third of the total labor force.

[34]   Let R be the number of reallocations. The Duncan index divides R by $2FM/(F+M)$ while reallocations as a percentage of the labor force are simply derived by dividing R by $(F+M)$, where F (M) is the size of the total female (male) labor force.

Table 3.6
Workers Who Would Have to Change Occupation
to Reach Equality in the Employment Distribution of Women and Men,
as a Percentage of the Total Labor Force

Country	Year	Percent Reallocated	Year	Percent Reallocated
All workers				
Argentina	1960	14.6	1980	16.8
Bolivia	1976	12.9		
Brazil	1970	16.3		
Chile	1952	16.4	1982	20.3
Colombia	1951	17.2	1964	16.7
Costa Rica	1963	16.4	1984	17.2
Ecuador	1962	13.5	1982	15.3
Guatemala	1950	13.9	1981	13.8
Honduras	1961	16.7	1974	17.4
Jamaica	1960	21.7	1970	24.8
Mexico	1970	13.0	1980	12.8
Panama	1950	16.3	1980	23.5
Peru	1961	10.6	1981	11.6
Uruguay	1963	15.8	1985	19.6
Venezuela	1961	16.6	1981	18.6
Self-employed				
Argentina	1960	8.4	1980	5.9
Bolivia	1976	14.3		
Brazil			1970	−
Chile	1952	13.8	1982	10.2
Colombia	1951	12.5	1964	10.6
Costa Rica	1963	8.0	1984	7.6
Ecuador	1962	11.8	1982	8.0
Guatemala	1950	13.2	1981	9.8
Honduras	1961	10.7	1974	16.9
Jamaica			1970	−
Mexico	1970	10.6	1980	11.0
Panama	1950	8.8		
Peru	1961	10.0	1981	9.4
Uruguay			1985	12.3
Venezuela	1961	10.9	1981	8.8

Continued

Table 3.6 (Cont).
Workers Who Would Have to Change Occupation
to Reach Equality in the Employment Distribution of Women and Men,
as a Percentage of the Total Labor Force

Country	Year	Percent Reallocated	Year	Percent Reallocated
Employees				
Argentina	1960	17.4	1980	19.6
Bolivia	1976	21.2		
Brazil			1970	—
Chile	1952	20.1	1982	20.0
Colombia	1951	23.6	1964	18.1
Costa Rica	1963	20.8	1984	18.8
Ecuador	1962	19.1	1982	20.2
Guatemala	1950	18.9	1981	19.8
Honduras	1961	25.6	1974	20.9
Jamaica			1970	—
Mexico	1970	14.5	1980	14.8
Panama	1950	24.0		
Peru	1961	17.9	1981	15.0
Uruguay			1985	21.6
Venezuela	1961	21.2	1981	18.3
Family workers				
Argentina	1960	6.3	1980	13.4
Bolivia	1976	4.6		
Brazil			1970	—
Chile			1982	10.7
Colombia	1951	9.3	1964	10.9
Costa Rica	1963	6.2	1984	7.7
Ecuador	1962	9.6	1982	4.2
Guatemala	1950	6.1	1981	6.1
Honduras	1961	4.1	1974	6.2
Jamaica			1970	—
Mexico	1970	13.5	1980	14.3
Panama	1950	3.7		
Peru	1961	3.4	1981	2.9
Uruguay			1985	12.9
Venezuela	1961	2.5	1981	15.1

— not available.

Source: Calculated from ILO, 1990, Table 2.

and the evidence suggest that the decline in occupational dissimilarity between women and men has not been fast enough to compensate for the rising numbers of working women in the labor force.[35] This finding has important policy implications to the extent that women's occupational status is not the result of genuine differences between the labor supply decisions of women and men, but are rather the direct or indirect result of possible discriminatory practices which result in an inefficient use of female labor in the economy.

10.   Comparison with Other Countries

Table 3.7 shows the dissimilarity between the occupational distribution of female and male workers in seven industrialized countries (excluding members of the European Communities, EEC, which are examined later).[36] The data upon which the calculations are based refer to one digit ISCO[37] level and refer to all workers. In this respect the data are comparable to those used in our estimates of dissimilarity for Latin America presented in the top panel of Table 3.4.

As a general observation the index of occupational dissimilarity in the industrialized countries is below the 0.49 mark. The index varies between 0.379 and 0.486 in all countries except in Japan where the value of the index is 0.224. In contrast, our estimates for Latin America (Table 3.4) reveal that in as many as eight of the 15 Latin American countries studied in this volume the value of the index is greater than 0.49. In only three of the Latin America countries (Bolivia, Mexico, and Peru) was the value of the index below the 0.40 mark, but even in these countries the value of the index was above 0.30. Therefore, occupational dissimilarity appears to be more severe in Latin America than in the industrialized world.

---

[35]   This finding is consistent with the experience in some industrialized countries. For example, in Britain occupational segregation, as measured by the Duncan index, has decreased by more than 10 percent since 1900 while the percentage of the labor force who should change occupation has increased by about 3 percent (Tzannatos, 1990). Also, our own estimates for the United States suggest that the value of the index has decreased by more than 20 percent while the percentage of the labor force which should change occupation to restore equality in the employment distributions of the two sexes has increased by more than 25 percent in the 1900-1970 period.

[36]   The table is taken from OECD *The Role of Women in the Economy: Report on Occupational Segregation by Sex*, Chapter II, Paris 1984.

[37]   International Standard Classification of Occupations.

Table 3.7
Dissimilarity Between Female and Male Occupational Employment
in Selected Industrialized Countries (1970-1982)

Country	Value of the Index (1982)	Annual % Change in the Index (1970-1982)	Structure Effect	Sex Ratio Effect
	(1)	(2)	(3)	(4)
Australia	0.479	0.1	+	-
Canada	0.379	-0.6	-	-
Japan	0.224	-0.9	-	-
Norway	0.478	-0.2	-	+
Sweden	0.422	0.5	+	-
United States	0.411	0.7	+	+

"+" ("-") indicates an increase (decrease) in the value of the index.

Note: Norway and Sweden (1981)
Source: Adapted from OECD (1984).

This conclusion is reinforced by observing that the present comparison refers to *all* workers.   Recall that the evidence for Latin America reveals that occupational dissimilarity is lower among the self-employed and family workers. These two groups employ a greater percentage of workers in developing countries than in industrialized countries.   In industrialized countries around three-quarters of all workers are employees.   If this difference is taken into account, then the dissimilarity among employees in Latin America should be even greater than among their counterparts in industrialized countries.

In terms of over time changes in occupational dissimilarity among industrialized countries, the evidence is mixed in that dissimilarity increased in three countries while it decreased in another three countries.   This finding is comparable to that for Latin America (last column in Table 3.4).   However, the sex ratio effect in industrialized countries appears to be negative more often than in Latin America. Recall that Table 3.5 showed that among the 13 Latin America countries where the identification of the two effects was possible, the sex ratio effect was positive in nine countries.   This means that, had changes in the relative employment of women and men *within* occupations been the only change in Latin America over time, the occupational dissimilarity index would have increased.   The increase in the value of the index was, however, averted by opposite and stronger changes in the occupational structure.   Hence, one may conclude that decreases in occupational dissimilarity during development come initially from structural changes and it is only after some critical point in time that "equal employment" effects become operative.

We finally examine the case of the Member States of the European Communities (EEC) in the 1980s. There are many advantages in focusing upon EEC countries alone. The region can be said to be subjected to more homogeneous forces than the group of all advanced countries taken together as there are no trade barriers within EEC and there are no restrictions on migration. In addition EEC has fairly common attitudes toward the social sector and has enacted legislation at Community level which outlaws sex discrimination and promotes sex equality. As there is no information for occupational dissimilarity in Europe, we concentrate on industrial data for both Europe and Latin America. The results for Europe are presented in the top panel of Table 3.8 and the results for Latin America in the lower panel.

What is striking is the substantial uniformity of results across Europe. First, the value of the index is only between 0.30 and 0.40 across the Communities (column 1): in seven countries the index registers a value of between 0.30 and 0.35 and in the other five countries the value of the index is between 0.36 and 0.39. Some reasons for this uniformity were mentioned in the previous paragraph. Another reason may be that the results are based upon the *harmonized* labor statistics held at Statistical Office of the European Communities in Luxembourg (EUROSTAT). Hence, discrepancies due to differences in the statistical treatment of employment should be minimal. Second, the uniformity of the European results also applies to changes over time. All Community countries have experienced a decline in dissimilarity over time; a negative structure effect; and a negative sex ratio effect (except in Germany in which the positive sex ratio effect was not strong enough to counterbalance the negative structure effect). In contrast, the results for Latin America are mixed. Industrial dissimilarity in the region varies from about 0.30 in Mexico and Peru to over 0.40 in Bolivia, Brazil, Ecuador, Jamaica and Colombia.[38] The structure effect in Latin America was positive in seven cases and the sex ratio effect was positive in three cases. Only in three countries, namely Bolivia, Colombia, and Jamaica, were the two effects in the same

---

[38] Note, however, that the estimate for Colombia refers to a relatively early year due to the unavailability of data in more recent periods.

Table 3.8
Dissimilarity Between Female and Male Industrial Employment[a]

A. European Community (1983-1989)[b]

Country	Value of the index (1989) (1)	% change in the index (1983-1989) (2)	Structure effect (1983-1989) (3)	Sex ratio effect (1983-1989) (4)	Reallocations[c] (1989) (5)
Germany	0.3355	-0.3	-	+	16.0
France	0.3059	-0.2	-	-	15.0
Italy	0.3224	-0.2	-	-	14.9
Netherlands	0.3650	-0.6	-	-	17.0
Belgium	0.3658	-0.2	-	-	17.1
Luxembourg	0.3958	-1.2	-	-	18.1
UK	0.3448	-0.6	-	-	17.1
Ireland	0.3326	-0.2	-	-	15.8
Denmark	0.3336	-1.1	-	-	16.6
Greece	0.3287	-1.0	-	-	14.8
Spain[d]	0.3602	--	--	--	15.5
Portugal[d]	0.3803	--	--	--	15.4

B. Latin America (Selected years)[e]

Country	Value of the index (latest years) (1)	% change in the index[e] (2)	Structure effect[e] (3)	Sex ratio effect[e] (4)	Reallocations[c] (latest years) (5)
Argentina 1970	0.3845	-0.5	+	-	14.5
Bolivia 1976	0.4275	1.9	+	+	15.0
Brazil 1980	0.4007	0.5	+	-	15.9
Colombia 1964	0.5524	-0.6	-	-	17.7
Ecuador 1982	0.4113	0.0	+	-	13.4
Jamaica 1982	0.4726	0.5	+	+	21.7
Mexico 1980	0.3062	-0.8	+	-	11.0
Peru 1981	0.3011	-0.6	+	-	10.6
Venezuela 1981	0.3803	-1.7	-	+	15.2

-- not available.

a.	"+" ("-") indicates an increase (decrease) in the value of the index.
b.	European results based on 11 industrial sectors uniformly defined across the Communities.
c.	Percentage of the total labor force who would have to change industrial sector to reach equality in the employment distributions of female and male workers.
d.	Spain and Portugal were not members of the European Communities in 1983.
e.	The base years for Latin America countries are those indicated in Table 3.4

Sources: Based on EEC Labor Force Survey (1983 and 1989).
Latin America: Calculated from Appendix Table A3.2.

direction. In Ecuador the two changes completely offset each other. In three of the remaining countries the sex ratio effect was the dominant one (Argentina, Mexico, and Peru) while the structure effect was stronger in Brazil and Venezuela.

The foregoing comparison with other regions implies a number of conclusions. First, employment dissimilarity in Latin America is still relatively high. Second, though there is some tendency for employment dissimilarity to decrease in Latin America, the tendency is not very strong. Third, the decrease in employment dissimilarity in Latin America is effected more by changes in the employment structure than by improvement in the sex ratios within given employment groups. Fourth, and finally, the assertion, that there are common factors operating during the process of development that lead toward some common patterns of women's employment, is not incompatible with the uniformity of results presented for European countries. Therefore it seems that women in Latin America are increasingly employed more "like men" but the process is slow and relies on structural (rather than "equal employment") effects. The issue becomes whether the "unbalanced" sex ratios reflect some kind of imperfection whose removal by appropriate policy measures can increase efficiency and accentuate the process of growth.

11.   Conclusion

This chapter has examined some characteristics of the distribution of female employment in Latin America and Caribbean countries. Within a developmental framework (initial conditions and changes over time) it tried to establish the importance of work status, industries and occupations in terms of female/male employment. Some facts emerged but equally a number of qualifications apply.

First, the service sector clearly stands out as an important employer for women. Manufacturing, rather than agriculture, is the next in the line. One relevant observation is that workers in agriculture may evade statistical enumeration more easily than workers in other sectors. Even so, the direction of employment change is known with fair a degree of certainty: during development the share of employment in the modern sector increases at the expense of agriculture/ traditional sector. Policies which facilitate this transition by making workers able to work in the modern sector may be preferred to corrective policies in the primary sector which are bound to be short lived and can even have adverse effects, if they are difficult to eliminate after the economic crisis is over.

Second, the distribution of women in paid employment (versus family work) has become more equal to that of men. Within paid employment, female employees (versus the self-employed) appear to have made most of the gains. This finding reinforces the significance of dependent employment for sex equality in the labor market. However, the role of the public sector upon these changes still remains unanswered and needs to be studied further, when appropriate data become available.

Third, despite the decline in dissimilarity among employees, the dissimilarity for this group of workers is still almost twice as high as the dissimilarity among the self-employed and family workers. Given this difference and the fact that dependent employment becomes successively more important during development, an examination of occupational choice in the formal sector may be particularly rewarding.

Finally, despite the gains achieved in paid and formal employment, the percentage of the total labor force who are potentially "misallocated" has increased (subject to the use of the term adopted in this chapter). The validity of this conclusion does not necessarily depend on the assumption that dissimilarity between the employment distributions of women and men reflects to a great extent some economic imperfection (of which discrimination may be one). It would also be valid if the extent of (whatever small) imperfection has remained constant over time. Of course, both statements are tentative, given the quality of the available data. This remains an area where more analysis needs to be undertaken.

Statistical Appendix to Chapter 3

The data reported in this Appendix exclude the members of the armed forces, the unemployed, those seeking employment for the first time and those not classified by either occupation/industry or employment status. These data were used in the sectoral analysis undertaken in this volume (Chapter 3). However, the aggregate analysis (Chapter 2 on the total size of the labor force) included these persons.

The classification by employment status was based on the International Classification of Employment by Status (ICSE) as recommended by the Population Commission of the United Nations in 1948 and amended by the Statistical Commission of the United Nations in 1958 (ILO, 1990, p. XXXV). The basic classification includes six status groups, namely employers, own-account workers, employees, unpaid family workers, members of producers' cooperatives and persons not classifiable by status. In the analysis undertaken in this volume the first two groups were considered and presented together under the heading "self-employed" workers while unpaid family workers were mentioned simply as family workers. The last two groups are numerically unimportant in most cases and were omitted from the analysis.

The industrial breakdown was based on the 1958 International Standard Industrial Classification of all Economic Activities (ISIC-1958) for the early period and on ISIC-1968 for the late period. Similarly, the occupational breakdown was based on the 1958 International Standard Classification of Occupations (ISCO-1958) for the early period and on ISCO-1968 for the late period. The correspondence between the 1958 and 1968 industrial/occupational classifications is as follows:

Correspondence Between the 1958 and 1968 Industrial Classifications

Industry	ISIC-1958 Division	ISIC-1968 Major Division
Agriculture, forestry, hunting and fishing	0	1
Mining and quarrying	1	2
Manufacturing	2-3	3
Construction	4	5
Electricity, gas, and water	5	4
Commerce	6	
Wholesale/retail trade, restaurants, hotels		6
Transport, storage, and communication	7	7
Services	8	
Finance, insurance, real estate, and business		8
Community, social, and personal services		9
Activities not adequately described	9	0

Correspondence Between the 1958 and 1968 Occupational Classifications

Occupation	ISCO-1958 Major Group	ISCO-1968 Major Group
Professional, technical, and related workers	0	0/1
Administrative, executive, and managerial workers	1	
Administrative and managerial workers		2
Clerical workers	2	
Clerical and related		3
Sales workers	3	4
Farmers, fishermen, hunters, loggers, and related workers	4	
Agriculture, animal husbandry, and forestry workers etc.		6
Miners, quarrymen, and related workers	5	
Workers in transport and communication occupations	6	
Craftsmen, production-process workers, and laborers	7-8	
Production workers, transport operators, and laborers		7/8/9
Service, sport, and recreation workers	9	
Service workers		5
Workers not classifiable by occupation	X	X
Members of the armed forces		

The minimum age for classifying a person as active/inactive varies between countries and has also varied within countries at different time periods. The table below shows the minimum age at which national censuses drew the distinction between activity and inactivity in the early and late periods under consideration.

Minimum Age for Inclusion in the Labor Force

Country	Period Early	Period Late
Argentina	14	14
Bolivia	10	10
Brazil	10	12
Colombia	10	10
Costa Rica	12	12
Chile	12	15
Ecuador	12	12
Guatemala	7	10
Honduras	10	10
Jamaica	14	14
Mexico	12	12
Panama	10	10
Peru	6	6
Uruguay	10	12
Venezuela	10	12

The industrial and occupational data were at times based on different minimum ages than those used in the calculation of the labor force participation action rates. The table below shows the minimum age for the industrial and occupational data.

Minimum Age for Classification by Sector

Country	Period	
	Early	Late
Argentina	15	14
Bolivia	10	10
Brazil	10	12
Colombia	10	10
Costa Rica	12	12
Chile	12	15
Ecuador	12	12
Guatemala	7	10
Honduras	10	10
Jamaica	14	14
Mexico	12	12
Panama	10	10
Peru	6	15
Uruguay	10	12
Venezuela	10	12

For more information see ILO *Year Book of Labor Statistics: Retrospective Edition on Population Censuses 1945-1989,* Geneva: International Labor Office, 1990.

Appendix Table A3.1a
Occupational Distribution of the Labor Force by Employment Status

ARGENTINA

1960	Total Labor Force		Self-Employed		Employees		Family Workers	
	(M)	(F)	(M)	(F)	(M)	(F)	(M)	(F)
Professional	185565	263619	56909	21723	122170	237662	173	278
Administrative	169394	13477	92391	5978	72708	6755	428	166
Clerical	579980	235393			576838	234149	627	577
Sales	582058	118220	370727	44188	196660	68975	7963	4534
Service	259127	426300	35042	31294	220655	390243	972	2770
Farmers	1263114	68705	481295	16183	656852	26938	121228	25291
Manual	2255276	365335	410492	106072	1797447	238370	9169	3867
Total	5294514	1491049	1446856	225438	3643330	1203092	140560	37483

1970	Total Labor Force		Self-Employed		Employees		Family Workers	
	(M)	(F)	(M)	(F)	(M)	(F)	(M)	(F)
Professional	306000	371500	109000	38150	190500	327750	1500	1000
Administrative	128350	9500	65150	3400	61750	5950	300	50
Clerical	660100	365300	3300	500	649600	360750	500	1150
Sales	816700	256100	458200	107100	331400	137950	18150	8950
Service	451300	685250	53150	43900	386800	603650	3550	19250
Farmers	1218150	77950	415750	25400	647700	27950	130500	23600
Manual	2743150	348200	510250	96000	2146550	236500	30150	9000
Total	6323750	2113800	1614800	314450	4414300	1700500	184650	63000

Appendix Table A3.1b
Occupational Distribution of the Labor Force by Employment Status

BOLIVIA

1976	Total Labor Force (M)	(F)	Self-Employed (M)	(F)	Employees (M)	(F)	Family Workers (M)	(F)
Professional	50183	35317	9607	1269	40081	33860	107	97
Administrative	7488	1604	3405	1128	4009	407	24	48
Clerical	41020	18589	928	225	39902	18241	31	49
Sales	41248	50137	33885	45837	6831	3259	377	913
Service	57153	71442	3671	6160	50061	64646	2812	296
Farmers	607950	89190	440334	41080	84791	3114	79387	44621
Manual	310073	60462	97783	44479	207355	10069	2122	5504
Total	1115115	326741	589613	140178	433030	133596	84860	51528

BRAZIL

1970	Total Labor Force (M)	(F)	Self-Employed (M)	(F)	Employees (M)	(F)	Family Workers (M)	(F)
Professional	575545	835201						
Administrative	440076	57021						
Clerical	1035150	526528						
Sales	1873448	320213						
Service	868018	2192291						
Farmers	11782384	1256765						
Manual	5560719	702852						
Total	22135340	5890871	—		—		—	

— not available.

Appendix Table A3.1c
Occupational Distribution of the Labor Force by Employment Status

CHILE

1952	Total Labor Force (M)	(F)	Self-Employed (M)	(F)	Employees (M)	(F)	Family Workers (M)	(F)
Professional	52019	40176	12955	4602	38773	35341		
Administrative	98400	39216	83313	32288	12709	2141		
Clerical	116100	44521	3577	1107	112214	42971		
Sales	40509	14292	21752	6197	18219	7227		
Service	81277	218791	6872	26531	74066	191593		
Farmers	570271	38119	155836	16648	392193	16203		
Manual	540996	124350	74185	53359	462839	69333		
Total	1499572	519465	358490	140732	1111013	364809	—	—

1982	Total Labor Force (M)	(F)	Self-Employed (M)	(F)	Employees (M)	(F)	Family Workers (M)	(F)
Professional	133370	148061	23952	8229	108773	139197	645	635
Administrative	73276	18850	49201	14314	23765	4312	310	224
Clerical	255778	163854	8366	3132	245885	158909	1527	1813
Sales	214653	101819	117824	46810	90121	50268	6708	4741
Service	127201	303457	9713	14536	116159	287636	1329	1285
Farmers	621661	18144	161854	4460	376908	10020	82899	3664
Manual	1049914	119177	170205	27479	865925	90156	13784	1542
Total	2475853	873362	541115	118960	1827536	740498	107202	13904

— not available.

Appendix Table A3.1d
Occupational Distribution of the Labor Force by Employment Status

COLOMBIA

1951	Total Labor Force (M)	(F)	Self-Employed (M)	(F)	Employees (M)	(F)	Family Workers (M)	(F)
Professional	54660	32416	16924	1881	33504	28246	273	219
Administrative or Admin./Clerical	247846	57603	134408	21822	103076	31820	3829	2314
Sales	42727	19832	11586	5029	29288	13739	778	624
Service	83018	313680	13688	15034	54553	291479	430	776
Farmers	1907900	86617	777160	44138	823813	24444	262213	15576
Manual	583770	184194	133185	98226	409989	66808	9080	14410
Total	2919921	694342	1086951	186130	1454223	456536	276603	33919

1964	Total Labor Force (M)	(F)	Self-Employed (M)	(F)	Employees (M)	(F)	Family Workers (M)	(F)
Professional	106174	95250	31530	6511	73711	87648	318	562
Administrative or Admin./Clerical	266922	104293	63256	11519	199550	90080	1755	1939
Sales	215157	73697	132716	33555	75927	34823	4917	4881
Service	146183	428297	20639	22988	122997	400351	1008	3242
Farmers	2320295	106404	974535	53106	994496	27728	343652	25354
Manual	897993	195028	240197	97444	626614	76048	13353	18223
Total	3952724	1002969	1462873	225123	2093295	716678	365003	54201

Appendix Table A3.1e
Occupational Distribution of the Labor Force by Employment Status

COSTA RICA

1963	Total Labor Force (M)	(F)	Self-Employed (M)	(F)	Employees (M)	(F)	Family Workers (M)	(F)
Professional	9067	11577	1378	152	7572	11051	115	373
Administrative	4595	548	1810	343	2728	185	53	20
Clerical	15022	5645	172	19	14770	5571	80	55
Sales	24336	5585	11713	1381	11255	3733	1365	471
Service	11457	26244	898	356	10362	25603	164	283
Farmers	183529	3040	50234	262	97266	2449	36018	329
Manual	64848	10181	9716	3159	53809	6765	1312	257
Total	312854	62820	75921	5672	197762	55357	39107	1788

1984	Total Labor Force (M)	(F)	Self-Employed (M)	(F)	Employees (M)	(F)	Family Workers (M)	(F)
Professional	44786	34251	6293	1320	38327	32811	166	120
Administrative	20017	3746	4325	732	15559	2965	133	49
Clerical	30093	28695	713	557	29266	28007	114	131
Sales	52486	15507	27805	5076	23816	9978	865	453
Service	41732	51638	2461	2448	38916	48410	355	780
Farmers	233670	5527	78682	581	123190	4595	31798	351
Manual	153606	24995	31186	3711	120717	21114	1703	170
Total	576390	164359	151465	14425	389791	147880	35134	2054

Appendix Table A3.1f
Occupational Distribution of the Labor Force by Employment Status

ECUADOR

1962	Total Labor Force (M)	(F)	Self-Employed (M)	(F)	Employees (M)	(F)	Family Workers (M)	(F)
Professional	24991	21982	5895	1011	17136	17837		
Administrative	4462	329	2000	170	2430	142		
Clerical	34661	13311			34488	13121	79	35
Sales	66466	19948	53685	13553	11105	4534	1654	1838
Service	32533	69642	7284	4841	24613	64206	221	189
Farmers	760763	39627	381419	18285	304909	13731	74256	7399
Manual	238950	66832	84561	47124	146997	14634	6906	4943
Total	1162826	231671	534844	84984	541678	128205	83116	14404

1981	Total Labor Force (M)	(F)	Self-Employed (M)	(F)	Employees (M)	(F)	Family Workers (M)	(F)
Professional	105797	77782	19041	4475	84378	71760	203	109
Administrative	9394	1729	3140	413	6103	1267	20	12
Clerical	72850	59075	1176	1044	70464	57213	253	96
Sales	146681	62699	107896	44647	33828	14952	2717	2061
Service	71222	108222	11584	13460	56713	83255	517	1871
Farmers	726050	58717	387166	27668	216418	9412	88167	18190
Manual	531900	69474	197114	31801	298047	30830	10971	2743
Total	1663894	437698	727117	123508	765951	268689	102848	25082

Appendix Table A3.1g
Occupational Distribution of the Labor Force by Employment Status

GUATEMALA

1950	Total Labor Force (M)	(F)	Self-Employed (M)	(F)	Employees (M)	(F)	Family Workers (M)	(F)
Professional	8910	6661	1976	326	6866	6299	68	36
Administrative	9147	5193	6440	4680	2524	289	183	224
Clerical	13441	3446	326	99	12979	3242	136	105
Sales	22419	9738	16702	6213	3801	2783	1916	742
Service	22214	44714	1565	2843	20483	41456	166	415
Farmers	635309	16493	292225	3014	189783	5597	153301	7882
Manual	129394	37204	41977	23047	80023	8891	7394	5266
Total	840834	123449	361211	40222	316459	68557	163164	14670

1981	Total Labor Force (M)	(F)	Self-Employed (M)	(F)	Employees (M)	(F)	Family Workers (M)	(F)
Professional	49490	31747	7980	1615	39687	28906	109	74
Administrative	16836	3281	3619	1194	12739	1807	31	32
Clerical	33121	23447	1065	562	31156	22118	72	71
Sales	66481	33035	42748	20127	20329	11192	1805	834
Service	38005	71843	2254	3883	34983	66154	112	354
Farmers	890628	20629	502366	5157	272805	11180	96260	3231
Manual	306635	43308	90821	22566	201866	16339	6146	2869
Total	1401196	227290	650853	55104	613565	157696	104535	7465

Appendix Table A3.1h
Occupational Distribution of the Labor Force by Employment Status

HONDURAS

1961	Total Labor Force (M)	(F)	Self-Employed (M)	(F)	Employees (M)	(F)	Family Workers (M)	(F)
Professional	6128	8172	895	139	5058	7966	8	11
Administrative	2975	367	519	139	2454	225	2	3
Clerical	8447	4186	87	13	8341	4100	18	73
Sales	14379	8029	9607	4956	4320	2501	449	570
Service	12392	32134	1071	1831	11224	30078	65	143
Farmers	371348	2874	183319	1545	98760	626	89262	703
Manual	52830	12431	10588	7597	41298	3605	927	1226
Total	468499	68193	206086	16220	171455	49101	90731	2729

1974	Total Labor Force (M)	(F)	Self-Employed (M)	(F)	Employees (M)	(F)	Family Workers (M)	(F)
Professional	16398	14584	1780	284	14556	14267	15	15
Administrative	5420	1592	873	622	4540	968	12	1
Clerical	22479	9305	9	21	22451	9226	12	46
Sales	27715	16192	17591	10968	9093	4312	999	892
Service	13376	36298	964	2021	12363	34186	33	78
Farmers	447153	5960	222126	1840	123629	2682	101214	1433
Manual	97985	33423	21376	21132	74124	9527	2281	2734
Total	630526	117354	264719	36888	260756	75168	104554	5199

Appendix Table A3.1i

Occupational Distribution of the Labor Force by Employment Status

JAMAICA

1960	Total Labor Force (M)	(F)	Self-Employed (M)	(F)	Employees (M)	(F)	Family Workers (M)	(F)
Professional	6871	12309	633	472	5998	11465	236	366
Administrative	9824	2182	7043	1913	2781	269	0	0
Clerical, Sales	27893	41052	7528	19788	19811	19133	550	2103
Service	12321	76252	861	3378	11353	71881	99	863
Farmers	194504	38702	104709	15990	78510	16623	11264	6087
Manual	128208	48887	20006	24970	100556	18749	7519	5141
Total	379621	219384	140780	66511	219009	138120	19668	14560

1982	Total Labor Force (M)	(F)	Self-Employed (M)	(F)	Employees (M)	(F)	Family Workers (M)	(F)
Professional	20518	29750						
Administrative	10904	8828						
Clerical, Sales	25243	51212						
Service	20747	45757						
Farmers	114956	13702						
Manual	117376	22108						
Total	309744	171357	—	—	—	—	—	—

— not available.

Appendix Table A3.1j
Occupational Distribution of the Labor Force by Employment Status

MEXICO

1970	Total Labor Force (M)	(F)	Self-Employed (M)	(F)	Employees (M)	(F)	Family Workers (M)	(F)
Professional	485268	247941	140529	39723	330134	201393	14605	6825
Administrative	267777	52051	128089	25378	139688	26673		
Clerical	579347	397832	66001	38408	503061	350750	10285	8674
Sales	698258	269009	393747	126475	247498	107515	57013	35019
Farmers	4724803	227397	1925262	84082	2347287	113024	452254	30291
Laborers	2415701	353079	430887	97342	1919688	234660	65126	21077
Transport	876173	684441	183476	156991	671861	499278	20836	28172
Total	10488800	2466257	3407562	645506	6411327	1643495	669911	176256

1980	Total Labor Force (M)	(F)	Self-Employed (M)	(F)	Employees (M)	(F)	Family Workers (M)	(F)
Professional	976039	622967	187989	49739	603263	436217	13541	11231
Administrative	202877	38647	81032	15794	98909	17025	877	802
Clerical	1133961	883519	58415	32693	870557	684020	21660	17229
Sales	1094760	517562	523872	231999	340023	147940	59255	51069
Farmers	4854926	678320	2396363	291044	1096114	96817	339288	75438
Laborers	4767377	871115	797075	152804	2972986	490596	201039	61329
Transport	471875	1101776	78493	190437	284500	545390	19400	91034
Total	15924806	6141278	4474365	1484327	7125648	2640863	776715	416276

Appendix Table A3.1k
Occupational Distribution of the Labor Force by Employment Status

PANAMA

1950	Total Labor Force (M)	(F)	Self-Employed (M)	(F)	Employees (M)	(F)	Family Workers (M)	(F)
Professional	4995	4896	1052	107	3931	4776	12	13
Administrative	6400	1109	4291	878	2072	188	37	43
Clerical	5648	4844	135	11	5501	4797	12	36
Sales	5979	3456	1724	521	3893	2557	362	378
Service	10729	17179	633	1403	10057	15726	39	50
Farmers	123057	7255	78267	2016	11692	226	33098	5013
Manual	38001	6246	7104	3233	30600	2540	297	473
Total	194809	44985	93206	8169	67746	30810	33857	6006

1980	Total Labor Force (M)	(F)	Self-Employed (M)	(F)	Employees (M)	(F)	Family Workers (M)	(F)
Professional	25574	28111						
Administrative	20162	4682						
Clerical	18195	37176						
Sales	22677	11738						
Service	35275	43902						
Farmers	135506	3838						
Manual	114721	10363						
Total	372110	139810	—		—		—	

— not available.

Appendix Table A3.11

Occupational Distribution of the Labor Force by Employment Status

PERU

1961	Total Labor Force		Self-Employed		Employees		Family Workers	
	(M)	(F)	(M)	(F)	(M)	(F)	(M)	(F)
Professional	55423	47289	12688	2491	41986	44129	66	86
Administrative	40338	4844	11106	2083	28739	2419	74	53
Clerical	91352	41993	1259	187	89479	41102	146	255
Sales	161116	65184	117088	49810	39679	10935	4123	4326
Service	111812	167450	8083	13311	103426	153654	303	485
Farmers	1321288	213488	720372	87838	413098	50088	187150	75417
Manual	535647	116947	152393	77394	376602	33329	4468	5698
Total	2316976	657195	1022989	233114	1093009	335656	196330	86320

1981	Total Labor Force		Self-Employed		Employees		Family Workers	
	(M)	(F)	(M)	(F)	(M)	(F)	(M)	(F)
Professional	254783	149690	38802	7786	211968	139329	268	277
Administrative	22031	1894	5357	423	16674	1471	0	0
Clerical	382307	184669	3492	1070	377857	182389	184	212
Sales	347166	180466	250657	141982	89460	28815	3115	6932
Service	184596	187135	17829	21652	164635	163609	387	1014
Farmers	1576719	263748	1152119	110519	291364	28489	106226	117114
Manual	903511	116897	290938	65110	591940	39446	3800	8320
Total	3671113	1084499	1759194	348542	1743898	583548	113980	133869

Appendix Table A3.1m

Occupational Distribution of the Labor Force by Employment Status

URUGUAY

1963	Total Labor Force		Self-Employed		Employees		Family Workers	
	(M)	(F)	(M)	(F)	(M)	(F)	(M)	(F)
Professional	24245	32739						
Administrative	12404	709						
Clerical	92071	34935						
Sales	75401	19355						
Service	52238	87222						
Farmers	175581	3413						
Manual	263911	55811						
Total	695851	234184	—		—		—	

1985	Total Labor Force		Self-Employed		Employees		Family Workers	
	(M)	(F)	(M)	(F)	(M)	(F)	(M)	(F)
Professional	43098	61969	11203	9173	30316	50935	505	536
Administrative	21808	5703	10498	2572	10855	2925	17	31
Clerical	75319	65326	1109	695	72582	63508	155	492
Sales	77334	40400	45832	19121	29505	18965	1241	1963
Service	54047	121634	4172	14253	49313	105809	199	565
Farmers	154874	10879	56494	4280	88767	2423	8514	4093
Manual	271945	60043	57598	16408	208121	41829	1411	397
Total	698425	365954	186906	66502	489459	286394	12042	8077

— not available.

Appendix Table A3.1n
Occupational Distribution of the Labor Force by Employment Status

VENEZUELA

1961	Total Labor Force (M)	(F)	Self-Employed (M)	(F)	Employees (M)	(F)	Family Workers (M)	(F)
Professional	63745	63430	9220	2849	52181	58518	3	2
Administrative	29798	3628	17143	2908	12533	697	7	
Clerical	102262	53120	1710	288	100165	52644	86	48
Sales	208740	20705	131092	10254	73411	9958	3718	433
Service	96925	167630	8510	24657	87823	141899	366	678
Farmers	736127	25215	396034	14981	245368	6974	93461	3206
Manual	556794	73666	122737	40313	430247	32628	1940	521
Total	1794391	407394	686446	96250	1001728	303318	99581	4888

1981	Total Labor Force (M)	(F)	Self-Employed (M)	(F)	Employees (M)	(F)	Family Workers (M)	(F)
Professional	262744	232291	22521	6019	228902	209781	158	177
Administrative	67523	8718	20761	1438	44568	6901	27	45
Clerical	236168	284316	6724	1992	217943	267053	229	495
Sales	381007	116789	183915	46311	185443	65907	1882	1544
Service	220800	332189	13465	24366	185905	144552	366	1655
Farmers	508373	15518	256640	6432	197674	6656	32484	1580
Manual	1637027	243982	284441	28702	978296	119940	4312	1431
Total	3313642	1233803	788467	115260	2038731	820790	39458	6927

Appendix Table A3.2a
Industrial Distribution of the Labor Force by Employment Status
ARGENTINA

1960	Total Labor Force (M)	(F)	Self-Employed (M)	(F)	Employees (M)	(F)	Family Workers (M)	(F)
Agriculture	1248624	75327	480487	16597	618260	30220	121140	25479
Mining	39341	1102	2399	92	36344	927	153	10
Manufacturing	1471339	384655	305631	108214	1135398	255074	7297	4017
Construction	420888	5537	102741	875	308574	4522	1202	32
Utilities	79816	2902	1048	22	77716	2812	55	4
Commerce	744020	169460	374486	45433	339157	115997	8285	4662
Transport	496819	24746	76192	620	412919	23943	1202	49
Services	733188	794939	122340	57393	599656	726388	1517	3291
Total	5234035	1458668	1465324	229246	3528024	1159883	140851	37544

1970	Total Labor Force (M)	(F)	Self-Employed (M)	(F)	Employees (M)	(F)	Family Workers (M)	(F)
Agriculture	1243150	87950	416050	25650	671250	36400	132200	24300
Mining	42850	1750	950	950	41050	1750	100	10
Manufacturing	1357500	413750	184000	93500	1139900	306500	10150	7200
Construction	699050	12250	161000	1100	518700	10850	6500	100
Utilities	90750	5800	1100	50	5650	50	50	1250
Commerce	1008500	316300	480450	110250	494550	192650	21750	10500
Transport	541450	51800	109500	4500	418700	45600	3250	1000
Services	1157500	1193900	215200	74700	919000	1077750	5850	19050
Total	6140750	2083500	1568250	309700	4291500	1677150	179850	62150

Appendix Table A3.2b

Industrial Distribution of the Labor Force by Employment Status

BOLIVIA

1950	Total Labor Force		Self-Employed		Employees		Family Workers	
	(M)	(F)	(M)	(F)	(M)	(F)	(M)	(F)
Agriculture	274772	397358	65698	9674	59675	12917	147537	373722
Mining	38969	4132	1564	168	37153	3636	184	309
Manufacturing	64539	44981	20274	24899	42183	8827	1361	11191
Construction	25131	869	1325	307	23574	554	45	7
Utilities	30588	10050	3102	121	27337	9702	92	204
Commerce	32736	24310	23812	14850	7285	2413	1531	7009
Transport	20492	782	2733	97	17558	668	90	16
Services	17513	52005	1567	2446	15864	48806	48	680
Total	504740	534487	120075	52562	230629	87523	150888	393138

1976	Total Labor Force		Self-Employed		Employees		Family Workers	
	(M)	(F)	(M)	(F)	(M)	(F)	(M)	(F)
Agriculture	604078	88971	440,206	40970	82310	3141	79331	44538
Mining	57194	3405	5,186	355	51749	3033	60	7
Manufacturing	88978	56426	35,019	42573	52244	8149	1047	5365
Construction	81918	529	23,033	66	58084	449	359	11
Utilities	1987	156	42	2	1937	153	2	1
Commerce	49650	57212	37,385	50259	11668	5746	475	1062
Transport	54250	1722	18,626	92	34586	1620	336	3
Services	176315	118537	30247	5965	140847	111540	3277	537
Total	1114370	326958	589744	140282	433425	133831	84887	51524

Appendix Table A3.2c

Industrial Distribution of the Labor Force by Employment Status

BRAZIL

1960	Total Labor Force (M)	(F)	Self-Employed (M)	(F)	Employees (M)	(F)	Family Workers (M)	(F)
Agriculture	10523225	1174573	5301878	264819	2774344	206461	2445994	703216
Mining Manufacturing Utilities	2813576	550656	399234	133303	2354167	372689	60020	44664
Construction	1579694	668547	171187	47932	1358777	585386	17283	28167
Commerce	1345301	174745	681660	35351	634501	132404	29063	6990
Transport	1044163	44635	216468	464	824193	44171	3109	393
Services	1291204	1440944	668275	443932	606744	982017	15939	14995
Total	18597163	4054100	7438702	925801	8552726	2323128	2571408	798032

1980	Total Labor Force (M)	(F)	Self-Employed (M)	(F)	Employees (M)	(F)	Family Workers (M)	(F)
Agriculture	11376454	1732961	5500588	477928	4466557	563595	1384747	688230
Mining Manufacturing Utilities	5790196	1733687	520300	109592	5234292	1607243	24571	12072
Construction	3095756	55338	855041	818	2228296	53942	5584	95
Commerce	2941586	1169721	1205397	293665	1701831	844863	29189	27471
Transport	1670831	144710	493931	1482	1168140	142549	5337	48
Services	5430825	6515945	1179744	1030288	4207943	5385286	30218	57037
Total	30305648	11352362	9755001	1913773	19007059	8597478	1479646	784953

Appendix Table A3.2d
Industrial Distribution of the Labor Force by Employment Status

COLOMBIA

1951	Total Labor Force (M)	(F)	Self-Employed (M)	(F)	Employees (M)	(F)	Family Workers (M)	(F)
Agriculture	1930229	93052	777817	44795	818726	28277	262513	15642
Mining	45256	15967	8738	8144	32762	2052	2111	5574
Manufacturing	303667	157240	88108	82389	195704	62744	5439	8547
Construction	131058	1864	16894	238	104683	1339	549	12
Utilities	9957	515	358	17	9176	474	1	
Commerce	158398	45376	94441	20960	54127	21019	3811	2470
Transport	123974	6109	21309	370	95781	5358	133	11
Services	235874	362219	33488	23903	169865	330611	691	1197
Total	2938413	682342	1041653	180816	1480824	451874	275248	33453

19??	Total Labor Force (M)	(F)	Self-Employed (M)	(F)	Employees (M)	(F)	Family Workers (M)	(F)
Agriculture	2311058	116001	975517	53631	984892	36446	343552	25715
Mining	61150	20129	12538	11520	44787	3144	3323	5429
Manufacturing	476643	179318	123700	75920	340945	90514	6793	11748
Construction	217234	3471	42720	594	168061	3428	1765	
Utilities	12248	1028	594		11550	1017	24	
Commerce	331862	108658	190627	44374	132289	57435	6603	6251
Transport	179485	12332	43753	626	131944	11497	1125	113
Services	374192	551754	57022	36214	312734	508525		
Total	3963872	992691	1446471	222285	2127202	712006	363185	49256

Appendix Table A3.2e
Industrial Distribution of the Labor Force by Employment Status

ECUADOR

1950	Total Labor Force (M)	(F)	Self-Employed (M)	(F)	Employees (M)	(F)	Family Workers (M)	(F)
Agriculture	552062	88517	279538	7764	193596	76481	78,556	4237
Mining	4760	199	1000	18	3683	176	76	5
Manufacturing	124958	108334	56825	17288	61675	85529	6,378	5149
Construction	25578	1224	2528	35	22639	1047	206	9
Utilities	1282	32	12	1	1270	31		
Commerce	49467	25658	33511	4559	14938	20789	974	302
Transport	25985	1388	5914	105	19853	1282	187	
Services	65525	75693	9211	3584	55456	70469	832	1614
Total	849617	301045	388539	33354	373110	255804	87209	11316

1982	Total Labor Force (M)	(F)	Self-Employed (M)	(F)	Employees (M)	(F)	Family Workers (M)	(F)
Agriculture	727880	59092	387573	27646	217721	9857	88144	18118
Mining	6912	494	1930	140	4697	315	101	23
Manufacturing	214063	72467	73665	30642	127451	36025	5091	2646
Construction	154683	3326	46300	458	96800	2654	2580	56
Utilities	11946	1237	510	23	11205	1197	18	
Commerce	185127	86787	118533	51004	60063	31762	3304	2511
Transport	96345	4976	45703	280	44539	4594	1681	13
Services	373492	225539	66004	16160	260138	182812	7582	3287
Total	1770448	453918	740218	126353	822614	269216	108501	26654

Appendix Table A3.2f
Industrial Distribution of the Labor Force by Employment Status

JAMAICA

1953	Total Labor Force (M)	(F)	Self-Employed (M)	(F)	Employees (M)	(F)	Family Workers (M)	(F)
Agriculture	225885	74402						
Mining	7572	220						
Manufacturing	40397	35097						
Construction	18698	1458						
Utilities	2490	270						
Commerce	19266	33107						
Transport	13143	2441						
Services	26141	79093						
Total	353592	226088		—		—		—

1982	Total Labor Force (M)	(F)	Self-Employed (M)	(F)	Employees (M)	(F)	Family Workers (M)	(F)
Agriculture	113306	14402						
Mining	4855	534						
Manufacturing	43649	13373						
Construction	20517	610						
Utilities	3757	605						
Commerce	23458	34495						
Transport	15534	5041						
Services	68910	93050						
Total	293986	162110		—		—		—

— not available.

Appendix Table A3.2g

Industrial Distribution of the Labor Force by Employment Status

MEXICO

1960	Total Labor Force		Self-Employed		Employees		Family Workers	
	(M)	(F)	(M)	(F)	(M)	(F)	(M)	(F)
Agriculture	5479642	663898	2560714	126119	2776360	520105	92645	8183
Mining	131928	9602	7291	941	124184	8555	109	15
Manufacturing	1306435	249656	217148	62661	1082953	185319	2161	618
Construction	394118	14161	47489	1106	345372	12954	299	13
Utilities	37542	3901	3616	356	33753	3501	34	6
Commerce	784837	290337	503252	157043	275578	130145	3565	2327
Transport	338105	18834	41470	779	295802	17957	92	15
Services	760161	767068	106014	36407	650993	724850	321	537
Total	9232768	2017457	3486994	385412	5584995	1603386	99226	11714

	Total Labor Force		Self-Employed		Employees		Family Workers	
	(M)	(F)	(M)	(F)	(M)	(F)	(M)	(F)
Agriculture	4958146	742714	2415701	313078	1195008	120435	469923	91903
Mining	353847	159492	85259	39013	219717	92557	16629	12294
Manufacturing	1898457	681742	303939	111792	1256134	427871	99834	46852
Construction	1093593	214174	193389	27785	689416	136808	46506	11809
Utilities	92144	24053	11490	2302	69825	18690	2262	726
Commerce	1151019	599509	475249	215457	434229	224852	66683	58954
Transport	605614	78026	125614	12302	367685	47154	22117	2570
Services	1490555	1372849	255009	169015	926701	796809	63078	250560
Total	11643375	3872559	3865650	890744	5158715	1865176	787032	475668

Appendix Table A3.2h

Industrial Distribution of the Labor Force by Employment Status

PERU

1961	Total Labor Force (M)	(F)	Self-Employed (M)	(F)	Employees (M)	(F)	Family Workers (M)	(F)
Agriculture	1340483	215077	721299	87922	431479	51557	187223	75430
Mining	64614	1799	1529	51	62899	1690	46	12
Manufacturing	294983	115997	103028	77501	187471	32455	4002	5824
Construction	103712	984	22312	138	80924	812	207	14
Utilities	8187	397	8072	317	115	80		
Commerce	202998	78849	120929	50426	77794	24151	4029	4140
Transport	89385	4586	29416	220	59515	4342	261	11
Services	242368	234346	23789	17500	217922	215767	657	1079
Total	2346730	652035	1022302	233758	1126076	331091	196425	86510

1981	Total Labor Force (M)	(F)	Self-Employed (M)	(F)	Employees (M)	(F)	Family Workers (M)	(F)
Agriculture	1596816	267192	1152794	111201	310430	31029	106226	117301
Mining	91532	5160	4852	219	85370	4736	80	26
Manufacturing	420366	136064	108659	64206	303146	59500	2301	8156
Construction	193503	3708	56241	395	132519	3177	442	24
Utilities	16123	1641	369	12	15585	1613	4	1
Commerce	412081	220425	260140	153503	143907	55722	3480	7822
Transport	195818	14189	74831	825	114477	13130	544	30
Services	750268	439092	103497	19094	641515	416449	939	677
Total	3676507	1087471	1761383	349455	1746949	585356	114016	134037

Appendix Table A3.2i
Industrial Distribution of the Labor Force by Employment Status

VENEZUELA

1961	Total Labor Force		Self-Employed		Employees		Family Workers	
	(M)	(F)	(M)	(F)	(M)	(F)	(M)	(F)
Agriculture	733320	26465	395265	15238	243185	7767	93479	3201
Mining	50660	2880	2187	92	48185	2768	55	1
Manufacturing	212988	74356	50236	39850	160600	33784	1355	517
Construction	129581	1420	34602	155	94173	1243	389	13
Utilities	22083	1243	274	12	21750	1225	7	2
Commerce	260181	37277	133181	10649	122660	26083	3761	440
Transport	112738	4910	42514	211	69621	4681	141	4
Services	298097	250201	26994	29931	269044	218284	429	718
Total	1819648	398752	685253	96138	1029218	295835	99616	4896

1981	Total Labor Force		Self-Employed		Employees		Family Workers	
	(M)	(F)	(M)	(F)	(M)	(F)	(M)	(F)
Agriculture	515484	19101	257436	6654	201968	9532	32948	1762
Mining	49231	5533	2802	77	43430	5162	16	3
Manufacturing	493542	145488	49129	19116	413313	117323	610	386
Construction	378216	21587	96917	895	259340	19313	766	29
Utilities	45015	8085	1434	49	40404	7529	18	3
Commerce	523668	208780	194363	52815	305475	143565	2610	2339
Transport	244965	31522	77705	1885	152090	27495	294	31
Services	698328	686682	75754	25629	580969	476491	744	1579
Total	2948449	1126778	755540	107120	1996989	806410	38006	6132

4

Potential Gains from the Elimination of Labor Market Differentials

1. Introduction

In the previous chapter, employment differentials were examined in a statistical way rather than an economic one, that is, the patterns and trends of the gender employment distributions were compared independently of pay. Pay, however, is the prime signal for the efficient functioning of the labor market. Consider, for example, two industries that are identical in all respects except in the ratio of female to male pay. If some part of the pay differential is due to non-competitive practices,[1] then the efficiency loss associated with this pay differential would be higher in the industry where relative female pay is lower.

In order to estimate the welfare loss arising from the differential treatment of women and men in the labor market, one has to consider both the dissimilarity in employment patterns of female and male workers as well as any associated difference in their respective pay. As there is no information about which part of the sex differential is justified, one can estimate the potential gain in efficiency and the effects on pay and employment only on the assumption that women and men are identical factors of production.[2] One can then adjust the

---

[1] A non-competitive outcome may be the result of pay and/or employment discrimination (by the employer, fellow employees, customers), protective or prohibiting legislation and social customs.

[2] In the words of an author sympathetic to women's reluctance to undertake some manual tasks "... women ... seem more likely to see real dangers in some blue collar work that men have accepted ... [M]en ... have lived with these conditions for years, but women may not be as willing to put up with them. Some of these very problems may be keeping other women from even trying these jobs" (O'Farrell, 1982, p. 155). Obviously,

results to the extent that these differences arise from different considerations by the individual suppliers of labor.

2. Theoretical Framework

The aim is to show how women's under payment in, or limited access to, some sectors (such as industries) would result in lower levels of production, even if women kept supplying the same amount of labor as if there were neither wage nor employment discrimination in the first instance. Obviously, to the extent that some women are discouraged from joining the labor market when rewards, in terms of either pay or employment prospects, are lower than what they should be, the loss of output will be even greater than that suggested by the present analysis.

The cost (welfare loss) of an unjustified pay or employment differential between working women and men can be shown in a simplified way as follows. First, assume that there are two industries employing two identical factors of production (women and men). For simplicity, assume further that (1) the two industries are identical in all respects relevant to the present study;[3] (2) the total factor supplies are fixed (perfectly inelastic) but can vary between the two industries; and (3) there are neither costs of adjustment nor any non-pecuniary differences associated with employment in the two industries.[4] Under competitive conditions there will be a common wage in both industries, and an efficient production and consumption will prevail.

Though one can proceed by imposing either a wage or an employment differential, let us assume the latter so that women are now excluded from the first industry and the displaced female workers seek employment in the second industry. This will lower wages in the second industry as employment has risen, while wages in the first industry will increase as employment has been reduced. The "male" industry has become more capital intensive while the "female"

"keeping from trying" is a supply decision quite different from "keeping out from a job," which appears as a demand determined condition in the labor market. Note, however, that both demand and supply can be affected by what is going on in the other side of the labor market.

[3]   This refers to the demand for the final product of the two industries as well as to available technology and the level of the capital stock.

[4]   Alternatively, if there are costs of adjustment and non-pecuniary aspects of employment, then they should be the same in the two industries.

industry is now more labor intensive. The labor market is characterized by both wage differentials and (most likely, partial) segregation.[5] Though this result is predicted from a hypothetical experiment, it conforms to common observations about women's and men's employment and wage patterns in practically all countries in the world.[6]

An interesting question arises as output in the second industry has increased while output in the first industry has dropped: what will be the net effect upon the total product of the two industries? The answer depends on whether the gain in output in the industry which provides refuge to women workers is greater than the loss in output in the discriminating industry. Assuming marginal productivity conditions, the answer is that the net effect will be negative. This is because the contribution of additional labor to production in the second industry will, at the margin, be less than the increase in output in the first industry. Though this analysis is based on partial equilibrium, its extension to a general equilibrium framework is feasible (though more cumbersome) and the basic results hold.[7]

So far, it has been established that there is bound to be an efficiency loss (lower level of total production, GDP) from a restriction in the labor market based on non-economic criteria (such as the sex of the worker). Unjustified differentials do, therefore, provide grounds for corrective policies from an economic (Pareto) point of view. However, the acceptability of any intervention depends also on its distributional effects, and one further question, therefore, needs to be answered -- that is, "who benefits and who loses" if an established differential is disturbed? This amounts to establishing who suffers the consequences of the employment restriction. Three groups are affected by such a restriction, though in different ways: female workers, male workers and employers. Workers are

---

[5]   Whether there is complete segregation will depend on the initial total factor supplies and the new size of employment in the two industries but, most likely, employment in the second industry will be mixed.

[6]   Of course, the observed differentials can be due to supply side decisions, a possibility which has been ruled out in the present paradigm by the assumption of homogeneity. However, supply side differences do not invalidate the present conclusions unless all differentials are due to supply factors -- and this is not likely to be the case.

[7]   See Tzannatos (1987a).

interested in wages while employers are concerned with profits.[8]   In the presence of discrimination of the type analyzed in this section, the only conclusion that has been demonstrated consistently in the literature is that women are always the losers.[9]   Therefore, the candidate beneficiaries are either male workers or employers or both.   Whether male employees and/or employers gain from discrimination has been a contentious issue and opinion is still divided.[10]   No attempt can be made to solve this issue here.   However, the results on welfare gains presented below, as well as the estimated effects upon male wages, can give some insight as to how strongly male workers (or male dominated unions) may react to measures promoting sex equality in the labor market.   In short, what is shown is that, if women competed with men on an equal footing, men would have a smaller share of the pie, but the size of the pie will be greater as the allocative mechanisms of the market will improve.   As a result, men's real pay need not suffer any adverse consequence in the longer run.

These considerations can be shown diagrammatically in the following simplified way.   In Figure 4.1 the left panel represents an industry which is initially exclusively male in terms of employment and the right panel represents an industry which is exclusively female.   The labor supply of men and the labor supply of women are assumed to be equal and perfectly inelastic.   The labor supply curves are shown in the respective panels of Figure 4.1 as the vertical lines MS^m and FS^f.   The negatively sloped curves, D, represent labor demand (value of marginal product) assuming that men and women are equally productive and perfect substitutes.   The model assumes that there are neither adjustment costs nor any non-pecuniary differences between employment in the

---

[8]   There are also employment effects which, for simplicity, are ignored in the present analysis.

[9]   For a review see Tzannatos (1990a).

[10]   According to the taste theory of discrimination, if observed differentials between workers are taken to reflect employers' preferences, the "remarkable agreement in the proposition that [employers] ... are the major beneficiaries of prejudice and discrimination ..." is dismissed as a "non-sequitur" (Becker, 1971, pp. 21-22).   The response to this assertion has been "if this deduction is correct ... do whites in South Africa ... have lower standards of living as a result of their discrimination?" (Thurow, 1969, p. 112).   Though employers may willingly pay a price for treating homogeneous labor in different ways, there is still considerable ambiguity about who gains.   Some empirical studies have shown that the elimination of sex differentials will also benefit at least some male workers (Pike, 1982) though other studies have shown losses for workers belonging to the "majority" group (Bergmann, 1971; Tzannatos, 1987b, 1988).

two industries. Under competitive conditions a common equilibrium wage, w^e, will prevail in the two industries. Let us introduced discrimination in the diagram in the form of either an arbitrary wage differential in favour of men (say, w^m-w^e) or an employment restriction in the male industry (say, from M to M*). As a result displaced workers from the male industry will seek employment in the female industry thus increasing employment (to $F+[M-M^*]$) and lowering wages (to w^f) in the latter industry. The welfare implications can be shown with the reference to the areas A, B and C. The reduction in employment in the male industry has reduced output by $A+B+C$. The gain in output from the additional employment in the female industry has increased output by only $A+B$. There has been a deadweight loss equal to the area indicated by the rectangle C in the male industry. Thus, the elimination of direct wage discrimination or indirect employment discrimination should lead to welfare gains, increases in female wages and decreases in male wages. It should, however, be noted that the welfare gain resulting from the elimination of gender differentials and productivity gains in the longer run may imply that the effect upon male wages need not be significant. The latter is in fact found to be the case in the simulations which we have undertaken and which are presented below.

For empirical purposes, one would require information about the level of female and male pay and employment by industry as well as production and product demand conditions.[11]   If these were known, one could work out the consequences of eliminating unjustified differentials and then compare the outcome to the prevailing one. As this type of information is unavailable, researchers have usually adopted an inverse strategy. They first evaluate the total product under the current conditions and then estimate the gain in output if employment differentials were eliminated, assuming factor homogeneity.[12] As in the case of employment dissimilarity and the Duncan index, this exercise provides long run upper bound estimates of the new level of output as well as female and male wages.

---

[11]   More precisely, to estimate the effects of the elimination of sectoral labor market differentials one needs to know (1) the labor demand and supply curves of women and men; (2) the currently available capital stock; (3) the nature of the production function; (4) the demand schedule for the final product(s); and (5) the elasticity of substitution between women and men.

[12]   See, among others, Bergmann (1971), Dougherty and Selowsky (1973), Pike (1982) and Tzannatos (1987b, 1988).

Figure 4.1

Effects of Sex-differentials in the Labor Market

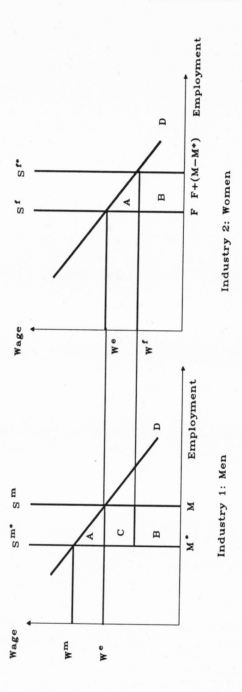

3. Data and Results

The data on pay and employment are the same as those used in the country studies in the companion volume. They refer to monthly earnings and persons employed by industry.[13] It is visualized that workers in each industry are employed in two distinct occupations, namely a high-pay one and a low-pay one. The male workers are assumed to be employed in the former occupation while women workers are assumed to be employed in the latter occupation. The aim is to examine the effects of allowing women to enter the high-pay occupation until wages are equalized within each industry.[14]

There is no information about the state of technology and the ease of substitution in production between female and male workers. In the absence of information about the nature of technology in the countries studied, the production function is assumed to be of a constant elasticity of substitution (CES) type. In theory, a high value (tending to infinity) of the elasticity of substitution would be appropriate for estimating the upper bound effects of the present simulation, as one wants to examine what would happen if women and men were equal in all respects.[15] Though estimates for this limiting case are presented, more modest values of the elasticity of substitution have been also used in order to accommodate the fact that there is some heterogeneity between female and male labor. Consequently, we also experimented with values of the elasticity of substitution (sigma) equal to 3, 6, 9 and 12.[16] Finally, the assumptions

---

[13]   In the case of Guatemala and Uruguay hourly wages are used. In addition, the sectoral distribution of employment and wages in Uruguay refers to occupations, not industries. The data for Ecuador were taken from Finn and Jusenius (1975).

[14]   Across industry differentials are allowed to persist as long as there are no within industry differences between women and men. Obviously, such differences should, at the limit, be eliminated as well, something which suggests that the empirical estimates of the present analysis understate the upper bound of welfare gains.

[15]   In practice, the complete exodus of women from the low-pay occupation was achieved (in the present data sets) when the elasticity of substitution reached a value between 40 and 80.

[16]   There is wide agreement in the literature that all pairwise elasticities of substitution are substantially greater than unity, ranging between three and nine (Bowles, 1970; Psacharopoulos and Hinchliffe, 1972; Dougherty, 1972; Hamermesh, 1986) and most studies have utilized the present range of values of the elasticity of substitution (Bergmann, 1971; Dougherty and Selowsky, 1973; Pike, 1982; Tzannatos 1987b, 1988).

Table 4.1

Results of the Within Industry Elimination of Occupational Differentials

Country	Year	Percentage Change in			
		Female Wage (1)	Male Wage (2)	GDP (3)	Labor Force[a] (4)
Argentina	1987	38.2	-8.9	4.0	25.3
Brazil	1980	96.6	-7.7	8.7	23.1
Chile	1987	40.5	-5.6	3.3	17.6
Colombia	1988	46.4	-7.6	4.6	20.2
Costa Rica	1989	34.8	-6.3	3.0	17.5
Ecuador	1966	58.6	-13.3	9.7	37.2
Guatemala	1989	25.2	-5.5	2.0	13.7
Jamaica	1989	60.7	-8.2	8.3	27.5
Uruguay	1989	29.6	-7.6	3.4	16.3
Venezuela	1987	23.6	-6.2	1.9	11.7

a. Percent of total labor force who would have to change occupation

underlying the present calculations are those implied by the competitive labor market model.[17]

Table 4.1 presents the results for the countries under consideration when the elasticity of substitution is assumed to be equal to three (the complete set of results is presented in Appendix Table A4.1). The first column indicates the average increase in the low-pay occupation (female earnings) as fewer workers will be employed in it. The second column provides the percentage reduction in the average wage in the high-paying occupation (male earnings) which would

---

[17]   These assumptions are: (1) that all workers, independently of their sex, are paid wages equal to the respective value of their marginal products before and after equality; (2) that adjustment is costless; (3) that the only reward to workers (cost to employers) associated with employment is the wage received (paid); and (4) that the capital stock (more importantly, utilization) is fixed. Though these assumptions are rather restrictive, especially if one wants to evaluate the labor market as a whole, they need not necessarily be so for comparative purposes. For example, even if wages are not equal to the value of their respective marginal products (one of the most argumentative issues in this area of research), this does not produce unacceptable results in the present analysis so long as the discrepancy between marginal products and wages is proportionately the same for women and men.

result from the increase in (female) employment in that occupation. The third column shows the welfare gain which would follow the influx of women into the high-pay sector in each industry. The fourth column shows the percentage of the labor force that needs to change occupation within industry for all these effects to be achieved.

The findings can be summarized as follows. First, the new level of wages in each industry suggests that the decline in male wages would, in general terms, be small and the increase in female wages large. Second, the net change in output which would result from the above changes in (real) wages would be positive and sizeable (unweighted average about 5 percent) even for low values of the elasticity of substitution (equal to 3 in Table 4.1). Third, around one-fifth of the total labor force would have to change occupations within industries for all these effects to take place (unweighted average 22 percent). Finally, and taking into account the complete set of results included in Appendix Table A4.1, the elasticity of substitution is a key parameter for the value of the results but is not so important as to render the simulation a wholly hypothetical exercise.

Particularly striking is the fact that, even at the lowest levels of the elasticity of substitution, the effects are more than suggestive. The welfare gain will be higher, the reduction in male wages lower, the increase in female wages higher, and the percentage reallocation of the labor force higher, the easier it is to substitute women for men as was expected. What is also interesting is that these effects are not proportional to the change in the value of the elasticity of substitution. As a summary statement, one may say that raising the value of the elasticity from 3 to its maximum value increases the gain in output by only 3 times, reduces the decline of male wages from approximately 10 percent to around 1 percent, and increases the rise in female wages by no more than 50 percent. The associated increase in the percentage of the labor force who should change occupations to achieve equality in wages within each industry rises from approximately 20 to 40 percent. In fact, in most cases the changes suggested from the maximum value of the elasticity of substitution are only marginally higher than those suggested by an elasticity of substitution equal to 9 and are practically indistinguishable from those derived when the value of the elasticity of substitution was set to 12.

The conclusion, therefore, is that even if most of the observed differentials were due to supply factors, and even if the easiness of substitution were not great, the gains in output and the rise in female wages could be sizeable at a trivial cost to male workers. One should also note that the number of reallocations required to achieve wage parity between women and men are greater than the

Table 4.2
Percentage Change in Female Wages

Country	If Women Had	
	Men's Wage Distribution	Men's Employment Distribution
Argentina	58.1	4.3
Brazil	129.4	-14.9
Chile	61.4	7.2
Colombia	63.3	4.7
Costa Rica	50.7	-18.0
Ecuador	103.0	9.0
Guatemala	39.3	-17.1
Jamaica	101.9	-3.9
Uruguay	50.5	-5.9
Venezuela	24.3	-15.4

Source: See text.

reallocations required to reduce the value of the Duncan index to zero. A straightforward implication of this is that employment dissimilarity as such is less damaging, in allocative terms, than wage differences. Expressed in a different way, policies which enhance the pricing mechanism of the labor market and let individuals adjust accordingly may have a more direct effect on female pay and women's position in the labor market than policies aiming at eliminating employment differentials. One such policy could be the introduction of employment quotas.

We can examine the last assertion in another simulation exercise.[18] Let us assume that women are employed in the same sectors as at present but are paid male wages. Alternatively, let us assume that women are paid as at present but their employment is distributed across sectors as the employment of men. The results of these two simulations are presented in Table 4.2. Column 1 shows the percentage increase in female wages, if women were paid as men in their current employment. Column 2 shows the corresponding change in female wages, if women had the male employment distribution but were still paid women's wages. The difference between these two results is impressive but

---

[18]   We use the same data on pay and employment as before, that is, industrial employment and wages.

comparable to that reported for other countries, both industrialized and developing ones.[19]   In short, the employment distribution of women has a modest effect on female pay. Much of the difference between female and male pay should be sought in women's low relative pay in the sectors in which they are employed.[20]

4. Qualifications and Discussion

The results of the previous analysis would be valid, if the underlying assumptions were true. This is not the case. However, the non-fulfillment of some of the assumptions biases the estimated effects upward while the non-fulfillment of others biases them downward. Therefore, the net effect of relaxing the non-realistic assumptions cannot be determined using available evidence. Only the direction of bias from selected factors is indicated below and precise estimates must await further research.

The results were based on the assumption that women and men have identical labor supply functions. However, empirical studies have documented that this is not true. In particular, women's responses to changing wages have been found to be highly elastic[21] while most studies imply that the male supply is totally or nearly perfectly inelastic.[22] Knowing that women's labor supply responds elastically to labor market conditions (so more women will be tempted to join the labor market when barriers are eliminated) and that the male labor supply

---

[19]   See Brown, Moon and Zoloth (1980a) for the United States, and Chiplin and Sloane (1976) and Miller (1987) for Britain. Similar evidence for developing countries is presented in the collection of studies in Birdsall and Sabot (1991).

[20]   Of course, our results may reflect to some extent the fact that broad employment categories have been used.

[21]   For a survey see Killingsworth and Heckman (1986) or the wide range of individual country estimates (which include the United States, Britain, France, Spain, Germany, Netherlands, Sweden, Italy, Australia, and Japan) provided in the *Journal of Labor Economics,* Vol. 3, No. 1, Part 2 (Special Issue), January.

[22]   For surveys see Pencavel (1986) or Fallon and Verry (1988).

will not react adversely to a decrease in their wages, one is confident that the welfare gain should be even higher than that suggested by the present results.[23]

Women's occupational choice, a key factor in the present analysis, is seen as more favorable to work which is compatible with family matters[24] and where productive skills do not depreciate much because of labor market interruptions (atrophy).[25] In addition, biological or attitudinal differences may also be important for some jobs.[26] In this respect, our estimates are upwardly biased. However, the following qualification may neutralize, or even reverse, this bias. One has in mind here the perennial chicken and egg question. That is the extent to which what appears to be a free occupational choice is not the result of a rational labor supply decision under labor demand constraints.[27] Consequently, the assumption of factor homogeneity may initially bias the estimates for efficiency gains upward but the (unavoidable) failure to account for the response of the female labor supply to the demand conditions[28] may well correct for this bias.

There are many refinements that could be mentioned in this context although little can be done in the context of the present study. Given the lack of informative data, this section is concluded with one more observation. The

---

[23]   Of course, the rise in female labor supply will eventually result in lower levels of average wages but this effect has not been found to be important in practice (Pike, 1982). In any case, the equalization of the occupational distribution of the sexes would be a continuous process over a number of years and, given the increase in labor productivity due to improvements in technology, the level of male real wages need not suffer at all.

[24]   Easterlin (1968); Lehrer and Stokes (1985).

[25]   Mincer and Polachek (1974); Mincer and Ofek (1974); Polachek (1975).

[26]   For example, in Britain shortly after World War I it was estimated that women's productivity was about 10 to 15 percent less than men's in tasks involving heavy manual work. See *Atkin Report* (War Cabinet Committee on the Employment of Women in Industry), London: HMSO, 1919.

[27]   Gronau (1982).

[28]   The constraints attributed to the labor demand side can well be the result of legislation (Kanowitz, 1969), informal mechanisms (Bernard, 1971), ideological/cultural factors (Williams and Best, 1982), men's interest in maintaining their privileges (Goode, 1982), union practices (Rubery, 1988), as well as consumer preferences (Becker, 1971).

simulations assumed that women's and men's pay and employment characteristics are equalized within but not across industries. This eclecticism was dictated by the fact that it is even harder to incorporate movements in employment across industries.[29] Even so, one is quite sure about the direction of bias from this omission: it has already been established in the previous chapter that industrial dissimilarity is almost as significant as occupational dissimilarity and, had one allowed for across industry equalization of employment, the gains would have been higher.

5.   Conclusions

One always faces a risk when trying to incorporate all eventualities in a rather simple economic framework -- as the one employed in this chapter.[30] Yet a number of conclusions may be relevant. In particular, even if only a small part of the observed sex differential in the labor market is due to demand factors or some (unspecified by the present analysis) imperfection, its elimination may result in sizeable gains in output (efficiency) which would in turn improve women's labor earnings (poverty). All this becomes possible from the more efficient use of any country's most abundant type of human capital. As women are disproportionately found in the low income segment of the population, the distributional effects are guaranteed. And, as real wages tend to rise with growth, the real wages of men need never suffer an actual reduction.

The (albeit tentative) nature of the present findings suggests that a rewarding direction of research would be the exploration of factors which cause the observed labor market differentials between women and men in the region. In a broader social cost-benefit framework, imperfections arising from causes other than legislation or labor market regulation are difficult to identify, even more so to quantify their effects. Hence, a relatively easy policy option may be to revise statutes which differentiate between the sexes and force individuals to accept one stereotype or another, either in the family or in the labor market.

---

[29]   One requires a substantial number of additional assumptions for this case such as cross-industrial (as well as occupational) elasticities of substitution.

[30]   Mason (1984, p. 157) notes that economists have given more attention to the consequences of female employment aggregates and occupational sex segregation than to their causes. However, this practice is changing as the study of Gronau (1982) and references therein indicate.

Statistical Appendix to Chapter 4

The table presents the simulation results of assuming that women are equally productive and have the same occupational distribution as men within each industry under different values of the elasticity of substitution.

Appendix Table A4.1
Results of the Within Industry Elimination of Occupational Differentials

Country/ Year	Elas. of Subst. (sigma)	Percentage change in			
		Female wage	Male wage	GDP	Labor force[a]
	(1)	(2)	(3)	(4)	
Argentina	3	38.2	-8.9	4.0	25.3
1987	6	45.0	-5.7	8.3	35.8
	9	48.8	-4.0	10.8	39.3
	12	51.1	-3.0	12.3	40.4
	max	56.4	-0.7	16.2	40.9
Brazil	3	96.6	-7.7	8.7	23.1
1980	6	112.0	-3.7	15.2	27.8
	9	118.0	-2.3	18.0	28.5
	12	121.0	-1.7	19.5	28.7
	max	126.6	-0.5	22.6	28.8
Chile	3	40.5	-5.6	3.3	17.6
1989	6	48.0	-3.3	6.7	24.1
	9	52.0	-2.2	8.6	25.9
	12	54.3	-1.7	9.7	26.5
	max	60.0	-0.3	12.6	25.9
Colombia	3	46.4	-7.6	4.6	20.2
1978	6	51.8	-4.5	8.4	29.8
	9	54.8	-3.1	10.4	34.5
	12	56.7	-2.3	11.6	36.5
	max	61.3	-0.7	14.7	38.2

(Continued)

Appendix Table A4.1 (Cont.)
Results of the Within Industry Elimination of Occupational Differentials

Country/ Year	Elas. of Subst. (sigma)	Percentage change in			Labor Force[a]
		Female Wage	Male Wage	GDP	
	(1)	(2)	(3)	(4)	
Costa Rica	3	38.8	-6.3	3.0	17.5
1978	6	40.1.	-4.0	6.0	24.2
	9	43.0	-2.9	7.7	26.7
	12	44.7	- 2.2	8.8	27.9
	max	49.3	-0.5	11.8	29.1
Ecuador	3	58.6	-13.3	9.7	37.2
1966	6	76.4	-7.3	19.7	51.8
	9	85.1	-4.7	25.1	54.3
	12	89.7	-3.4	28.1	54.7
	max	97.3	-1.4	33.4	54.9
Guatemala	3	25.2	-5.5	2.0	13.7
1989	6	29.0	-3.7	4.3	20.4
	9	31.5	-2.6	5.9	22.8
	12	33.0	-1.7	7.0	23.1
	max	38.1	2.4	11.8	21.9
Jamaica	3	60.7	-8.2	8.3	27.5
1987	6	77.4	-4.4	15.7	35.3
	9	84.7	-2.9	19.4	38.1
	12	88.7	-2.2	21.4	39.5
	max	94.0	-1.2	24.3	40.6
Uruguay	3	29.6	-7.6	3.4	16.3
1989	6	34.7	-4.9	6.9	24.2
	9	37.8	-3.4	9.0	29.2
	12	39.9	-2.6	10.4	33.3
	max	48.1	-0.5	15.2	40.3
Venezuela	3	23.6	-6.2	1.9	11.7
1987	6	26.7	-4.4	4.1	21.5
	9	29.0	-3.3	5.6	27.1
	12	30.6	-2.6	6.6	30.1
	max	36.4	-0.4	10.3	32.9

a. Percent of total labor force who would have to change occupation
Source: See sources to Table 4.2.

5

Gender Differences in the Labor Market:
Analytical Issues

1. Measuring and Interpreting Gender Wage Differentials

Female labor is, on average, rewarded less than male labor. This is, and has been, true for all countries for which data exist, irrespective of the mechanism used in allocating economic resources (from market to plan) or the developmental stage of the country (from basic agrarian to mature industrialist). What is less common is agreement on the reasons giving rise to this. In previous studies a sizeable part of the pay gap remains unexplained even after accounting for differences between the employment characteristics of women and men (such as occupation and industry, whether they are employed in the public or private sector, or in rural, urban or metropolitan areas) and the personal characteristics of workers (such as education, labor market experience and unionization).[1]

From an economist's point of view, any observed difference in pay can be seen as the interaction of labor demand and labor supply schedules that differ between women and men. In other words, if women and men are identical factors of production, women's inferior position in the labor market may be the result of

---

[1]   For a survey see Cain (1986). One author's summary statement of the empirical findings attributes up to two-thirds of the pay gap to differences in workers' characteristics (Killingsworth, 1990, p. 57) though this seems to be a rather high figure (Duncan, 1984, Chapter 1, Table 1). However, these studies relate primarily to advanced economies and it is probable that different considerations apply to countries characterized by large informal sectors and excess supply of labor. In fact, the present results are more in line with earlier studies in developed countries where differences in characteristics appeared to account for only a small part of the total wage gap between women and men (Oaxaca, 1987).

some form of discrimination against them in the workplace (labor demand side).[2] Alternatively, if the pricing and allocation of women's work in the labor market is gender blind, the observed differences may be the result of women's own choices and efforts to compromise their willingness to work with domestic activities (labor supply side).[3] However, even if it were possible to determine that the initial reason for a particular differential was more on the supply than the demand side, or vice versa, the observed differential would most likely be a mixture of the two -- as individuals attempt to maximize their welfare and employers their profits subject to their own constraints and the constraints imposed by the behavior of other parties. For example, if women perceive it as unlikely that they will end up in a senior position, they will underinvest in education as rewards will be lower compared to men's. In this respect, it would be wrong to argue that women's low achievement in the labor market is the result of their free choice to underinvest in their human capital. Alternatively, if employers expect women to drop out of the labor market during family formation, they will underinvest in women's training as the expected benefits will be lower than in the case of men. In this respect, employers can be seen as rational agents (rather than discriminators) who balance their decisions between different current costs and expected returns.[4] Given the difficulty in isolating which part of the female/male wage differential is due to demand reasons and which part is due to supply reasons, what one hopes to do is to

---

[2]   One should note that what appears as discriminatory practice in the labor market need not necessarily be, wholly or in part, the result of employers' practices. Fellow employees' attitudes ("men do not like to be led by women"), unions' practices ("most union members are men"), customers' preferences ("surveys have shown that air travellers prefer female hosts"), government regulations (protecting or prohibiting) and social norms ("a woman's place is at home") can all contribute to different treatment of women and men in the labor market. See Boserup (1970), Cain *et al.* (1979), Easterlin (1968), England (1982), Hofstede (1980) and Lehrer and Stokes (1985).

[3]   Of course, observed differentials in the labor market can be due to differences in productivity between women and men as well as difference in "fixed costs" associated with the decision to supply/demand labor in the market (Oi, 1962; Nickell, 1978; Cogan, 1980a).

[4]   This behavior of employers has been labelled "statistical discrimination" (Phelps, 1972; Thurow, 1975; Aigner and Cain, 1977).

differentiate between the systematic relationship between earnings and workers' productive characteristics in general and the "gender effect" upon earnings.[5]

For practical purposes one can bypass the long list of theoretical arguments and address the issue in a way susceptible to empirical investigation. There are two different approaches. First, one can examine whether there is a *fixed* premium/disadvantage associated with the sex of the worker. Second, one can investigate whether *individual characteristics* of female workers are rewarded differently in the labor market than the corresponding characteristics of men. The former approach relates to a "shift" in the earnings function and the latter to a "difference in the slope coefficients" of the earnings function.

The first approach consists of running a regression of earnings upon the characteristics of all (male and female) workers including a separate variable which indicates the sex of the worker.[6] This can be shown as follows:

$$\ln(W_i) = C + (X_i)a + b(F_i) + e_i \tag{5.1}$$

where $\ln(W_i)$ is the logarithm of the ith worker's pay,[7] C is a constant term, X is a vector denoting whatever measurable personal characteristics of relevance are utilized by the researcher, a is the vector of the estimated coefficients/effects of these characteristics upon pay, F is a (dummy) variable taking the value of 1 if the worker is female and 0 if the worker is male, and e refers to unobserved or unmeasurable characteristics.[8] The interpretation of equation 5.1 is that individual earnings depend on the worker's observed characteristics (X's), the

---

[5]   Economists have conventionally referred to the sex effect as the "upper bound of discrimination," irrespective of origin, or "the extent of our ignorance" (Sloane, 1985; Siebert, 1990).

[6]   See Beller (1984), Fallon and Verry (1988, Chapter 5) or Killingsworth (1990, Chapter 3). For applications and extensions of this approach to measuring wage differentials in other areas of research see Smith (1977), Oswald (1985) and Ehrenberg and Schwarz (1986).

[7]   The logarithm of earnings, rather than the level of earnings as such, is considered to be the appropriate regressand both on theoretical grounds (Mincer, 1974) and also on empirical grounds (Dougherty and Jimenez, 1991).

[8]   The error term is assumed to be normally distributed with zero mean.

worker's sex (F), and unobserved characteristics (the error term) assuming that e is not correlated to F at given X.[9]

The coefficient of interest is that on the variable representing the sex of the worker, which shows whether women receive on average lower pay than men ($b < 0$) other things being equal (after adjusting for whatever the X's account for). This approach constrains, however, the values of the coefficients on the other explanatory variables, such as education and experience, to be the same for women and men. Given that sex specific earnings functions have produced coefficients on female characteristics that are significantly different than those for men,[10] a finding confirmed also by the present studies, this approach is bound to yield, in general, biased results.

The second approach consists of running two regressions separately on women's earnings and men's earnings and comparing the outcome. This method requires the two regressions to have a strictly comparable specification, that is, the number and type of variables should be the same in both the female and male earnings functions. Thus the estimation can start with the following two regressions (omitting subscripts for notational simplicity):

$$\ln(W_m) = C_m + (X_m)m + e_m \qquad (5.2)$$
$$\ln(W_f) = C_f + (X_f)f + e_f \qquad (5.3)$$

where C_s (s=male or female) is the constant term, X_s is the vector of male or female characteristics, m and f are the respective coefficients on these characteristics, and e_s is the error term. Then, the "adjusted" pay gap can be estimated in the following way: the difference in the *average* logarithms of male and female pay $[\ln(W_m)-\ln(W_f)$ - no subscripts] can be shown[11] to be equal to the percentage difference of male to female average pay (W_m and W_f):

---

[9]   If the error term is negatively correlated to F, then the coefficient on discrimination will be biased upwards as women will possess fewer unobservables than men with the same X's. This bias arises because the characteristics which are unobserved and affect women negatively will register an effect via the coefficient on the dummy variable measuring sex in addition to the pure effect of sex upon pay.

[10]   Psacharopoulos (1985); Tilak (1987); Sahn and Alderman (1988); Schultz (1989b); Bustillo (1989).

[11]   Oaxaca (1973).

$$\ln(W_m) - \ln(W_f) = \ln[(1 + (W_m - W_f)/W_f] \qquad (5.4)$$
$$= (W_m - W_f)/W_f$$

Given the previous two equations and utilizing the regression property that the error term has a mean value of zero, one can rewrite the right hand side of equation 5.4 as:

$$\ln(W_m) - \ln(W_f) = (C_m - C_f) + [(X_m)m - (X_f)f] \qquad (5.5)$$

where the first bracket refers to the respective constant terms in the male and female earnings functions, and X_m and X_f are the average values of the male and female characteristics in the sample. Adding to and subtracting from equation 5.5 the term $(X_f)m$ or $(X_m)f$ and rearranging produces the following two "decompositions" of the gross differential in average pay:

$$\ln(W_m) - \ln(W_f) = [(C_m - C_f) + (X_f)(m-f)] + [(X_m - X_f)m] \quad \text{or} \qquad (5.6)$$
$$= [(C_m - C_f) + (X_m)(m-f)] + [(X_m - X_f)f] \qquad (5.7)$$

Thus, the percentage difference in pay can be seen to come from two different sources. First, the differential rewards to male and female characteristics (m-f) in the labor market including the difference between the constant terms and, second, the differences in the quantities of these characteristics held by men and women $(X_m - X_f)$. In this approach, the portion of the wage gap due to differences between the endowments of productive characteristics held by women and men can be considered to be nondiscriminatory (or "justified" discrimination).[12] On the other hand, the portion of the wage gap which is due to differences in the values of the coefficients, including the constant term, can be thought of as the upper bound of ("unjustified") discrimination. Obviously, this approach (equations 5.6 and 5.7), which utilizes two separate earnings functions, encompasses the previous one (equation 5.1) which is based on a single regression and examines, in effect, only the difference in the constant terms. This explains the popularity of the decomposition based on separate earnings functions for women and men in applied research.[13] This is the approach followed here.

---

[12]   Blinder (1974).

[13]   It should be noted that, in practice, the two approaches (equation 5.1 and equations 5.6 or 5.7) may yield similar results as the constrained single equation estimation is, in effect, a matrix-weighted average of the results produced by the two equation method (see also Killingsworth, 1990, p. 96).

One should note that equations 5.6 and 5.7 do not produce the same results. The former decomposition evaluates the justified and potentially discriminatory components of the pay gap if women were paid as men. The latter decomposition assumes that men are paid like women. This is a common problem with index numbers and is shown in Figure 5.1.[14] The horizontal axis measures education (schooling in years) which can be considered a typical individual characteristic. The vertical axis measures wages. The lower line represents the earnings function for women, that is, it shows that female wages increase by f (the slope of the line) for an additional year of schooling. The upper line is the earnings function for men and m is the corresponding slope coefficient. Let S_f and S_m be the average level of schooling attained by women and men respectively. The way the diagram is drawn suggests that women have on average lower wages than men ($W_f < W_m$) because (1) they are less educated ($S_f < S_m$), (2) their education is rewarded less than men ($f < m$), and (3) uneducated women have been assumed to receive a lower wage in the labor market than men (the constant term for women, C_f, is lower than the constant term for men, C_m). Assuming that the difference in educational attainment is the result of women's free choice, one is interested in finding which part of the gross wage gap ($W_f W_m$) is justified, that is, can be explained by the fact that women are less qualified than men in the sense that they possess a lower amount of schooling than men (the difference arising from $S_f < S_m$). If "no discrimination" is taken to mean that women should be paid as men (f should be equal to m and C_f should be equal to C_m), then women's average pay should increase to W; hence $W_f W$ is the unjustified part of the wage gap. Alternatively, if "no discrimination" means that men should be paid as women (m equal to f and C_m equal to C_f), then the unjustified part of the wage gap becomes $W W_m$.

The two decompositions in Figure 5.1 produced dramatically different results. This was purely for expository purposes. In practice, it is not certain if a decomposition based on female means will produce a higher or lower estimate for justified or unjustified discrimination than a decomposition based on male means. It all depends on the relative "flatness" of the two earnings functions (that is, the curvature of the lines around the region of the average female and male characteristics) which is not captured in the simple linear specification adopted in Figure 5.1. However, both decompositions have produced similar results in applied research -- including the present country studies.

---

[14]   Some authors have taken the average of the estimates of the two approaches (Greenhalgh, 1980) but, as explained later in the text, this makes practically no difference to the results as the "slope" effect typically dominates the "endowment" effect.

Figure 5.1
Decomposition of the Gender Wage Gap

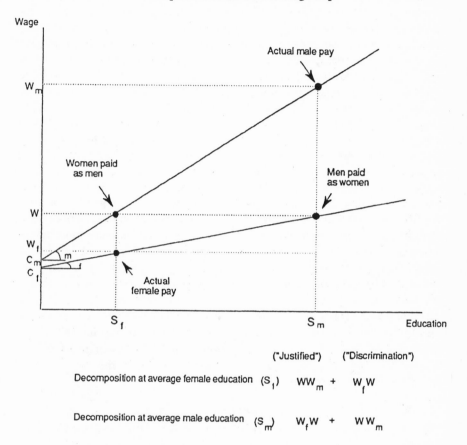

		("Justified")	("Discrimination")
Decomposition at average female education	(S_f)	WW_m +	W_fW
Decomposition at average male education	(S_m)	W_fW +	WW_m

The role of the constant term needs further clarification as its value changes depending on how qualitative (dummy) variables are specified. Assume that a variable suggesting "residence" (urban/rural) is included in the earnings functions to capture the fact that pay in urban areas is typically higher than pay in rural areas. If this variable takes the value of zero for rural residence and unity for urban residence, then the regression will produce a positive coefficient on residence. In this specification the constant term will have a relatively low value as it refers to the pay of rural residents. Conversely, if the variable proxying residence takes the value of unity for rural areas and zero for urban areas, it will produce a negative coefficient while the constant term will be higher as it refers to the pay of urban residents. Nothing else will change in this regression and the two specifications are formally equivalent. However, this innocuous change may have an effect on the results of the decomposition to the extent that rural/urban residence affects women's pay and men's pay in different ways. With reference to equation 5.6 or equation 5.7, the second term (difference in endowments) will remain unchanged and the percentage of the pay gap attributed to endowments will be as much as before. The first term (difference in rewards) will again be the same if considered together but the relative importance of differences in the constant terms will be different compared with differences in rewards. As a result, attempts to separate the effect of the constant term from the total effect of rewards may result in arbitrary conclusions.[15] Despite this difficulty, most modern studies on discrimination have conventionally examined the effect of the constant term separately within the "rewards part" of the gender wage gap.[16] In what follows, the nature of our results necessitates the separation of the effects from the difference in the constant terms and the differences between rewards but the previous qualifications should be borne in mind.

2.   Earnings Functions

So far the analysis has proceeded along very general lines. One has to be more specific with respect to the "earnings functions" summarized in the form of equations 5.2 and 5.3. The most common formulation of earnings functions comes from the seminal work of Mincer (1974). At the cost of some abstraction, the basic model can be summarized as follows.

First, assume that education (1) lasts for a given number of years (denoted by S), (2) is of a given "type" (for example, there is no distinction between arts, humanities, science and so on) and (3) is full-time (that is, an individual either works or studies). Thus to become educated is an all or nothing decision.

Second, assume that individuals are *ex ante* identical in all respects (such as tastes, ability, financial endowments, access to capital markets, parental

---

[15]   This point was raised by Jones (1983) who noted that up to 20 percent of the gender wage gap may shift from the constant term component to the other rewards component when qualitative variables are specified in different forms.

[16]   See among others, Shapiro and Stelcner (1986); Behrman and Wolfe (1986); Birdsall and Behrman (1983); Birdsall and Fox (1985); Knight and Sabot (1982) and the collection of papers in Birdsall and Sabot, eds. (1991).

influence and socio-economic background). This and the previous assumption result in two different wages in the labor market: one for educated labor and another for uneducated labor. Then the difference between these two wage levels can be taken to be a common compensating differential for all individuals. It is immediately obvious that under the assumptions of the model the role of demand in this type of labor market is simply to determine the percentage of the labor force who are educated. Now, the question becomes what the difference between these two wages would be in such an environment. To answer this question a few more assumptions are required.

Third, assume that there are no direct costs to education (such as fees, expenditure on books, etc.) and that the only (indirect) cost to education is foregone earnings (the cost of not being employed in the labor market).

Fourth, assume that all workers have the same total working life (T years) irrespective of whether they undertake education or not. Thus educated workers retire from the labor market S years after the uneducated ones have retired.

Fifth, assume that there is no on-the-job training and no other kind of investment in human capital after the completion of formal education. In other words, the difference in the wages between educated and uneducated labor is due to differences only in formal schooling undertaken in early life.

Sixth, assume that with the exception of the wage rate, other characteristics of jobs requiring educated and uneducated labor are identical. This assumption implies that observed wages differ because some workers have education and others have no education at all.

Seventh, and finally, assume that the market is perfect in terms of information and adjustment costs, and that there is a given rate of interest (r).

This model is shown in a diagrammatic manner in Figure 5.2. The individual is at the start of what can be his working life (he is, for example, 15 years old). If he joined the labor market at that age, his wage would be W^U and his lifetime earnings would be equal to the sum of the areas A plus C. If he carried on studying for S years, he would forfeit the earnings indicated by area C ("cost") but would enjoy a higher wage, W^e. His post-education earnings would be equal to the sum of the areas A plus B (B is the benefit that results from more schooling).[17]

---

[17]   Strictly speaking, area B should extend beyond retirement age by S years (this is so because of the fourth assumption) but this part of the diagram is omitted for simplicity.

Figure 5.2
Costs and Benefits of Investment in Education

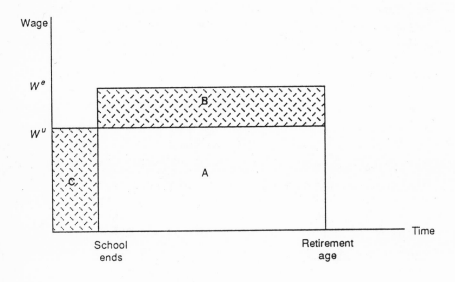

On the assumptions of the model, the present values (PV) of the lifetime wages (W) of uneducated and educated workers (superscripts *u* and *e* respectively) at the point they start working are respectively:

$$PV^u = W^u/r \ (1 - e^{-rT})$$

$$PV^e = W^e/r \ (1 - e^{-rT}) \ e^{-rS}$$

where *e* is the basis of the natural logarithms (approximately equal to 2.72).

The interpretation of the right hand side of these two equations is as follows. The ratio of wages to the interest rate (W/r) is simply the present value of an annuity paid forever. The term in parentheses is the finite life correction factor, that is, it corrects the previous ratio for the fact that people retire after T years of work. And the third term which appears only in the second formula is another adjustment for the fact that those who become educated will have no wage until their education stops and work starts. In other words, those who contemplate starting work immediately discount to today, while those who undertake education discount everything to S years ahead.

With individuals *ex-ante* identical, the two present values should, at a competitive equilibrium in a perfect market, be equal. Equating the right hand sides of the two equations above, eliminating the term in the bracket from both sides, and rearranging we obtain:

$$W^e = W^u \, e^{rS}$$

and taking the logarithms on both sides:

$$\ln(W^e) = \ln(W^u) + rS$$

because $\ln(e^x)$ is simply x.

Thus the theory is compatible with the common sense result that the educated should have greater wages than the uneducated ($W^e > W^u$) -- given that both r and S are positive. In addition, this simple model provides a convenient (semi-logarithmic) relationship between annual earnings and length of schooling (in years) which is capable of being used in econometric work. In particular, one can run a regression of the log earnings of individual workers upon a constant term and their length of schooling. In this context, the constant term should be approximately equal to the logarithm of the wage for non-educated labor while the coefficient on schooling should be roughly equal to the rate of interest. In fact, and as the underlying assumptions necessitate, in a perfectly competitive environment the market rate of interest should be equal to the rate of time preference in the society and also to the rate of return to an additional year of schooling.

The merit of this approach is that it is derived from an explicit economic foundation that dictates the functional form (log annual earnings on years of schooling) that econometric estimation should take. One disadvantage of the "earnings function" derived as above is that it ignores all other aspects of human capital formation and especially on-the-job training. In fact, in many jobs employer provided training or simply experience may be more significant forms of human capital and more important determinants of earnings than formally acquired education. The flat age earnings profile depicted in Figure 5.2 contradicts the typically observed age earnings profiles. In particular, age-earnings profiles increase at first, reaching a peak sometime in the working life of an individual until they eventually flatten out or even decrease (after the age of, say, 50 or 55 years). This pattern is suggestive of the fact that other types of human capital are formed during a person's working life. These observations can be accommodated by including into the model some proxy for post-education human capital formation on the right hand side of the last equation. The most popular version of earnings functions is by far the following one:

$$\ln(W^e) = \text{Constant} + rS + aE + bE^2$$

where E (E^2) is years of post-school work experience (and its square) and a (b) are coefficients. In theoretical terms the quadratic (in experience) formulation of earnings functions can be derived by assuming that investment in human capital declines linearly with time.[18]   In practical terms, the inclusion of experience and its square as an explanatory variable has been found to "belong" to the earnings functions in the sense that regression analysis returns coefficients on experience which have the correct sign, are statistically significant and are "intuitively" of reasonable size.

The earnings functions thus specified have proven to be the most stable econometric relationship in the area of applied economics.[19]   They have been estimated for practically all countries for which individual (cross-section) data exist. Their popularity rests partly on the very few variables that are required, namely education and experience. The former variable is usually available from many sources (labor force surveys or household surveys). The latter variable, namely labor market experience is relatively easily proxied, at least in the case of men, as follows:

Experience = Age - Schooling - (school entry age)

as most men are in the labor force after the completion of their formal education and throughout their prime age. Experience thus calculated is in effect *potential* experience (or, as referred to by some authors, Mincerian experience).

---

[18]   The proof can be found in many labor economics textbooks such as Fallon and Verry (1988), p.149-150.

[19]   Griliches (1977).

A number of issues have been raised with respect to the use of Mincerian functions and the previously described decomposition in the attempt to identify the gender effect on pay. The arguments relate to whether the parsimonious formulation of earnings functions is sufficient and appropriate for the task in hand on both theoretical and empirical grounds. We do not dwell on the former as it is beyond the scope of this study and the relevant literature is rich.[20] With respect to the latter, applied research may encounter measurement and omitted variables errors as well as endogeneity, selectivity and specification problems. Such effects have a complex impact on the decomposition results whose interpretation may not be immediately obvious. These aspects are examined below.

3.   Errors of Measurement and Omitted Variables

Education. Errors of measurement and omitted variables problems are both common and interrelated issues in the earnings functions approach. For example, the effect of formally acquired human capital is captured by the coefficient on the education variable, the latter being usually measured as years of schooling. The shortcomings associated with this approximation are, first, that it assumes an extra year of schooling augments earnings irrespective of whether it was acquired at an elite or deprived school, or whether it is added to 2 or 12 years of schooling, or whether education relates to studies in arts, social sciences or engineering.[21]   Second, there is also evidence that parents usually invest in higher quality education for boys than girls.[22]   Hence, the nature of the schooling variable in the men's regression may be different from that in the women's regression. Third, formal schooling is not the only type of education

---

[20]   For the theoretical foundation and the common form of the earnings function see Mincer (1974) and Griliches (1977) and for surveys on the debate which has followed see Siebert (1985) and Willis (1986).

[21]   Welch (1966); Behrman and Birdsall (1983); Birdsall and Behrman (1983).

[22]   Becker and Tomes (1979) suggest that parents could distribute investment among their children with different characteristics differently and empirical evidence from developing countries confirms that, if such differential treatment is practiced (in areas such as health care, nutrition or expenditure on education), it favors boys (see Visaria, 1971, on India; Chen *et al.*, 1981, on Bangladesh; Aird, 1984, on China; Blau, 1984, on Nicaragua; Martorell *et al.*, 1984, on Nepal; Amin and Pebley, 1987, and Schultz, 1982, on India; and Bardhan, 1984, for an overview).

one can have; nonformal education is also important.[23]   Consequently, education may not be measured precisely while its coefficient may be affected by the absence of variables (omitted/unobservable) which relate to the quality of education. The only way we could have taken into account some of the differences between women's and men's type and quality of education was by separating, on the one hand, general from vocational secondary education and, on the other hand, "soft" and "hard" subjects at university level (such as arts and social sciences versus engineering and science).   However, even in the seven countries for which such information existed, the number of identifiable cases was minute for women, especially in terms of vocational education.[24] When a further breakdown was attempted (for example, by region or age) the number of useful cases dropped to single figures -- no more than two observations in some countries. The paucity of information in this respect is at the same time reassuring that the bias in our estimates may not be significant: too few women opt for vocational education and their enrollment in tertiary education is still low. In fact, one in ten of all females aged 15 to 24 years in the region were illiterate in the early 1980s and as many as one in four of those aged 35 to 44 years.[25]   Given that specialized studies do not generally start before the beginning of upper secondary education, men and women workers in the region should have more homogeneous education than their counterparts in advanced countries.

Experience for men. Similar considerations apply to the other human capital variable -- "experience" -- typically included in the earnings functions. Information about actual work history rarely exists in data sets. The usual strategy is to use potential experience (age minus schooling minus school entry age) and its square as right hand variables in the earnings functions in order to proxy the effect of the informal acquisition of human capital.[26] The experience

---

[23]   Though the distinction between formal and nonformal education is far from clear (La Belle, 1986), nonformal education can be defined as the knowledge acquired outside the conventional primary/secondary/tertiary education system (Coombs, 1968).

[24]   The countries for which such information exists are Argentina, Colombia, Guatemala, Honduras, Panama, Uruguay, and Venezuela.

[25]   UNESCO (1990).

[26]   The inclusion of experience thus specified has been proposed on theoretical grounds (Mincer, 1974) and though this specification and its interpretation has been the subject of debate (Psacharopoulos and Layard, 1979; Griliches, 1977) it is still considered to be an appropriate simplification for estimating the returns to human capital

variable so constructed has been routinely assumed to be a good proxy for the labor force experience of men. This might have been the case when the first earnings functions were tried using data sets in the 1960s in advanced countries following the post-war economic prosperity.[27] However, unemployment has increased considerably from the mid-1970s onward and the assumption of continuous work record is less accurate today than before.[28] In addition, neither the incidence nor the duration of unemployment is distributed equally among the various groups of workers. There are some workers who do not, in practice, experience unemployment (in tenured posts) while others may have an unemployment spell only rarely (the more educated and the more skilled). The bulk of those responsible for a 5 or 10 percent unemployment rate come from the lower end of the employment distribution, the less qualified workers.[29] As a consequence, the regression result will be inefficient and biased downward since potential experience in the sample will be greater than actual experience.

Experience for women. In the case of women, the use of potential rather than actual experience is even more problematic. Women generally leave the labor market during their family cycle and, when reliable data exist, their unemployment rates are usually higher than those of men. Hence, the measurement error is more serious and a decomposition of the pay gap based on potential experience would suggest a higher estimate for discrimination than the actual one. We cannot answer the question how the inclusion of potential rather than actual experience affects the estimates in this volume because there is no information on actual experience in the current data sets. However, the evidence from a few studies addressing this issue using cross-section or longitudinal data

---

(Willis and Rosen, 1979; Heckman and Hotz, 1986).

[27] Mincer's original application related to a sample of prime age men in 1959 — the unemployment problem was negligible in the United States during that period.

[28] A recent study for Britain (Main and Elias, 1987) utilizing data from the *National Training Survey 1976* shows even at that time, when the unemployment was less than half its level today, as many as 20 percent of the men in the sample did not have continuous work histories.

[29] A comprehensive study of the incidence and duration of unemployment among male workers of different characteristics was performed by Nickell (1980) who confirms the broad patterns of the duration and incidence of unemployment described in the text.

suggests that the estimated effect of potential experience upon female pay may be as low as 50 percent of the effect of actual experience.[30]

Proxied and unobserved human capital characteristics. The standard human capital variables (schooling and experience) may serve only as proxies for other unobserved individual characteristics and education can be seen as a signal for these unobserved characteristics.[31] In this context, if men have higher mean values of the proxy variables, the regression result for discrimination will be biased downward.[32] In addition, education and experience are not the only attributes rewarded in the labor market. There are also individual differences stemming from innate ability, motivation -- perhaps related to different family circumstances -- and formal and informal training. These are unmeasured or unmeasurable aspects whose exclusion from the earnings function will again produce biased results.[33]

Endogeneity. Even if information on actual labor market experience for women were available, one could not use it as such in the earnings equation. The reason for this is endogeneity. Experience is nothing more than a measure of "accumulated" participation, and participation depends on pay. For men, this is not perhaps a very important issue as the inelasticity of male labor supply to wages can be interpreted as an indication of the fact that men participate and

---

[30]   Malkiel and Malkiel (1973), Mincer and Polachek (1974), Zabalza and Tzannatos (1985) and Miller (1987). These studies conclude that the earnings increment associated with *actual* labor market experience among females is comparable to that received by male workers. In fact one study (Levine and Moock, 1984) found that almost half of the wage gap between husbands and wives could be attributed to the fluctuations in the labor force attachment of wives, especially to depreciation of female skills during interruptions in employment. However, their sample was drawn from a suburb of New York City in the late 1980s and may not be a representative one for other areas even within the United States. Wright and Ermisch (1991) estimated that the inclusion of actual experience in the earnings functions of women increases the part of the gender wage gap in Britain attributed to differences in endowments from 12 percent to only 17 percent – the latter being the estimate derived from using potential experience. Thus, in the present context one may argue that bias arising from proxying actual experience by potential experience may not be that great.

[31]   Berg (1971); Arrow (1972).

[32]   Hashimoto and Kochin (1980); Roberts (1980).

[33]   Unless, of course, the unobserved characteristics of relevance are distributed randomly among individuals – not a very realistic scenario (Polachek, 1975).

accumulate experience independently of their earnings.[34]   However, for women, especially married women, the elasticity of labor supply to their prospective pay has generally been found to be positive and sizeable.[35] Therefore, by focusing on one equation only, we ignore a more extensive (multi-equation) model where past and present female pay and work exhibit strong endogeneity.[36] This point has been forcefully made before and the endogeneity problem is clearly documented in the empirical literature.[37] In fact, one study, which corrected for the endogeneity of female participation and used actual female labor market experience, estimated that the returns to experience in the case of women are significantly greater (by as much as 50 percent) than the corresponding returns for men.[38] A possible explanation for this is that more "experienced" women (women who are permanently attached to the labor force) are a relatively scarce factor of production compared to men. Another explanation, of course, is that those women with a long labor market history may be superior to the average man in the labor force. This issue relates in part to the selectivity problem addressed below.

Selectivity. The use of earnings functions in the study of discrimination may have an additional complication, namely selectivity. Selectivity relates to the bias which results from the omission of unobserved variables from the analysis and can be highlighted with the use of the following example. Assume that all men work irrespective of their unobserved innate ability and their average pay is $100. This level of pay reflects the reward to the work of an average man. Assume that only half of women work and their average pay is $60. Finally

---

[34]   See among others Rosen (1969, 1976), Brown, Levin and Ulph (1976), Atkinson and Stern (1980), MaCurdy (1981), Blundell and Walker (1982). For a survey see Pencavel (1986) or Fallon and Verry (1988).

[35]   Though the labor supply elasticities for women have been estimated to be as high as 14 or more (Heckman and MaCurdy, 1980; Dooley, 1982), a value of around 1.5 to 3 could be considered quite typical. This range is also typical for a number of countries in Latin America (ECIEL, 1982).

[36]   In fact, the seriousness of failing to account for the endogeneity of female participation can be shown by reference to a study which reconciled the micro-evidence (cross-section data) with the observed patterns and trends in female participation (time-series data) only after correcting for (endogenizing) the experience of married women (Iglesias and Riboud, 1985).

[37]   Blinder (1973) and Mincer and Polachek (1974).

[38]   Zabalza and Arrufat (1985, p. 86, Table 5.4).

assume that men and working women have the same *observable* characteristics of relevance to the earnings function. The decomposition described earlier will attribute all the pay difference to discrimination. This result will be correct if innate ability is shared equally between working and non-working women. However, if women workers are more able than non-workers, then discrimination would amount to more than $40, as the average female worker is more able than the average male worker (=average man).

In the present context, in which the focus is on the economic aspects of women's work, wages are observed for working women but not for non-workers. Hence, a sample of working women can be taken as representative either of all (working and non-working) women, or only of those women who can attract a high offered wage, or only of women who have a low asking wage. Intuitively, it may be more reasonable to assume that women in the labor force are more likely to be a combination of women with high potential labor market rewards and low tastes for staying at home. Consequently, the sample is drawn from a self-selected group of women who are not likely to be representative of prospective female workers. The implication for the study of discrimination is that wage *offers* may constitute a more appropriate variable upon which the decomposition should apply, and not the *actual* wages that are, in effect, derived from the offered wage distribution *that is acceptable to job seekers*.[39]

A counterargument could be that women who are not currently in the labor force may be simply at a different stage of their lifecycle and they may not be different from women who do work: at another time, non-workers may enter the labor force when childrearing is over while workers may drop out of the labor force for reasons of family formation. If this is the case, there should be no concern for selectivity and restricting the basis of comparison to the sample of working women only should not overstate the value of the wage offers to women.[40] Whether this observation is more relevant than the one mentioned in the previous paragraph is an empirical question which has been addressed by the so called "second generation" models of labor supply whose rationale can be seen in the following analogy.[41]

---

[39]   Gronau (1974).

[40]   Gronau (1973), Cogan (1980b).

[41]   The second generation models are invariably based upon the procedure suggested by Heckman (1974, 1979) and are surveyed/expanded in Lee (1978), Willis and Rosen (1979), Wales and Woodland (1980), Killingsworth (1983), Heckman and MaCurdy (1980, 1982) and Borjas (1987).

Assume that a driver sets off for a journey between two points. He does not know the distance between the two points and the car mileometer is not working. He wants to find out the distance between the two points. Under normal circumstances this should present little problem. If the car travels at a constant speed of 50 miles per hour (mph) and gets to the destination in two hours, then the distance should be 100 miles. If traffic conditions are variable, then one can work out the implications. However, apart from the faulty mileometer there is another catch: the speedometer is sticky at 50 mph, that is, it stays at 50 mph whenever the car reaches a speed higher than this and up to the maximum of 100 mph the car is capable of doing. Fortunately, the driver is accompanied by a helpful passenger, who happens to be a statistician. They set themselves up to find out the distance in the following way: the driver will inform the passenger about the speed of the car and any changes in the speed while the passenger will keep a note of the speed and will monitor the time.

At the end of the journey their information consists of the following. First, the journey took 1 continuous hour of driving. Second, they travelled at an average speed of 40 mph for 51 minutes, when the speedometer oscillated between 0 and 50 miles per hour. On this information, they know for certain that they covered 40 miles while the distance covered during the remaining 9 minutes of high speed (more than 50 mph) is to be guessed. The driver suggests the assumption that during the time the car was driven in excess of 50 mph the speed was 75 mph (half-way between 50 mph and 100 mph). This would bring the total distance to ([1/60][51x40+9x75]) 45.25 miles. The statistician passenger considers this to be too high: he does not think they exceeded the legal limit that often (the driver is prepared to accept this). The passenger asserts that, since the observed average speed was 40 mph during the 51 minutes for which reliable information exists, the average speed should be around 42 mph and the total distance 42 miles. The driver is initially mystified but, after listening to the statistician's explanation - which is repeated in the next section, agrees. Let us get the basics for establishing this assertion.

In Figure 5.3 a standardized normally distributed variable is depicted for which information exists up to point T (truncation) but not above. In line with the previous example, T corresponds to 50 mph. The left hand side of the distribution corresponds to the 51 minutes for which information exists. The shaded right hand side of the distribution corresponds to the observations that have been lost during the 9 minutes that the car speed exceeded 50 mph (due to the faulty speedometer). In other words, there exists information for 85 percent of the observations but not for the remaining 15 percent.

Denoting

$\overline{\mu}$	=	estimated mean from the sample (40 mph for 51 minutes)
μ	=	true mean of the distribution (unknown)
σ	=	known standard deviation (say, 7 mph)
X_k	=	kth observation of the variable (speed in any minute)
n	=	number of useful observations (51 minutes)
$\phi(\delta)$	=	height of the distribution at the standardized truncation point (50 mph)
1-I	=	percentage of observations which are known (51/60 minutes or 85 percent)

one can establish the relationship between the calculated (sample) mean from the useful observations and the true mean as follows. The sample mean is:

$$\overline{\mu} = \Sigma X_k/n$$

Obviously this is lower than the true mean as information on high speeds is lost. To correct for this (selectivity) bias something has to be added. The "correction" (or "adjustment") factor needs to take into account how *thick* the missing tail of the distribution is *at the truncation* point. The "thickness" depends on the standard deviation of the distribution (or, equivalently, its height) at the truncation point. The truncation point relates to how much is "lost" as one moves along the horizontal axis (note that the truncated normal distribution is summarized completely by its mean, standard deviation and the truncation point). Hence, to calculate the correction factor one needs information on the thickness of the distribution and the location of truncation.

The derivation of the adjustment factor can be found in advanced econometric textbooks (see, for example, Greene, 1990, Chapter 21) but, for present purposes, what has to be added to correct for the selectivity bias is the product of the standard deviation times "lambda" (λ), that is:

correction factor	= standard deviation	x	λ
	= σ	x	$[\phi(\delta)/(1-I)]$

and the true mean becomes:

$$\mu = \overline{\mu} + \sigma[\phi(\delta)/(1-I)]$$

Let us put some numbers into the last formula. The driver and the passenger estimated that the speed averaged 40 mph for 51 minutes. They know that 15 percent of time (observations) is lost, hence $(1-I)=1-0.15=0.85$. The standard deviation is assumed to be known and equal to 7 mph. The final thing to calculate is the height ($\phi(\delta)$, called "abscissa") of the distribution at the

Figure 5.3
A Truncated Distribution

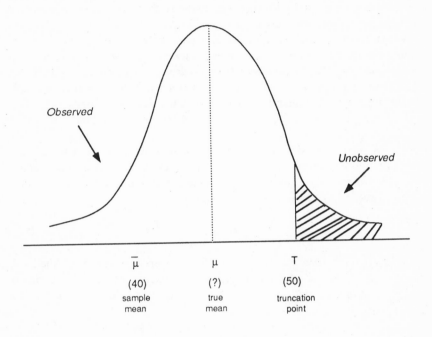

$\bar{\mu}$	μ	T
(40)	(?)	(50)
sample	true	truncation
mean	mean	point

truncation point: from the standard normal tables $\phi(\delta)=0.2323$ when $I=0.15$. Putting these numbers together implies that the (estimated) true average speed of the car was:

$$\mu = 40 + 7[0.2323/0.85] = 40 + 1.91 \approx 42$$

The faulty speedometer analogy in the context of selectivity bias shows two things. First, when one utilizes information which relates to only part of the sample, one obtains estimates which will in the general case be biased. Second, adjustment for sample selection is possible only when one is prepared make a "distributional assumption." In our example, the driver assumed that the distribution of speed above 50 mph had zero variance (constant speed at 75 mph) while the passenger assumed a normal distribution. Though one might feel that the passenger's guess was more realistic, one has to bear in mind that selectivity correction is not "something for nothing." The benefit is that one can work even with truncated distributions. The cost is the price one pays in the distributional assumption.

The similarity of the faulty speedometer to the study of female labor supply is obvious. One can get information on wages from existing workers, establish the known part of the wage distribution and make an informed guess about the unknown part, that is, the *ex ante* wages of non-working women. We are now in a position to compare the econometric models which did not take into account selectivity in the estimation of earnings functions with those which explicitly accounted for it. The former models are conventionally called "first generation" labor supply models while the latter are called "second generation" models.

The earlier models considered the market wages of working women only. In terms of regression analysis, these models postulate that the observed (market) wage of a woman relates to her characteristics in the following way (omitting individual subscripts for notational simplicity):

$$W_M = Xa + e_M \qquad (5.8)$$

where W_M is the market wage, X refers to characteristics relevant to the labor market, a is the vector of their respective coefficients, and e_M is a normally distributed error term with zero mean.[42] The expected value of market wages thus specified is:

$$E(W_M) = E(Xa) + E(e_M) = Xa \qquad (5.9)$$

under the assumption that the error term has zero mean. This specification is very much in accordance with the simplified earnings functions presented earlier in this chapter.

The second generation models note that market wages are observed only for women who have already decided to work. For these women the market wage should be higher than their shadow wage at home, W_H, otherwise women would stay at home where rewards are higher than in the market.[43] As in the case of

---

[42]   For simplicity we do not specify explicitly the constant term which can be assumed to be contained in vector X.

[43]   Note that this does not imply that wage offers among working women are on average necessarily greater than wage offers among non-working women. Neither does this imply that productivity at home is necessarily greater for non-working women than working women. It is therefore possible that women who can fetch a high wage in the

market wages, the value of the shadow wage can be thought as determined by women's personal characteristics, call them Z.[44] Hence,

$$W_H = Zb + e_H \tag{5.10}$$

where b is the corresponding vector of coefficients and e_H is another error term with the conventional properties. A woman's market wage is observed if:

$$I = W_M - W_H = Xa - Zb + e_M - e_H > 0 \tag{5.11}$$

where I is the difference between the market wage and the value of work at home. I is a continuous variable and can be considered to be an index representing a woman's propensity to participate in the labor market. In the present formulation (equation 5.11) when the value of the index for a particular woman is positive, the woman decides to work.[45] Consequently, the expected value of a woman's market wage is not dependent only on her labor market characteristics, X, as was assumed in the first generation models (equation 5.9), but on:

$$E(W_M) = Xa + E(e_M | I > 0) \tag{5.12}$$

which depends also on her personal characteristics, Z, because equation 5.12 incorporates the arguments in the right-hand side of inequality 5.11. A comparison of the last equation with equation 5.8 reveals that not correcting for selectivity amounts to another omitted variables problem, that is, we omit the second term in equation 5.12 (the "sample selection rule") which indicates whether a woman would be in the labor market. The sample selection rule

---

market do not work as they are also more productive at home than workers. In other words, the truncation point varies with the characteristics. This amounts to extending the car experiment to more than one car whose speedometers get sticky at different speeds: we do not know which car is faster than the others.

[44]   The vector of personal characteristics (Z) which determine women's productivity at home is assumed to include all the characteristics of relevance to the labor market (X) plus others but not vice versa. This assumption appears to be intuitively correct as there are many personal characteristics which do not affect productivity in the market but not vice versa. For example, being able to drive may augment home production but very few employers would care about it.

[45]   In fact, the critical value of I at which a woman decides to join or not the labor market does not have to be zero. However, without loss of generality, one can normalize the critical value to zero as we have done in the text for expository purposes.

consists of two terms: it is the product between a scalar, σ, and a variable (called lambda or the inverse Mill's ratio). The former term, σ, is a function of the standard deviations of the error terms in the market wage equation (5.8) and the home wage equation (5.10), and their correlation.[46] The latter term, lambda, is the ratio of the ordinate of the standard normal density divided by the standard normal distribution both evaluated at (I). In other words, its value depends on where the critical point (truncation) lies and the height of the distribution at that particular point.[47] Lambda can be calculated from another regression of a woman's decision to participate in the labor market upon her personal characteristics (this regression is called the participation function).[48] Then lambda can be included in equation 5.12 in order to solve, at least in theory, the problem of omitted variables as far as selectivity is concerned and it should attract a coefficient equal to σ:

$$E(W_M) = Xa + \sigma(lambda) \qquad (5.13)$$

Equation 5.13 is representative of the earnings functions used in the present studies.   Two more observations need to be added.   First, the theory as presented here does not unambiguously predict the sign of σ, the coefficient on lambda (that is, the outcome of the interplay between the standard deviations of and the correlation between the errors terms).[49] For example, the coefficient

---

[46]   The value of the scalar, σ, is equal to $\sigma_{e(h)}[\sigma_{e(m)}/\sigma_{e(h)} - r_{e(h),e(m)}]$, where $\sigma(.)$ stands for the standard deviation of the appropriate error term and r for the correction between the two error terms.

[47]   Because the problem arises from the "truncation" of the distribution of a particular characteristic, economists have habitually referred to this situation as a "truncated" regression instead of the more accurate term "censored." In the present context, truncation would occur if there are observations only for working women. However, what we are presented with is censorship which occurs when there is information, though incomplete, about non-working women -- though not, of course, with respect to their market wages. The correction consists in effect of predicting the missing information from whatever information is available in the censored data set.

[48]   The dependent variable in this case is a binary variable which takes the value of 1, if a woman is in the labor market, and the value of 0, if a woman is inactive.

[49]   In the early literature the expectation was that the coefficient on lambda would be positive. In fact, studies which reported negative coefficients were more or less dismissed as an "anomalous" result (Killingsworth and Heckman, 1986, commenting on the results for selectivity among Canadian women estimated by Nakamura *et al.*, 1979b). However, subsequent studies have often reported either insignificant or negative and

on lambda will be positive (and significant), if the unobserved factors which induce women to work are also directly related to female pay.   However, rewards to home activities may be more dispersed than those in the market and unobserved variables which boost productivity at home may relate positively to returns to market work. If these two conditions are met, then women who decide to join the labor market would be those who are least productive in terms of the unobservables[50] and the coefficient on lambda will be negative (and significant). These remarks suggest that the inclusion of lambda in an earnings function may solve[51] the econometric problem that arises when the error terms do not have the expected optimal properties but there is no "correct sign" or unique interpretation of its coefficient.[52]

Second, in many studies the coefficient on lambda proved to be statistically insignificant. This insignificance can be interpreted as no evidence of self-selection.[53] This can, in turn, be taken to imply that women as a group are more homogeneous than initially perceived and they are, in general, expected to work as much as men do. In fact, all country studies in this volume confirm that, after controlling for other factors, women have a greater tendency to work as they enter prime age.   Along these lines, the observed differences in participation are simply a reflection of household specialization during family

---

significant coefficients on lambda. See Heckman and MaCurdy (1980) and Stelcner and Breslaw (1985). Behrman, Wolfe and Blau (1985) also find a negative coefficient on lambda for Nicaraguan women in rural areas.

[50]   For a more detailed exposition of this argument see chapter on Venezuela by Cox and Psacharopoulos in the companion volume.

[51]   The simplified exposition of the sample selection effect and its correction adopted in our presentation masks the complexity of selection models and a number of difficult to resolve specification issues.   More specifically, the conventional error distribution assumptions have been questioned by Lee (1982), Olsen (1980) and Duncan and Leigh (1985).   In addition, problems of heteroscedasticity have not been fully resolved (Nelson, 1984). Finally, the assumed additivity in the effects of variables in the various equations in the model may not hold (Little, 1985).

[52]   Dolton and Makepeace (1987).

[53]   Cogan (1980b) shows that lack of adjustment for self-selection bias does not change the parameter estimates of the labor supply model for U.S. married women, who are the group for which the bias might be thought *a priori* to be more serious (for example, the corrected return to schooling increases to only 8.8 percent from 8.5 percent).

formation. Thus, at a point in time some women are in and others out of the labor force. At another point in time those who were previously in are out and vice versa.[54] This relates to a "quantity" interpretation of women's labor supply and, in effect, challenges the "qualitative" view derived from the observation that not being in the labor force at a given time is highly correlated with not being in the labor force at any time.[55] Though there is no ambition in the present volume to study whether "persistence" and "habit formation"[56] is a more appropriate explanation for the pattern of female participation during the life cycle than the "intertemporal substitution" models of labor supply,[57] one may feel tempted to accept that the forces determining women's roles within the family still dominate decisions about market employment in the developing countries. This may imply that selectivity may not be present in developing countries until the social groups are sufficiently differentiated -- when some critical level of per capita GDP is achieved.

One should also add that results derived only from a sample of working women may well produce biased estimates even for working women. The reason that bias creeps into the estimation is that both asking and offered wages depend on unobserved variables (an educated woman may well have a lower taste for home chores). As a result, the error terms in the structural model (the decision to work, to work at what wage, and to work for how long) are correlated with other variables assumed to be exogenous to the model, and are also correlated between themselves across the different equations in the model.[58]

---

[54] Though in a different context, Nakamura, Nakamura and Cullen (1979a) find that the occupational and industrial distribution is the same for both married and unmarried women and this supports the view that the factors affecting women are common in the two groups.

[55] Ben-Porath (1973); Heckman and Willis (1977); Keeley (1981).

[56] Clark and Summers (1982); Blanchard and Summers (1988). According to these authors, the persistence in female participation should be greater than in the working population as a whole. Cross and Allen (1988) echoed this theme at a macro-level and Behrman, Wolfe and Blau (1985) confirm that "there is a strong serial correlation in labor force participation because of differences across individuals in tastes, needs and returns from paid labor market participation" (p. 8).

[57] Lucas and Rapping (1969); Altonji (1982).

[58] Killingsworth and Heckman (1986).

The implications of selectivity are usually visualized to be more important for women, as we usually observe only a fraction of women in the labor force while male participation is taken to be nearly universal. Although economists do not address the issue of male non-participation explicitly, especially for men in their prime age, one can be reasonably sure that some selectivity bias may be present even in the estimates for men. For example, during the process of development, life expectancy increases and older groups have lower labor force participation rates than prime age people. At the other end of the age distribution, the participation rates of younger men are also declining, though for other reasons such as rising school enrollment. Thus selectivity may also affect the estimates for men and its importance may be increasing over time.[59]

Having assessed, corrected, and interpreted the effect of selectivity bias, one can go back to the original question, that of discrimination. The correction in women's earnings functions allows us to estimate the wage offers of all women irrespective of current labor force status. Such knowledge can help us establish the productive potential of the country's womanpower, an important consideration in development strategies. However, one may argue that the kind of difference one wants to study is that arising *in* the labor market from *demand* factors. Under these circumstances, one needs to know what is paid in the labor market to those who work. Even if working women are a self-selected group with better than average characteristics than the whole group of women, these are the ones whose productive characteristics are evaluated in the labor market. Can or should the market pay non-working women with inferior attributes as much as women who are better qualified and actually working? In this respect, the appropriate decomposition of the pay gap should apply to the coefficients of the female wage equation uncorrected for selectivity and to the average value of characteristics held by working women only. This is, however, a procedure that practically all studies of discrimination have bypassed instead routinely using selectivity corrected wages for the sample characteristics of working women. If one wants to expand the notion of discrimination to include the pay potential of non-working women, one should use the selectivity corrected wage estimates and evaluate the adjusted pay gap at the value of the average characteristics of *all*

---

[59]   Nine of the country studies which follow report selectivity corrected results for men (Brazil - both studies, Chile, Colombia 1979, Guatemala, Honduras, Panama, and Peru - both studies). The findings suggest that the labor supply of men may be more affected by the presence of selectivity than the labor supply of women. This is not an unexpected finding: non-working men are less likely to be representative of all men. Therefore, we are somewhat reluctant to assign a great significance to selectivity for men in comparing wage offers between women and men because the typical non-working man may be not comparable to the typical non-working woman.

women in the sample, both working and non-working. For reasons of completeness, and as a contribution toward this new direction of research, the country studies have evaluated the decomposition using both uncorrected wages cum working women means as well as corrected wages cum all women's means.

Finally, one can add that the mechanics of selectivity correction is subject to the reservations raised in the case of earnings functions. (For example, is the participation function correctly specified? Are the explanatory variables good proxies of the theoretical variables they are assumed to represent?) In addition, the estimates would be affected not only by omitted variables and measurement errors and so on, but also by optimization errors, preference errors and budget constraint errors.[60] The net effect of these errors is as yet unknown to practitioners.

The "chicken and egg" question. Even if the functional form of the earnings function is the appropriate one, and there are neither specification errors nor omitted or poorly measured variables, one cannot be certain that the decomposition results reflect accurately a properly standardized difference between female and male pay. This is because it is hard to distinguish to what extent endowments are the effect of past or expected discriminatory practices, something which can be said to constitute indirect discrimination.[61] For example, women may suspect or know that they are less likely to enter a high-wage and/or senior position and as a result they are discouraged from acquiring human capital of the size and/or type they would have opted for, had they perceived equality of opportunity in the labor market.[62] In this respect, the

---

[60] Optimization errors refer to discrepancies in the measurement of optimal and actual values of the variables concerned; preference errors refer to unobservable differences in utility functions across individuals; and budget constraint errors refer to unobserved differences in the budget constraints across individuals. These issues are not pursued further in this volume since they are still at a theoretical stage (see, Killingsworth and Heckman, 1986).

[61] In this case one has a different kind of endogeneity that is in the earnings function (earnings versus investment in human capital) compared with endogeneity in the participation function (employment versus wages). However, Griliches (1977) argues that accounting for the endogeneity of schooling typically does not alter significantly the coefficients in the estimated earnings functions.

[62] England (1982); Weiss and Gronau (1981); Gronau (1982).

measured wage discrimination would be underestimated more often than not by the present decomposition.[63]

What is "pay"? With respect to the dependent variable, the current approach assumes by necessity that the only reward to a worker from selling his/her labor, and the only cost from employing a worker, is what we observe as *reported* labor earnings at a point in time. This is deficient as, theoretically, one should use permanent earnings and, in practice, one should include fringe benefits and all other aspects of pay. Again, the implications are different for the male and the female results, but little can be done to accommodate them in practice.

Another issue which relates to pay is what variables, other than education/schooling and potential experience/training, can be used in the earnings equation if the objective is to measure discrimination. As already argued, the semi-logarithmic formulation views the relationship between individual earnings and human capital characteristics as the result of an individual's willingness to maximize his/her lifetime earnings.[64] This is a supply side story. However, here one is interested in identifying demand discrimination. The argument is, therefore, about rates of pay for comparable work and not earnings which are the product of wage rates and labor supply. This implies that either earnings on the left hand side of the regression equation should be adjusted by the amount of labor supply that generated them (such as weekly earnings divided by weekly hours of work), or one should include hours as an additional explanatory variable on the right hand side. Although the inclusion of hours in the right hand side of the earnings function equation can be labelled agnostic on theoretical grounds,[65] it has usually been justified as a useful device for the study of sex wage differentials as discrimination is more meaningfully analyzed in terms of rates of pay among homogeneous groups.

---

[63]   For the difficulty in distinguishing between the causes and effects associated with unequal endowments see Zabalza and Tzannatos (1985), Chapter 1.

[64]   Mincer (1974); Blinder and Weiss (1976).

[65]   Alternatively, the inclusion of variables other than human capital ones (that is, mainly education and experience) may be interpreted in many ways. For example, assume that the earnings equation relates to manual workers where the physique of the worker matters. Thus, the inclusion of hours as an additional regressor can somehow reduce the bias arising from omitted variables, as the two sexes are heterogenous in this respect, but this has little to do with the original justification offered for the conventional semi-log human capital specification of the earnings functions.

What is "comparable characteristics"? The attempt to make the two groups homogenous before the gross wage differential is broken down into its constituent components can go beyond controlling for differences in the amount of labor supplied by women and men. For example, men could be paid more because they work in certain occupations and industries rather than because they are paid more than women who may also work in those sectors.[66]

Consequently, one may be tempted to include explanatory variables relating to employment status in order to adjust for the effect of the different employment distributions of women and men on pay. To ask an employer to pay women in one industry or occupation as much as men in another industry or occupation may not sound immediately obvious.[67]   The same considerations apply to the effect upon pay of differences arising from the regional employment distribution of women and men. Therefore, the standardization of certain differences in the earnings equation before one attempts to establish the discriminatory part appears prima facie necessary. However, it makes a lot of difference if women choose to become nurses (instead of doctors) or employers do not promote women to managers and let them stay in junior administrative tasks. If restriction of entry is a determinant factor for the employment distributions of the sexes, the inclusion of employment variables will result in more standardization than needed for establishing the unjustified wage gap between women and men.   This will be so because that part of the wage differential which is due to employment status would be attributed to differences in characteristics although it is really due to discrimination in the form of unequal opportunities in employment. On the other hand, if occupational choice is unconstrained and the occupational wage structure reflects compensating differentials, ignoring the occupational structure would lead to an exaggeration of the extent of discrimination.

---

[66]   The evidence suggests that women are predominantly found in low-pay sectors and are also paid less than men within these sectors.

[67]   There are countries where such cross-establishment comparisons are allowed "in the same trade or industry" in the context of sex equality legislation if due to segregation in the employment of women and men, the comparability principle cannot readily apply at firm level (this provision is made by the Dutch Equal Pay Act of March 20, 1975; see Hepple, 1984).

In the absence of clear theoretical guidelines for the specification of the earnings equation in the study of discrimination, the contributors to the country studies have omitted the employment structure.[68] In effect, this approach amounts to the purest application of the human capital theory in the study of labor earnings.[69] There were also two practical considerations for this eclecticism. First, in some countries there was no information on either the occupational or the industrial status of those working. Second, the coding practices differ between countries. If industrial/occupational variables were included in some of the present studies but excluded in others, this would have limited to a significant extent the comparability of the findings.

4.   Summary of the Methodology Adopted in the Present Study

There are considerable unresolved theoretical and empirical problems in estimating which part of the gross difference between female and male earnings can be attributed to discrimination. Despite the analytical nicety of the distinction between demand and supply, in practice it is difficult either to define what constitutes a discriminatory practice or to disentangle it from what may be a rational individual choice. Further, one cannot be sure whether the mechanics of estimation result in the net over- or underestimation of discrimination. The existing empirical literature in developed countries has provided varying pictures of the situation depending on the time period examined, the specification of the model, the steps taken to correct for selectivity, the extent to which endogeneity was accounted for, and the type of data used.[70] Bearing these reservations in mind the authors of individual country studies were asked to:

---

[68]   There have been some recent studies which attempt to account for the wage effect of occupational segregation (Brown, Moon and Zoloth, 1980, for the United States, and Chiplin and Sloane, 1976 and Greenhalgh, 1980, for Great Britain). Brown *et al.* merge behavioral models of occupational attainment and of gender wage distributions and then derive a more accurate decomposition of the pay gap between women and men. However, it was deemed that the data requirements for such approaches was beyond the limits of the present study. This may not be a serious problem as Miller (1987) notices that eliminating differences by sex across occupational groups will have little impact on women's wages unless it is accompanied by changes in relative wage rates between occupations.

[69]   Mincer (1974).

[70]   For reviews see Lloyd and Niemi (1979), Treiman and Hartmann (1981), Sloane (1985), Cain (1986), Killingsworth (1990).

1.   Give an aggregate picture of women's relative position in the labor market;

2.   Estimate a female labor force participation function in order to show the impact of certain variables upon women's decisions to participate in the labor market and also to produce the selectivity correction variable for inclusion in the earnings functions;

3.   Evaluate the determinants of pay using a relatively parsimonious, but also comparable across country studies, specification of the earnings functions; and

4.   Decompose the pay gap, if women were paid as men and if men were paid as women both in respect to actual wages and also in terms of wage offers.

The results are summarized in the following chapter.

6

Summary of Empirical Findings and Implications

1. Introduction

This chapter gives representative results from the country studies included in the companion volume. Two warnings apply. First, the reader should note that some of the results may not be strictly comparable across countries. This point can be clarified with reference to the following case. There was no information in the Chilean and Mexican data sets about weekly hours of work. As a result, this particular variable does not appear in the earnings functions for these two countries and the effect of differences in hours worked by women and men is not reported in the corresponding summary table. The omission of hours may have also affected the coefficients of other variables included in the regression. Throughout the summary presented below we have, therefore, selected the most representative results that are susceptible to an analysis in a comparative context within the scope of the present study. The interested reader can always refer to the individual country studies for more detailed information.

Second, our results as summarized below refer to all working women in the economy, that is, the distinction between employment in the formal and informal sector is not pursued in this section in great detail. We felt that any generalization about the informal sector could be misleading as (1) the informal sector is very much country specific (with respect to aspects such as racial composition of the population and regional pluralism) and not susceptible to easy categorizations; (2) even if the informal sector were comparable among countries which are at the same stage of economic development, it is not necessarily comparable across the countries examined in this volume. These remarks can be examined with reference to the few individual country studies which were able to tackle these differences. For example, Stelcner et al. conclude that Brazil's regional/economic/social diversification may preclude the consideration of the country "as a whole" and note that the urban/rural residence is an important one for employment in the formal sector and the earnings of employees but not for the self-employed. They also argue that education not only enhances earnings but "sorts" individuals among different types of labor force activity (dependent employment, self-employment and family work). Tenjo also notes that the decomposition results for Colombia are sensitive to the inclusion or not of domestic servants. If the latter are excluded from the analysis then the unexplained part of the gender wage gap is reduced from 77 percent to 10 percent. He is, however, careful to add that there are employment "ghettos" for women and there are more opportunities for occupational advancement for men than for women. In contrast, Gill's distinction between self-employment and wage/salaried employment in Peru produced insignificant results. These remarks suggest that as far as the formal/informal distinction is concerned, it may be better to refer to the country studies directly rather than attempt to produce a synthetic profile of the informal sector across the region.[1]

We present the results in the following order. First, we look at some factors which affect the decision of a woman to participate in the labor force. Second, we present the aggregate results of the decomposition analysis, that is, the estimates for the percentage of the wage gap which can be attributed to differences in the average values of the characteristics between women and men ("differences in endowments" or "justified" part of the pay gap) and to differences in the rewards of these characteristics in the labor market ("upper bound of discrimination" or "unjustified" part of the pay gap). Finally, we attempt to identify the contribution of some variables included in the earnings functions to the observed pay gap the pay gap.

2.   Participation

Table 6.1 summarizes the effects of some key variables on women's decision to participate in the labor market.

Education has a significant effect on participation. For example, in Argentina the observed average participation of all women is 36 percent. However, a woman with less than primary education has a *ceteris paribus* probability of participation of only 22 percent compared with a probability of 58 percent of a woman who is a university graduate. In Venezuela the probability of participation for the corresponding education groups rises from about 30 percent to more than 85 percent. These estimates compare to an average female labor force participation rate in Venezuela of approximately 40 percent.

---

[1]   For some aspects of the diversity of women's labor market characteristics and treatment in the informal sector see Berger and Buvinic, eds. (1989).

Table 6.1
Female Participation by Selected Sample Characteristics
(percent)

Characteristic	Argentina 1985	Chile 1987	Colombia 1988	Costa Rica 1989	Ecuador 1987	Guatemala 1989	Panama 1989	Peru 1990	Uruguay 1989	Venezuela 1987
Education										
Less than Primary	21.7	–	11.0	16.9	44.0	21.4	10.0	38.6	28.9	31.8
Primary	31.4	23.7	20.0	21.6	46.0	22.4	14.1	38.7	34.7	34.4
Secondary	32.6	32.5	34.0	30.9	47.0	40.7	33.6	40.0	46.9	62.8
University	57.6	60.7	53.0	38.1	49.0	47.2	47.7	63.2	54.1	87.4
Marital Status										
Single	55.9	40.8		40.4		33.0		47.3		56.2
Married	24.5	13.9		17.7		14.1		33.1		34.3
Number of Children										
None	37.2	28.6	25.0	25.2	49.0	22.3	26.7	42.6	39.8	
One	33.6	23.0	}20.0	24.4	45.0	21.3	23.7	38.2	32.5	
Two	30.2	18.0	}	23.5	42.0	20.3	20.1	34.0	25.9	
Household										
Head		37.8	47.0	34.1	65.0	30.3	57.2	57.9	65.8	64.7
Not Head		–	21.0	22.7	43.0	19.6	20.4	–	34.2	41.7
Residence										
Rural	17.9	17.9		19.9		15.6	17.8			32.7
Urban	–	–		28.9		29.7	29.6			45.6

– not available.

Source: Based on case studies reported in Volume II.

Women's family characteristics also exercise a strong effect on participation. Married women's probability of labor force participation is about half the probability for single women. For example, the probability for married women in Chile drops to 14 percent compared to 41 percent for single women. In Costa Rica the corresponding decrease is from 40 percent to 18 percent, in Venezuela from 56 percent to 34 percent and in Guatemala from 33 percent to 14 percent.

Being head of household increases the probability of participation in all countries under consideration. In fact, this demographic aspect seems to be one of the strongest determinants of female labor force participation. For example, in Colombia the probability for a woman who is head of household jumps to 47 percent (from 21 percent for non-heads of household), in Panama to 57 percent (from 20 percent), in Uruguay to 66 percent (from 34 percent), in Venezuela to 65 percent (from 42 percent) and in Guatemala to 30 percent (from 20 percent).

The effect of children is mixed depending on their age. As a general rule, results from countries which could not take into account the age of children suggest that the probability of participation drops by about three to five percentage points for each child. When the age of children could be taken into account, the results for young children (aged less than 6 years) suggest that the effect is even stronger.[2] However, the presence of older children increases the probability of female participation in some countries.[3] This can be explained by the fact that older children may be substitutes for women's services at home, as older children can both supervise their younger siblings and contribute toward other areas of family production.[4]

Individual country studies also report effects of variables which are country specific. For example, in Bolivia the probability of Spanish speaking women to be in the labor market is 42 percent while the corresponding probability for indigenous women is only 22 percent.[5] Also, variables relating to the physical health of a woman have the predicted effect that is, ill-health affects adversely

---

[2]   See chapters on Chile, Panama and Uruguay in the companion volume.

[3]   See chapters on Jamaica and Peru in the companion volume.

[4]   Boserup (1970) and Standing (1981).

[5]   Indigenous women have a lower probability of participation in the labor force in Guatemala and in Brazil there are substantial differences in the participation probabilities of women belonging to different racial groups (white, black, Asian and Mulatto).

the probability of participation.[6] In addition, the presence of adult non-workers in the household decreases the probability of female participation.[7] This may suggest that there is higher demand for domestic services when older people are in the household and this translates into an increase in women's shadow wage at home.[8] Finally, residence is another significant factor for women's decision to participate. As a general rule women in urban areas have a much higher probability of participation than their counterparts in rural areas.

In conclusion, the country studies confirm that women's decisions to participate in the labor market depend on education and on their demographic characteristics. As explained in the methodological section, these results are derived from the assumption that these characteristics are exogenous to the labor supply model estimated in our country studies, and this assumption is not necessarily appropriate. However, the magnitude and consistency of results are sufficiently clear for the limited generalizations presented in the introductory chapter to this volume with respect to policy implications.

3.   Bird's Eye View of the Aggregate Pay Differential

Table 6.2 presents the percentage of the pay gap which can be attributed to differences in the labor market endowments held by women and men and to differences in the labor market rewards associated with these characteristics.[9]

---

[6]   See chapter on Bolivia in the companion volume.

[7]   See chapters on Ecuador and Jamaica in the companion volume.

[8]   These estimates may understate the effect of the presence of non-working adults in the household upon the probability of female participation as such adults may also assist in some household tasks performed by women.

[9]   The information presented in the Table 6.2 is derived from Appendix Table A6.1 where we report results which are standardized on female means (women paid as men: columns 2-3 and 6-7) and also on male means (men paid as women: columns 4-5 and 8-9).   We also report separately the results obtained from coefficients which were uncorrected (columns 2 to 5) or had been corrected for selectivity bias (columns 6 to 9). In some countries where selectivity did not appear to be statistically significant, the authors did not report separately results for uncorrected coefficients.   In other countries, the authors reported coefficients uncorrected for selectivity for illustrative purposes. When the coefficient on the selectivity correction variable was statistically insignificant, the results for corrected and uncorrected coefficients were practically identical.

Table 6.2
Decomposition of the Male Pay Advantage in the Region
(percent)

Selectivity Correction	Pay advantage due to	Evaluated at	
		Female means	Male means
No	Endowments	3.2	2.9
	Rewards	96.8	97.1
Yes	Endowments	11.7	13.7
	Rewards	88.3	86.3
	Total[a]	100.0	100.0

a.   The overall male pay advantage is 30 log percentage points.

Source: Appendix Table A6.1

A number of clarifications need be made in order to correctly interpret the summary decomposition results. First, the pay gap is shown as log percentage points of the male pay advantage.[10] This corresponds closely to the ratio of average male earnings to average female earnings in the sample.[11] Second, differences in endowments refer to the difference in the average values of a particular characteristic in the sample between *men and women.*[12]   Third,

---

[10]   The reason for expressing the pay gap in terms of male advantage is that the decomposition is formulated in this way. Recall that our decomposition refers to the difference in the average logarithms of earnings between men and women, that is, $\log(W_m)-\log(W_f)$. See equation 5.6.

[11]   For example, in Argentina the pay gap is indicated as 43.2 percent and this should be taken to mean that men earn on average 43.2 percent more than women. In other words the pay differential is not expressed in one of the more conventional ways - - such as in terms of the relative female/male wage (which is 69.8 percent) or the underpayment of women (which is 30.2 percent).

[12]   Again with reference to Argentina working women have on average 9.4 years of schooling compared to 8.8 years of schooling for men (see Appendix Table A6.3). In this case the relevant difference is -0.6 years of schooling and the negative sign suggests that, had women and men been equally endowed in terms of schooling, the male pay advantage would have been even greater.

differences in rewards refer to the difference in the corresponding coefficients as reported in the earnings functions. Again this difference is calculated between *men and women.*

According to the data, the male pay advantage in the present data set varies between about 15-20 percent (in Colombia, Mexico and Peru) and 40-50 percent (in Argentina, Bolivia, Ecuador and Jamaica). This gives an unweighted average of male pay advantage in the region of about 30 log percentage points (or female/male pay of about 75 percent). The two most obvious conclusions that can be drawn from Table 6.2 are the following.

First, the selectivity corrected estimates for the part of the pay gap attributable to differences in rewards (upper bound of discrimination) are lower than the results derived from the uncorrected estimates. Correcting for selectivity reduces the upper bound of discrimination from 97 percent to around 87 percent. The reason that selectivity correction reduces the unexplained part of the wage gap in the region is because in most country studies the coefficient on lambda was negative.[13] This implies that the difference in the *wage offers* of women and men is smaller than the difference in *actual wages.* Though it is not strictly appropriate to calculate averages from percentages, especially when these percentages refer to countries which differ in population size (and characteristics) as much as Jamaica differs from Brazil, the magnitude of the corrected and uncorrected results may be taken to suggest that only a small part of the difference in the actual wages between women and men reflects self-selection of women in the labor force. Our figures imply that, if the average female worker had the characteristics of the average woman in the population, then the observed pay gap would decrease by approximately 10 percent (or about 3 percentage points).[14]

---

[13] The coefficient on lambda was positive and significant only in the case of Uruguay. Insignificant positive coefficients are reported for Ecuador, Peru (1986) and Bolivia. Insignificant negative results are reported for Argentina, Colombia (1979), Costa Rica, Peru (1990) and Venezuela (1989). See Appendix Table A6.6.

[14] This was derived by taking the difference between the uncorrected estimates for the part of the pay gap attributed to rewards (97 percent) and corresponding part suggested by the corrected coefficients (about 87 percent). Given that the male pay advantage is about 30 percent, this implies that $(0.1 \times 0.3 =)$ 3 percentage points would be eliminated from the actual wage gap, if working women were representative of all women in the economy.

A second conclusion is that, irrespective of whether the results are based on corrected or uncorrected coefficients, only a small part of the pay gap is attributable to differences in endowments. Even in the case of selectivity corrected results almost four-fifths of the pay gap is due to differences in rewards. This finding warrants further inspection in order to see which variables in the earnings functions give rise to such an impressive result.

Contribution of specific variables to the decomposition. The decomposition was calculated from separate earnings functions for women and men. In particular, the earnings functions had the following simplified general form (omitting subscripts i for notational simplicity):

$$\ln(W_m) = C_m + a_m S_m + b_m E_m + c_m \ln(H_m) + (X_m)m + e_m$$
$$\ln(W_f) = C_f + a_f S_f + b_f E_f + c_f \ln(H_m) + (X_f)f + e_f$$

where W stands for weekly earnings, C is the constant term, S refers to education measured in years of schooling, E is *potential* experience also in years (age minus years of schooling minus school entry age), H is weekly hours worked and X is a vector representing whatever other variables might have been included in the earnings functions of individual country studies. Lower case letters attached to these variables stand for their respective coefficients, subscripts m and f refer to men and women, and e is an error term assumed to have the usual properties.

Let us now dissect the contribution of each of the variables explicitly specified in the last two equations upon the observed pay gap. For brevity, we report results for coefficients derived from the sample of women workers only, that is, uncorrected for selectivity. As noted in the previous sections the difference between corrected and uncorrected coefficients was not that great. Also, uncorrected results are more comparable across countries than corrected results because the variables used in the participation functions (in order to estimate the lambda) varied between countries. In addition, recall that women workers are the appropriate reference group for explaining the observed (actual) gap in wages (rather than the gap in wage offers). Finally, the coefficient on lambda was found to be statistically insignificant in half of the countries studied.[15] As noted earlier, our regional averages were calculated from percentages and their sums do not match exactly the observed pay gap. In addition, there are effects from other variables which have not been taken explicitly into account.

---

[15]   See Appendix Table A6.6.

Table 6.3
Contribution (in log percentage points) of Selected Variables
to the Male Pay Advantage in the Region

| Variable | Due to Difference in | | Total Explained by |
	Endowments	Rewards	these Variables
Hours	6.6	-32.1	-25.5
Education	-11.1	-12.3	-23.4
Experience	9.9	10.2	20.1
Total excl. constant term	5.4	-34.2	-28.8
Constant term		52.2	52.2
Total incl. constant term	5.4	18.0	23.4
	(22%)	(78%)	(100%)

Source: Appendix Tables A6.1 to A6.5.

Table 6.3 shows which part of the pay gap can be attributed to differences in endowments and which to differences in rewards with respect to each of the main variables in the earnings functions. In terms of endowments, women appear to be disadvantaged with respect to hours and also experience (though men have longer experience because of fewer years of schooling). These two variables taken together explain just over half of the pay gap (16.5 log percentage points). However, women's advantage in schooling reduces the pay gap and, in fact, schooling has the strongest effect of these three variables in terms of endowments. As a result, the part of the pay gap that can be attributed to difference in endowments is only 22 percent.

In terms of rewards, women seem to benefit significantly from education and hours (though the latter may be taken as an unfavorable result because women work fewer hours than men).[16] These two factors would have more than

---

[16] This is an appropriate point to raise a specific methodological issue in the present decomposition analysis. Can the greater female coefficients on hours be interpreted as discrimination *against men?* In fact, this is what a "mechanical" interpretation of the Oaxaca decomposition would suggest. However, we do not think this interpretation is correct. Another way of interpreting the female advantage in the rewards of weekly hours is the following: women are penalized in the labor market because working fewer hours than men reduces their pay proportionately more than men working shorter hours. In this respect, what the present decomposition assigns as a female advantage in terms of rewards is in effect a disadvantage because endowments are systematically lower for women than men.

eliminated the pay gap had it not been for the opposite effect from the difference in the coefficients on experience. However, the contribution of experience is not that important and the net effect of these three variables suggests a reversal of the pay gap (pay advantage for women). When the constant term is taken into consideration, the effect from the difference in rewards is inflated in the opposite direction to the point that differences in rewards account for 78 percent of the male pay advantage.

These results may be subject to two different interpretations. First, ignoring the effect of differences between the constants terms,[17] one can argue that in many of the countries studied in this volume only a small fraction (if any) of the gross pay differential can be attributed to different wage structures (differences in rewards).[18] However, this interpretation may be biased by the fact that formal sector employees are heavily represented in our samples. For example, in Guatemala the female participation rate is originally reported as 29 percent but the percentage of women with positive incomes and positive hours is only 24 percent. One suspects that the 20 percent of women missing in the second figure are women engaged in family work or other activities in the informal sector. Also, public sector employment accounts for a significant proportion of female workers in the formal sector and appears to be paying its female workers substantially more than women employees in the private sector. In fact, women's pay in the public sector is found to be higher than that in the private sector in many of our studies.[19] To some extent this finding reflects the higher educational attainment of women workers in the public sector. However, the study on Ecuador confirms that women workers in the public sector have a wage premium of almost 25 percent (compared to the private sector) even after

---

[17]   The role of the constant term in measuring discrimination is questionable, if the constant term is taken to proxy the average effect on earnings of productivity characteristics omitted from the analysis. However, if the earnings functions are correctly specified, then the constant term should be included in the decomposition formula.

[18]   This is not an uncommon finding in the literature on discrimination for developing countries. Knight and Sabot (1982) report that in Tanzania in 1971 only 5-17 percent of the gross pay differential between women and men can be attributed to different wage structures when evaluated at male means while it is negative (-3 to -45 percent) if evaluated at female means. Similar results are reported in many of the studies included in Birdsall and Sabot (1991).

[19]   See chapters on Costa Rica, Guatemala, Honduras, Panama, and Uruguay in the companion volume and Table 6.4.

controlling for the effects of human capital and other variables.[20] Similarly, the study on Uruguay suggests a corresponding premium of 15 percent again after controlling for other characteristics.[21] The overrepresentation of public sector employees in our databases and the high wages paid to women workers in the government sector make us skeptical about the "no or little discrimination" results suggested by the decomposition analysis in some of our countries. In addition, as argued below, it might be true that the constant term cannot be considered separately from the other "rewards" in the decomposition analysis but there is no practical objection that its place is among the "rewards" part of the gender wage gap.

The second interpretation stems from the last observation, that is, that the part of the wage gap attributed to the difference in the constant terms falls well within the *potential* discrimination aspect of the results. The constant term represents the "reward to the sex of the worker" when all other characteristics are set equal to zero. In other words, the constant term can be interpreted as the earnings of an uneducated worker who is just about to enter the labor market. However, we are not prepared to say that the difference in constant terms represents *actual* discrimination because information is lacking. In particular, as noted earlier, the value of the constant term is affected by factors pertaining to both labor demand and labor supply. With respect to labor demand, one can mention genuine differences in productivity between the sexes or imperfect information while on the labor supply side there may be genuine differences in tastes between women and men. This is as pessimistic a conclusion to the present analysis as the light that was shed into the economists' "black box" (differences in rewards) which revealed another black box inside it: the constant term is another black box on its own.

A more optimistic interpretation may, however, be relevant to our findings. The constant terms can be seen as a pure premium that is independent of a worker's other wage determining characteristics. Hence, if women are undervalued in the market when they have few characteristics (zero endowments) but recoup almost half of the lost ground because of the effects of schooling, hours of work and, possibly, experience, then one may have a policy prescription to the problem of growth and the feminization of poverty: if women's education increases and their labor force attachment and experience

---

[20]   See Table 17.4. The same study suggests that there is no corresponding premium for men working in the public sector.

[21]   See Table 25.5. It is interesting to note that the premium to male workers in the public sector is negative and significant (-7.6 percent).

also increases, women's pay will increase proportionately more. In fact, we believe that this is the way the present findings should be interpreted.

4.   Evaluation of Results

The present volume added some information to the growing area of research on "women in development." We make no claim that our study has solved the problems associated with women's role in the economy. There are significant methodological issues and practical problems which remain unresolved. The reader had the opportunity to assess the merit and limitations of the preceding discussion and evidence. Below we attempt a synthesis, albeit aggregate and tentative, of we believe that can serve as a basis for some limited generalizations and potential policy implications. Most of the discussion derives directly from the previous chapters but is supplemented by additional information in some instances.

Female participation/employment. Initially our analysis was based on one of the "grand ratios" in economics, namely the labor force participation rate. Conventionally defined, the participation rate refers to those who are engaged in an economic activity. Economic activity is taken to be one which results in an "economic = financial" reward. In advanced economies where production is very much monetized this interpretation of an economic activity may not be inappropriate. In these economies most workers are employees, thus, they are engaged in tasks that result in pay in one form or another. Also, if one were to focus on men, the value of men's household production can be thought to be low in the sense that few men, especially in developing countries, spend much of their time at home. As most "value" is deemed to derive from labor, even a relatively single minded approach to men's contribution to economic/social welfare may not lead to grossly misleading conclusions. This is not, however, the case for women, especially in developing countries.

Women spend a substantial part of their time in and around the house. Analyses of women's issues that adopt the conventional dichotomy (between "work" and "leisure = non-working time") are bound to miss some significant aspects of economic and social welfare. The reason is that non-working time includes activities such as meal preparation (from purchasing, if not growing, the basic inputs for meals to serving meals on a plate and cleaning the dishes); looking after and improving the mental well-being of persons (in the sense of providing informal education to younger members of the family -- home economics has been the earliest subject taught much before the appearance of schools and its formal inclusion in the curriculum); and a wider range of activities, all of which are necessary for human existence and survival -- such activities extend from the purely "mechanical" activities (such as the "passive" supervision of minors -- if it could ever be passive) to the extremely "sophisticated" ones (such as the administration of medicines). In short a narrow interpretation of what constitutes an economic activity can easily lead to a practically meaningless measurement of women's contribution to societal output. To assume that women's work at home has zero value does not make sense.

It must be obvious to the reader that we have not made such an assumption. The value of production at home, especially women's home value, is a prerequisite for all economic (monetized) activities. With this in mind we examined the female participation rate. We found that there has been an underlying upward trend in women's work in the market which, though we had no ambition to analyze it and offer explanations, suggests that where "other regions are already today" (the industrial economies), Latin America "will be there tomorrow." The question becomes whether Latin America is catching up with the rest of the world in an efficient and distributionally appropriate manner. "Efficient" means simply "can a rearrangement of existing resources produce a pie of greater size?" "Distributionally" means "does the resulting growth from a more efficient allocation of resources ensure that benefits accrue successively to a greater part of the population?"

We found that female participation rates in Latin America are among the lowest in the world. If this is the result of women's or households' free choice and assuming that women are free to chose within households, then the issue of (in)efficiency does not arise. However, if female participation rates are low because of a market failure, then social policy may have something to offer. Let us clarify the relevant concepts and the conditions under which a market failure may arise. Efficiency implies that as much output as possible is created out of a given resource base at any given point in time (technical efficiency) and that output is also exchanged at the right relative prices (allocative efficiency). A third aspect of efficiency arises when intertemporal comparisons are made in which case dynamic efficiency refers to the maximum or optimal rate of growth. Distributional aspects have been often but erroneously considered to be independent of efficiency considerations and, at times, they are assumed to constitute a conflicting objective to wealth creation. However, it is more appropriate to think of "distributional efficiency," that unique initial allocation of resources among economic agents which will lead to the greatest feasible amount and most desirable product mix of output.[22] In other words, in the

---

[22] The first fundamental theorem of welfare economics postulates that a perfect competitive market economy will of its own eventually reach a Pareto optimal equilibrium. The second fundamental theorem postulates that a given Pareto optimal equilibrium can be achieved only under a certain initial distribution of resources. In other words, that unique Pareto equilibrium which maximizes social welfare will not and cannot be achieved unless resources are distributed in a particular way.

present framework it may be possible to achieve a superior outcome by changing the present distribution of resources among the sexes. It is in this context that we interpret our results by observing that initial conditions are different for women than for men (Table 1.2 showed that women's literacy rates were substantially lower than those for men); female labor force participation rates are also substantially lower than those for men (Table 2.2); and the decision of women to participate in the labor market is only determined to a small extent by what one can consider economic variables (Table 6.1). Do these findings suggest that there is a market failure somewhere?

The answer is not an easy one in that what appears as a result may well be the cause. This is already covered ground (recall the relevant "chicken and egg" discussion in Chapter 5). However, we believe that on balance the biological asymmetry that has destined women and men to the "traditional" roles is becoming successively less relevant for determining the functional roles of the sexes in the context of modern production. Today working for the market is characterized by more complex and capital intensive modes of production and by greater demand for coordination that calls for an expansion of the service sector. In this respect a market failure may consist of "less than perfect" information in the sense that roles and functions that are perceived today as appropriate by a girl and her family/parents may prove counterproductive later in life. The reason these expectations do not materialize is that *until the steady state is reached* present conditions are not representative of what would prevail in the future. The inability to see far enough in the future ("myopia") can easily divert the economy from its optimal path. In addition, the absence of perfect capital markets, even in industrialized economies, results in investment in human capital to be less than optimal: human bodies do not provide the kind of collateral for borrowing purposes that lenders are readily prepared to accept.

We must next consider whether there exists anybody else other than individuals or households who is better equipped to reach more rational and non-myopic judgements.[23] The answer is that the general trend that economies follow

---

[23]   In technical terms the optimality properties of the perfect competitive market model breaks down if there is "irrationality" and "myopia." Irrationality means that the future is discounted at a higher rate than it should be discounted. For example, a sufferer from the severe results of smoking at the age of 50 would have in most cases decided against smoking earlier in life, had he "discounted properly" at the age of 20 how bad the quality of life would be 30 years later. This explanation of irrationality holds assuming that the smoker knew in advance the danger of smoking. If he did not know about the dangers of smoking but the information existed, then the market failure is due to imperfect information. In either case, there may be good grounds for policy intervention, if the benefits from reducing smoking outweigh the necessary costs of the policy.

during development is better known to governments than to individuals. For example, individuals may assume that their employment conditions and family roles will continue to be in the future as they are at present. However, governments know that, even if conditions remained unchanged for some individuals, on average the employment conditions will move in certain directions (such as toward urban based activities in the services sector). Consequently, governments can undertake policies within a probabilistic context while, of course, individual actions will be decided by individual considerations.

The relevance of these remarks to women's employment in the labor market is that it is possible that the currently observed low female participation rates in Latin America may well reflect a sub-optimal outcome in the sense that the developmental changes have not been correctly anticipated or have not been properly discounted by women or by their parents some time ago. As a result, it is probable that more women would have liked to be in the labor force today but find that they are not in possession of the right amount or mix of human capital. Failure of capital markets to ensure an optimal investment in human capital is also relevant in this respect.

One does not have to engage in heavy theorizing in order to determine the role and effectiveness of social policy in market economies (such as those in Latin America) vis-a-vis actions undertaken by what *is assumed to be* "well informed" individuals. Irrespective of persuasion, one is certain that Latin America is moving toward economic and family structures which are currently observed in industrialized countries. There are many and at times contradictory explanations about the "catching up" or "converging" process evident in many economies. The fact remains that in the longer historical perspective women become more like men in all aspects of life and the implications of the biological asymmetry of the sexes diminishes due to technical change. Those individuals and countries which can envisage these movements and adjust to them earlier rather than later are bound to find themselves in a better position to grasp the opportunities when changes occur. Of course, preparing for the future involves costs that have to be paid at present. For example, a campaign of information dispelling myths such as "the longer the hair, the smaller the brain"[24] has costs and, perhaps,

---

[24]   This phrase was obviously coined before the advent of long hair for men. It can be found in Weineger (1906) whose analysis led to the conclusion that "even the malest (sic) woman is scarcely worth more than 50 percent of men." Further back in history Aristotle wrote "the male is by nature (sic) superior and the female inferior: the one rules and the other is ruled" (Aristotle, *Politiks*, bk. I, ch. 5) and the *Book of Leviticus* (27:1-7) prescribed that the value of a woman shall be assessed at three-fifths the value of a man.

not only economic ones.   Also, the elimination of sex specific protective or prohibiting legislation would benefit some persons/groups but may result in costs for others.   Those costs must be evaluated in comparison to the benefits before decisions are made that whatever involves costs is not desirable.   In terms of female participation in Latin America, an optimist may argue that this could not have been any better in the past: the rate of increase in female participation has been remarkable by all accounts.   A pessimist may want to point out that female participation is still lower than in other regions.

Female pay.   Pay is the price of labor.   If pay accurately reflects competitive market conditions, then nothing more can or should be said or done.   The concern arises when there are imperfections and less than competitive conditions either in the product market or in the labor market.   If so, individuals and households do not supply the optimal amount of labor while employers do not utilize labor in the most efficient way.   In this case total product is lower than it could be (inefficiency) while there are significant implications for the distribution of personal/household incomes (and poverty).

Our study showed that women in the Latin American labor market are paid less than their male counterparts.   This was not unexpected: so far we are unaware of any country study at any point in time that has come to an opposite conclusion when *average* female pay was compared with *average* male pay.   As argued in the main text, the value of the present analysis rests on its comparison with other areas.   In this respect it was established that a sizeable part of the gross wage differential between women and men in Latin America remains unaccounted for by some common economic characteristics.   We repeatedly labelled the unexplained part as "upper bound" of discrimination and we consistently stated that the true extent of discrimination should in all country cases be lower than its "upper" bound.   Still, the summary results presented in Table 6.2 and the detailed results presented in Appendix Table A6.1 are out of line with results from advanced countries.   For example, the "discriminatory" part of the sex wage gap was found to be between half and three-quarters of the gross pay differential in Britain and the United States or even less.[25]   The country studies in the companion volume typically suggest that the discriminatory part in Latin America accounts for "three-quarters and up."

It is possible that the present estimates of potential discrimination in Latin America are greater than those found for other countries because studies undertaken in other countries and world regions have used more accurate data

---

[25]   Wright and Ermisch (1991) for Britain and Killingsworth (1990) for the United States.

or have accounted for more factors in deciding what determines earnings. This may be true. However, we expressed our skepticism about the practice to go on adding explanatory variables to the right hand side of the earnings equation in order to standardize for the difference between women's and men's pay. The inclusion of additional factors in the analysis (such as occupational or industrial types of employment) may bias the estimates of potential discrimination downward. Still, the uniformity of the results in Latin America with respect to the extent of potential discrimination is sufficiently clear to suggest that a greater part of the gross sex wage differential in Latin America (compared with results for other countries) is due to factors that are not immediately obvious. The identification of these factors (such as country specific legislation) requires a different and more in depth analysis than the regional study we have undertaken.

One particular aspect of female pay in Latin America requires attention. This does not relate to the *decomposition* of the gender wage differential upon which our study has focused but on the pay differential *per se*. Sex wage differences in Latin America are by comparison to other regions small. The unweighed average of female relative pay comes to about 70-75 percent -- women workers even in many industrialized countries are still short of this figure in terms of their average remuneration in the labor market.[26] If this is taken at face value it may suggest that, though a good part of the pay gap in Latin America can be discriminatory in its origin, the labor market rewards women on average more like men than in other regions. We do not think so and the reasons are explained below.

First, in our data sets there may be an overrepresentation of the earnings of workers engaged in activities in the formal sector. Such workers are more easily detected and included in databases than workers in the informal sector. In addition, the earnings of formal sector workers are less easily understated. The case of many informal sector workers reporting positive hours of work and zero labor incomes has already been discussed. As a result, our estimates may overstate the level of average female pay because women in the informal sector are not well represented (especially family workers). In contrast, in industrialized countries where most workers are employees such a bias either is smaller than in developing countries or does not arise at all. The implication is that, if women in the formal sector are overrepresented in our data sets and if reported pay is statistically greater in the formal sector than in the informal sector, then female average pay would be artificially greater than what a female worker would fetch on average in the formal *and* informal labor market.

---

[26]   Gunderson (1989).

Second, and related to the previous point, women workers in the formal sector are primarily employed in the public sector. Consequently, not only are women in the formal sector overrepresented, but women workers in the formal sector tend to be dominated by public sector employees. The issue becomes whether Latin American women are paid more in the public sector than their counterparts in the private sector. An answer to this question is given in Table 6.4 (columns 1 and 2). To accommodate the fact that women employed in the public sector tend to be more educated than those in the private sector we broke down the information on pay by education level. The evidence suggests that women in the public sector are paid twice as much as women in the private sector -- especially at lower levels of education. The difference tends to narrow at tertiary education level (save for Panama) but, as few women possess university qualifications, the average pay of all female workers is little affected by them.

Third, we are not aware of any country in Latin America whose government or related organizations practice overt pay discrimination.[27] Consequently, one expects female pay *relative to* male pay in the public sector to be higher than that in the private sector. The last two columns in Table 6.4 show that women are paid more like men in the public sector than in the private sector -- indeed, women are paid more than men in the public sector in Guatemala. A more sophisticated way of establishing the role of the public sector in determining the average pay of women workers is through the use of earnings functions. As mentioned earlier in this chapter women in the public sector enjoy a *ceteris paribus* pay premium (after controlling for other factors, such as human capital variables, hours worked and location). There is no statistical evidence that such a premium exists in the case of male workers. Consequently, the role of the public sector in Latin America may distort the overall estimates of female relative pay. In contrast, the difference between public and private sector pay is not that important in advanced market economies. If anything, the public sector in the latter group of countries is generally considered to be a low-pay employer because of the other non-pecuniary benefits it provides. Such benefits include job security, social benefits, longer holidays and better pensions.

The foregoing provides some explanation why, somewhat unexpectedly, female relative pay in Latin America appears to be on the high side compared with women's relative pay elsewhere. This explanation has significant policy implications. In particular, it is probable that the public sector is paying "distortionary" wages, that is, wages in excess of what a clearing labor market

---

[27]   It is, however, possible than indirect (employment) discrimination may be taking place in the sense that there is a prior expectation about the sex of workers in particular jobs and certain administrative ranks.

Table 6.4
Female Wages (in local currency) and Female Relative to Male Wage (percent)
in the Private and Public Sectors
(selected countries)

Country (pay)	Educational Level	Female Wages		F/M Wage	
		Private	Public	Private	Public
Guatemala (quetzals/hour)	Primary	1.03	2.11	69	128
	Secondary	2.03	4.07	79	127
	Tertiary	3.90	4.26	72	96
Panama (balboas/hour)	Primary	0.62	1.28	56	77
	Secondary	1.52	2.13	85	77
	Tertiary	1.03	1.83	58	71
Uruguay (pesos/hour)	Primary	551	695	79	91
	Secondary	646	853	71	94
	Tertiary	1211	1268	56	89
Costa Rica (colon/month)	All levels	10928	24954	66	91

Source: Country studies in the companion volume.

would have established. The reasons for public sector pay being out of line with the competitive wage are well known. The public sector is not necessarily governed to by immediate cost constraints but is relatively free to pay wages which conform to other considerations, even the satisfaction of group interests. Consequently, the public sector may not be a price taker. On the contrary, the public sector make act as a price maker given its size in terms of employment. In this respect, more detailed information and a deeper analysis is required before a concrete conclusion is reached.

5. Concluding Remarks

Given the empirical results reported in this volume we believe that the labor market is quite well equipped to sort out a number of problems. We have noted the rise in female labor force participation which appears to have occurred during less than ideal macro-economic conditions. We also found that the employment distributions of women and men in the region have become more alike over time. In terms of wages women in Latin America appear to be paid relatively more than even in some advanced countries -- though a number of qualifications may apply. However, the percentage of the sex wage gap that is unaccounted by differences in the human capital characteristics held be women and men in Latin America is sizeable and greater than in other countries. We are not prepared to pinpoint the actual extent of wage (=price) discrimination against women in Latin America. But economics is not only about prices. Economics is also about *constraints*. Are the constraints that women workers and employers face "real" constraints? By "real" we mean either genuine economic constraints (for example, limited consumer income or producers' resources) or "unavoidable" ones (such as the state of technology). In the case of real constraints nothing much can be done. However, if the constraints are "removable" and were indeed removed, then the economy could achieve a superior outcome. Such constraints may relate to labor market legislation or family law. They can also be the result of distortionary price setting by the public sector. Finally they may derive from limited rationality, myopic perceptions, capital market failure and externalities in the sphere of human capital. Many examples of these constraints have already been given in this volume. One feels certain that, if these constraints were removed, women would improve their position both at home and also in the labor market. Then inefficiency and poverty issues would become less acute in the region.

Statistical Appendix to Chapter 6

The tables in this appendix show representative results from the country studies included in the companion volume. When means are reported, they are calculated as unweighted means of the countries for which information exits.

Appendix Table A6.1
Percentage of Male Pay Advantage Attributed to Differences in Endowments (E) and Rewards (R)

Country	Year	Male Pay Advantage[b]	Selectivity Uncorrected				Selectivity Uncorrected[a]			
			Evaluated at				Evaluated at			
			Female Means		Male Means		Female Means		Male Means	
			E	R	E	R	E	R	E	R
		(1)	(2)	(3)	(4)	(5)	(6)	(7)	(8)	(9)
Argentina	1985	43.2	22.0	78.0	32.0	68.0	26.0	74.0	38.0	62.0
Bolivia	1989	47.3	14.9	85.1	24.1	75.9	14.9	85.1	24.1	75.9
Brazil[c]	1989	35.7	–	–	–	–	19.0	81.0	11.0	89.0
Chile	1987	33.8	–	–	–	–	-14.9	114.9	-13.7	113.7
Colombia	1988	16.7	12.3	87.7	22.1	77.9	8.0	92.0	14.8	85.2
Costa Rica	1989	21.3	-3.6	03.6	-3.2	103.9	5.5	94.5	6.7	93.3
Ecuador	1987	41.6	26.4	73.6	33.2	66.8	37.8	62.2	57.2	42.8
Guatemala	1989	26.4	-1.8	101.8	0.4	99.6	45.3	54.7	55.4	44.6
Honduras	1989	21.1	-69.2	169.2	-81.9	181.9	-50.6	150.6	-46.5	146.5
Jamaica	1989	55.1	–	–	–	–	-13.7	113.7	-19.1	119.1
Mexico	1984	15.7	–	–	–	–	28.1	71.9	20.0	80.0
Panama	1989	22.1	-22.9	122.9	-40.6	140.6	13.9	86.1	14.7	85.3
Peru	1990	17.7	19.5	80.5	15.1	84.9	19.5	80.5	15.1	84.9
Uruguay	1989	29.5	24.0	76.0	26.0	74.0	23.0	77.0	23.0	77.0
Venezuela	1989	25.5	14.0	86.0	5.0	95.0	14.0	86.0	5.0	95.0
Average[d]		30.2	3.2	96.8	2.9	97.1	11.7	88.3	13.7	86.3

– not available.

a. Selectivity correction statistically insignificant in Argentina, Bolivia, Costa Rica, Peru and Venezuela.
b. Measured in log-percentage points. It refers to hourly pay in Brazil, Ecuador and Peru and weekly/monthly pay in other countries.
c. The figures for Brazil refer to married women working as employees.
d. Unweighted average.

Source: Based on results reported in the corresponding country cases in the companion volume.

Appendix Table A6.2a

Average Hours per Week and Coefficients on Log (hours) by Sex

Country	Year	Average Hours per Week		Male Advantage in Hours (percent)	Coefficient on Log (hours)		Male Advantage in Coefficients (percent)
		M	F	(1)/(2)	M	F	(4)/(5)
		(1)	(2)	(3)	(4)	(5)	(6)
Argentina	1985	46.31	37.48	23.6	0.391	0.659	-40.7
Bolivia	1989	51.30	44.12	16.3	0.354	0.424	-16.5
Colombia	1988	49.90	46.10	8.2	0.426	0.458	-7.0
Costa Rica	1989	47.64	40.53	17.5	0.626	0.718	-12.8
Guatemala	1989	48.12	42.27	13.8	0.344	0.475	-27.6
Honduras	1989	45.73	43.75	4.5	0.301	0.438	-31.3
Panama	1989	42.76	40.14	6.5	0.660	0.600	10.0
Uruguay	1989	48.44	37.31	29.8	0.587	0.685	-14.3
Venezuela	1989	43.71	38.48	13.6	0.541	0.554	-2.3
Average		47.10	41.13	14.9	0.470	0.557	-15.8

Source: Based on results reported in the corresponding country cases in the companion volume.

Appendix Table A6.2b
Contribution of Differences in Hours to the Male Pay Advantage

Country	Year	Evaluated at				Total Effect of Hours Upon the Pay Gap (7)+(8) or (9)+(10)	% of Male Pay Advantage Explained by Differences in Hours
		Female Means		Male Means			
		Effect Due to Differences in		Effect Due to Differences in			
		Endow.	Coeff	Endow.	Coeff		
		(7)	(8)	(9)	(10)	(11)	(12)
Argentina	1985	0.083	-0.971	0.139	-1.028	-0.888	-205.8
Bolivia	1989	0.053	-0.265	0.064	-0.276	-0.212	-44.8
Colombia	1988	0.034	-0.123	0.036	-0.125	-0.089	-53.2
Costa Rica	1989	0.101	-0.341	0.116	-0.355	-0.239	-112.2
Guatemala	1989	0.045	-0.490	0.062	-0.507	-0.446	-169.2
Honduras	1989	0.013	-0.518	0.019	-0.524	-0.504	-239.3
Panama	1989	0.042	0.222	0.038	0.225	0.263	119.3
Uruguay	1989	0.153	-0.355	0.179	-0.380	-0.201	-68.4
Venezuela	1989	0.069	-0.047	0.071	-0.049	0.021	8.4
Average		0.066	-0.321	0.080	-0.335	-0.255	-85.0
% of pay gap explained		23.4	-114.2	28.6	-119.4	-90.8	

Source: Based on results reported in the corresponding country cases in the companion volume.

Appendix Table A6.3a
Average Years of Schooling and Estimated Coefficients on Schooling by Sex

Country	Year	Average Years of Schooling		Male Advantage in Schooling (percent)	Coefficient on Schooling (x100)		Male Advantage in Coefficients (percent)
		M	F	(1)/(2)	M	F	(4)/(5)
		(1)	(2)	(3)	(4)	(5)	(6)
Argentina	1985	8.80	9.41	-6.5	9.1	10.7	-15.0
Bolivia	1989	9.50	8.97	5.9	7.1	6.3	12.7
Brazil	1980	4.86	6.96	-30.2	14.7	15.6	-5.8
Colombia	1988	7.60	8.70	-12.6	12.0	11.2	7.1
Costa Rica	1989	6.66	8.47	-21.4	10.1	13.1	-22.9
Ecuador	1987	9.70	9.05	7.2	9.7	9.0	7.8
Guatemala	1989	3.90	4.72	-17.4	14.3	16.4	-12.8
Honduras	1989	4.89	6.29	-22.3	15.4	17.8	-13.5
Jamaica	1989	7.37	7.84	-6.0	12.3	21.5	-42.8
Mexico	1984	6.26	7.56	-17.2	13.2	14.7	-10.2
Panama	1989	9.21	10.45	-11.9	9.7	11.9	-18.5
Peru	1986	8.21	9.01	-8.9	11.5	12.4	-7.3
Uruguay	1989	8.34	9.06	-7.9	9.9	11.1	-10.8
Venezuela	1989	6.93	8.52	-18.7	9.1	11.1	-18.0
Average		7.30	8.22	-12.0	11.3	13.1	-10.7

Source: Based on results reported in the corresponding country cases in the companion volume.

Appendix Table A6.3b
Contribution of Differences in Schooling to the Male Pay Advantage

Country	Year	Evaluated at Female Means		Male Means		Total Effect of Schooling Upon the Pay Gap (7)+(8) or (9)+(10)	% of Male Pay Advantage Explained by Differences in Schooling
		Effect Due to Differences in		Effect Due to Differences in			
		Endow.	Coeff	Endow.	Coeff		
		(7)	(8)	(9)	(10)	(11)	(12)
Argentina	1985	-0.141	-0.065	-0.151	-0.056	-0.206	-47.7
Bolivia	1989	0.076	0.033	0.072	0.038	0.109	23.2
Brazil	1980	-0.044	-0.328	-0.063	-0.309	-0.371	-130.2
Colombia	1988	0.061	-0.123	0.070	-0.132	-0.062	-37.4
Costa Rica	1989	-0.200	-0.237	-0.254	-0.183	-0.437	-204.7
Ecuador	1987	0.068	0.058	0.063	0.063	0.126	30.4
Guatemala	1989	-0.080	-0.134	-0.099	-0.117	-0.216	-82.1
Honduras	1989	-0.117	-0.249	-0.151	-0.216	-0.367	-173.9
Jamaica	1989	-0.678	-0.101	-0.721	-0.058	-0.779	-141.5
Mexico	1984	-0.094	-0.191	-0.113	-0.172	-0.285	-181.5
Panama	1989	-0.203	-0.148	-0.230	-0.120	-0.350	-158.6
Peru	1986	-0.074	-0.099	-0.081	-0.092	-0.173	-95.2
Uruguay	1989	-0.100	-0.080	-0.109	-0.071	-0.180	-61.1
Venezuela	1989	-0.139	-0.176	-0.170	-0.145	-0.315	-123.7
Average		-0.111	-0.123	-0.129	-0.105	-0.234	-92.3
% of pay gap explained		-40.4	-44.7	-47.0	-38.1	-85.1	

Source: Based on results reported in the corresponding country cases in the companion volume.

Appendix Table A6.4a
Average Years of Potential Experience and Coefficients
on Potential Experience by Sex

Country	Year	Average Years of Potential Experience		Male Advantage in Experience (percent)	Coefficient on Experience (x100)		Male Advantage in Coefficients (percent)
		M	F	(1)/(2)	M	F	(4)/(5)
		(1)	(2)	(3)	(4)	(5)	(6)
Argentina	1985	24.19	21.30	13.6	4.9	3.8	28.9
Bolivia	1989	18.44	20.49	-10.0	5.0	2.8	78.6
Brazil	1980	26.31	21.01	25.2	4.2	3.9	7.7
Colombia	1979	7.04	5.56	26.7	2.5	2.2	13.6
Costa Rica	1989	22.45	19.10	17.5	3.5	3.1	12.9
Ecuador	1987	23.60	22.80	3.5	3.1	1.4	121.4
Guatemala	1989	24.90	22.16	12.4	4.5	4.1	9.8
Honduras	1989	23.81	21.33	11.6	5.2	5.0	4.0
Jamaica	1989	21.35	22.64	-5.7	7.7	8.2	-6.1
Mexico	1984	20.76	16.91	22.8	8.6	6.6	30.3
Panama	1989	20.36	18.36	10.9	7.9	10.3	-23.3
Peru	1986	19.22	15.86	21.2	5.5	7.6	-27.6
Uruguay	1989	24.47	22.48	8.9	5.8	4.2	38.1
Venezuela	1989	23.05	19.55	17.9	3.5	2.8	25.0
Average		21.4	19.3	12.6	5.1	4.7	22.4

Source: Based on results reported in the corresponding country cases in the companion volume.

Appendix Table A6.4b

Contribution of Differences in Potential Experience to the Male Pay Advantage

Country	Year	Evaluated at				Total Effect of Experience Upon the Pay Gap (7)+(8) or (9)+(10)	% of Male Pay Advantage Explained by Differences in Exper.
		Female Means		Male Means			
		Effect Due to Differences in		Effect Due to Differences in			
		Endow.	Coeff	Endow.	Coeff		
		(7)	(8)	(9)	(10)	(11)	(12)
Argentina	1985	0.266	0.110	0.234	0.142	0.376	87.1
Bolivia	1989	0.406	-0.057	0.451	-0.103	0.348	73.7
Brazil	1980	0.079	0.207	0.063	0.223	0.286	100.2
Colombia	1979	0.021	0.033	0.017	0.037	0.054	19.0
Costa Rica	1989	0.090	0.104	0.076	0.117	0.194	90.7
Ecuador	1987	0.401	0.011	0.388	0.025	0.412	99.2
Guatemala	1989	0.100	0.112	0.089	0.123	0.212	80.4
Honduras	1989	0.048	0.124	0.043	0.129	0.172	81.4
Jamaica	1989	-0.107	-0.106	-0.113	-0.099	-0.213	-38.6
Mexico	1984	0.415	0.254	0.338	0.331	0.669	426.3
Panama	1989	-0.489	0.206	-0.441	0.158	-0.283	-128.0
Peru	1986	-0.404	0.255	-0.333	0.185	-0.148	-81.4
Uruguay	1989	0.392	0.084	0.360	0.115	0.475	161.3
Venezuela	1989	0.161	0.098	0.137	0.123	0.259	101.8
Average		0.099	0.102	0.093	0.108	0.201	76.6
% of pay gap explained		32.6	33.9	30.9	35.5	66.4	

Source: Based on results reported in the corresponding country-cases in the companion volume.

Appendix Table A6.5
Contribution of Differences in the Constant Terms to the Male Pay Advantage

Country	Year	Male Pay Advantage	Constant Term		Difference in Constant Terms (2)-(3)	% of Male Pay Advantage Explained (4)/(1)
			Male	Female		
		(1)	(2)	(3)	(4)	(5)
Argentina	1985	0.43	8.34	7.07	1.27	294.1
Bolivia	1989	0.47	1.58	1.35	0.23	48.7
Brazil	1980	0.29	2.40	1.75	0.65	227.9
Colombia	1988	0.17	5.66	5.66	0.00	0.0
Costa Rica	1989	0.21	4.53	3.69	0.84	393.6
Ecuador	1987	0.42	3.58	3.48	0.10	24.0
Guatemala	1989	0.26	2.01	0.97	1.04	394.7
Honduras	1989	0.21	1.25	0.33	0.92	436.5
Jamaica	1989	0.55	1.61	-0.44	2.05	372.3
Mexico	1984	0.16	6.66	6.58	0.08	51.0
Panama	1989	0.22	0.72	0.48	0.24	108.7
Peru	1990	0.18	2.10	1.78	0.32	180.5
Uruguay	1989	0.29	1.11	0.42	0.69	234.3
Venezuela	1989	0.25	3.92	3.52	0.40	157.1
Average		0.30	3.52	2.62	0.63	208.8

Source: Based on results reported in the corresponding country cases in the companion volume.

Appendix Table A6.6
The Value and Significance of the Coefficient on the Sample Selection Variable
(Lambda)
in the Earnings Functions

Country	Year	Coefficient	t-value
Argentina	1985	-0.08	1.7
Bolivia	1989	0.07	1.2
Brazil	1980	-0.30	6.5
Chile	1987	-0.82	9.9
Colombia	1979	-0.09	1.3
Costa Rica	1989	-0.05	1.1
Ecuador	1987	0.03	0.5
Guatemala	1989	-0.29	7.5
Honduras	1989	-0.59	11.3
Jamaica	1989	-0.39	4.3
Mexico	1984	-1.45	6.7
Panama	1989	-0.39	12.3
Peru	1990	-0.05	1.0
Uruguay	1989	0.06	2.0
Venezuela	1989	-0.14	1.6

Source: Based on results reported in the corresponding country cases in the companion
volume.

Appendix A

A companion to this Volume will be published and contains the following studies:

"Female Labor Force Participation and Gender Earnings Differentials in Argentina", by Y. C. Ng.

"Women in the Labor Force In Bolivia: Participation and Earnings", by K. Scott.

"Labor Force Behavior and Earnings of Brazilian Women and Men, 1980", by M. Stelcner, J. B. Smith, J. A. Breslaw and G. Monette.

"Female Labor Force Participation and Wage Determination in Brazil, 1989", by J. Tiefenthaler.

"Is There Sex Discrimination in Chile? Evidence from the CASEN Survey", by I. Gill.

"Labor Markets, the Wage Gap and Gender Discrimination: The Case of Colombia by J. Tenjo.

"Female Labor Market Participation and Wages in Colombia", by T. Magnac.

"Women's Labor Force Participation and Earnings in Colombia", by E. Velez and C. Winter.

"Female Labor Force Participation and Earnings Differentials in Costa Rica", by H. Yang.

"Why Women Earn Less Than Men in Costa Rica", by T. H. Gindling.

"The Effect of Education on Female Labor Force Participation and Earnings in Ecuador", by G. Jakubson and G. Psacharopoulos.

"Female Labor Participation and Earnings in Guatemala", by M. Arends.

"Women's Labor Force Participation and Earnings in Honduras", by C. Winter and T. H. Gindling.

"Female Labor Force Participation and Earnings: The Case of Jamaica", by K. Scott.

"Women's Participation Decisions and Earnings in Mexico", by D. Steele.

"Female Labor Force Participation and Wages: A Case Study of Panama", by M. Arends.

"Women's Labor Market Participation and Male-Female Wage Differences in Peru", by S. Khandker.

"Is There Sex Discrimination in Peru? Evidence from the 1990 Lima Living Standards Survey", by I. Gill.

"Women's Labor Force Participation and Earnings: The Case of Uruguay", by M. Arends.

"Female Participation and Earnings, Venezuela 1987", by D. Cox and G. Psacharopoulos.

"Female Earnings, Labor Force Participation and Discrimination in Venezuela, 1989", by C. Winter.

Appendix B

The Authors of the Companion Volume

Mary Arends is a Consultant for the World Bank's Latin America and Caribbean Technical Department, Human Resources Division.

Jon A. Breslaw is Associate Professor in the Department of Economics, Concordia University, Montreal.

Donald Cox is Associate Professor of Economics, Economics Department, Boston College at Chesnut Hill, Massachusetts.

Indermit Gill is Assistant Professor in the School of Management at the State University of New York at Buffalo.

T.H. Gindling is Assistant Professor in the Department of Economics, University of Maryland, Baltimore County.

George Jakubson is Associate Professor in the School of Industrial Labor Relations at Cornell University.

Shahidur Khandker is a Research Economist in the Women in Development Division, Population and Human Resources Department, The World Bank.

Thierry Magnac is associated with INRA, ESR Paris, France and the Department of Economics, University College of London, United Kingdom.

Georges Monette is Associate Professor in the Department of Mathematics, York University, Toronto.

Ying Chu Ng is Assistant Professor at Hong Kong Baptist College.

George Psacharopoulos is Senior Human Resources Advisor, Technical Department, Latin America and the Caribbean Region, The World Bank.

Katherine Scott is a Consultant for the World Bank's Latin America and Caribbean Technical Department, Human Resources Division.

J. Barry Smith is Associate Professor in the Department of Economics, York University, Toronto.

Diane Steele is an Analyst at the American Institutes for Research, Washington D.C.

Morton Stelcner is a Professor in the Department of Economics at Concordia University, Montreal.

Jaime Tenjo is Assistant Professor in the Department of Management and Economics at the University of Toronto, Scarborough Campus.

Jill Tiefenthaler is Assistant Professor in the Department of Economics at Colgate University.

Zafiris Tzannatos is a Labor Economist in the Education and Employment Division, Population and Human Resources Department of the World Bank.

Eduardo Velez is an Education Specialist in the Human Resources Division of the Latin American and Caribbean Region of the World Bank.

Carolyn Winter is a Human Resources Specialist in the Women and Development Division, Population and Human Resources Department of the World Bank.

Hongyu Yang is a Consultant in the Human Resources Division of the Latin American and Caribbean Region of the World Bank.

References

Adelman, I. "Development Economics: A Reassessment of Goals." *American Economic Review,* Vol. 65 Papers and Proceedings (1975). pp. 302-309.

Ahluwalia, M.S., N. Carter, and H. Chenery. "Growth and Poverty in Developing Countries." *Journal of Development Economics,* Vol. 6, No.3 (1979). pp. 299-341.

Aigner, D.J. and G.G. Cain. "Statistical Theories of Discrimination in the Labor Market". *Industrial and Labor Relations Review,* Vol. 30, No.2 (1977). pp. 175-187.

Aird, J.S. "The Preliminary Results of China's 1982 Census." *China Quarterly,* Vol. 96 (1984). pp. 613-640.

Amin, S. and A.R. Pebley. "The Impact of a Public Health Intervention on Excess Female Mortality in Punjab." Mimeograph. Princeton, New Jersey, 1987.

Anker, R., M. Buvinic and N. Youssef (eds.). *Women's Roles and Population Trends in the Third World.* London: Croom Helm, 1982.

Altonji, J.G. "The Intertemporal Substitution Model of Labor Market Fluctuations: An Empirical Analysis." *Review of Economic Studies,* Vol. 49, No.5 (special issue) (1982). pp. 783-824.

Arrow, K.J. "Higher Education as a Filter." Institute for Mathematical Studies in the Social Sciences. Technical Report No. 71. Palo Alto, California: Stanford University, 1972.

Ashenfelter, O. and R. Layard (eds.). *Handbook of Labor Economics.* Amsterdam: North Holland, 1986.

Atkinson, A.B and N.H. Stern. "On the Switch from Direct to Indirect Taxation." *Journal of Public Economics,* Vol. 14, No. 2 (1980). pp. 195-224.

Bardhan, P.K. *Land, Labor and Rural Poverty: Essays in Development Economics.* New York: Columbia University Press, 1984.

Becker, G.S. *The Economics of Discrimination.* The University of Chicago Press, 1971 (2nd edition).

-----. *A Treatise on the Family.* Cambridge, Mass.: Harvard University Press, 1981.

Becker, G.S., E.M. Landes and R.T. Michael. "An Economic Analysis of Marital Instability." *Journal of Political Economy,* Vol. 85, No. 6 (1977). pp. 1141-1187.

Becker, G.S. and N.Tomes. "An Equilibrium Theory of the Distribution of Income and Intergenerational Mortality." *Journal of Political Economy,* Vol. 87, No. 6 (1979). pp. 1141-1187.

Behrman, J.R. and N. Birdsall. "The Quality of Schooling: Quantity Alone is Misleading." *American Economic Review,* Vol. 73, No. 5 (1983). pp. 928-946.

Behrman, J.R. and B.L. Wolfe. "Labor Force Participation and Earnings Determinants for Women in the Special Conditions of Developing Countries." *Journal of Development Economics,* Vol. 15 (1985). pp. 259-288.

Behrman, J.R., B.L. Wolfe and D.M. Blau. "Human Capital and Earnings Distribution in a Developing Country: The Case of Prerevolutionary Nicaragua." *Economic Development and Cultural Change.* Vol. 34, No. 1 (1985). pp. 1-29.

Beller, A.H. "Trends in Occupational Segregation by Sex and Race, 1960-1981" in B.F. Reskin (ed.). *Sex Segregation in the Workplace: Trends, Explanations, Remedies.* Washington DC: National Academy Press, 1984. pp. 11-26.

Beller, A.H. and Han, K.K. "Occupational Sex Segregation" in B.F. Reskin (ed.). *Sex Segregation in the Workplace: Trends, Explanations, Remedies.* Washington DC: National Academy Press, 1984. pp. 91-114.

Ben-Porath, Y. "Economic Analysis of Fertility in Israel: Point and Counterpoint." *Journal of Political Economy*, Vol. 81, No. 2 (Part 2) (1973). pp. S202-S233.

Berg, I. *Education and Jobs: The Great Training Robbery.* Boston, Mass.: Beacon Press, 1971.

Berger, M. and M. Buvinic (eds.). *Women's Ventures: Assistance to the Informal Sector in Latin America.* 1989. West Hartford, Conn.: Kumarian Press.

Bergmann, B. "The Effect on White Incomes of Discrimination in Employment." *Journal of Political Economy,* Vol. 79, No. 2 (1971). pp. 294-313.

Bernard, J. *Women and the Public Interest.* Chicago: Aldine-Atherton, 1971.

Birdsall, N. and J.R. Behrman. "Does Geographical Aggregation Cause Overestimates of the Return to Schooling?" Washington DC: The World Bank, DEDPH, 1983.

Birdsall, N. and M.L. Fox. "Why Males Earn More: Location and Training of Brazilian Schoolteachers". *Economic Development and Cultural Change.* Vol. 33, No. 3 (1985). pp. 533-556.

Birdsall, N. and R. Sabot (eds.). *Unfair Advantage: Labor Market Discrimination in Developing Countries.* The World Bank, 1991.

Bishop, J. "Jobs, Cash Transfers and Marital Instability: A Review and Synthesis of the Evidence." *Journal of Human Resources.* Vol. 15, No. 2 (1980). pp. 301-334.

Blanchard, O.J. and L.H. Summers. "Hysteresis and the European Unemployment Problem" in R. B. Cross (ed.). *Unemployment, Hysteresis, and the Natural Rate Hypothesis.* Oxford: Basil Blackwell, 1988. pp. 306-364.

Blau, D.M., J.R. Behrman and B.L. Wolfe. "Schooling and Earnings Distributions with Endogenous Labour Force Participation, Marital Status and Family Size." *Economica,* Vol. 55, No.219, (1988). pp. 297-316.

Blau, F.D. "Occupational Segregation and Labor Market Discrimination" in B.F. Reskin (ed.). *Sex Segregation in the Workplace: Trends, Explanations, Remedies.* Washington DC: National Academy Press, 1984. pp. 11-26.

Blau, F.D. and W.E. Hendricks. "Occupational Segregation by Sex: Trends and Prospects." *Journal of Human Resources,* Vol. 14, No. 2 (1979). pp. 197-210.

Blinder, A.S. "Wage Discrimination: Reduced Form and Structural Estimates". *Journal of Human Resources,* Vol. 8, No.4 (1973). pp. 436-455.

-----. *Toward an Economic Theory of Income Distribution.* Cambridge Mass.: MIT Press, 1974.

Blinder, A.S. and Y. Weiss. "Human Capital and Labor Supply: A Synthesis". *Journal of Political Economy,* Vol. 84, No. 3 (1976). pp. 449-472.

Blumberg, R.L. "A General Theory of Gender Stratification" in R. Collins (ed.). *Sociological Theory.* San Francisco CA: Jossey Bass, 1984. pp. 23-101.

Blundell, R. and I. Walker. "Modelling the Joint Determination of Household Labour Supplies and Commodity Demands." *Economic Journal,* Vol. 92, No. 366 (1982). pp. 351-364.

Borjas, G.J. "Self-selection and the Earnings of Immigrants". *American Economic Review.* Vol. 77, No.4 (1987). pp. 531-553.

Boserup, E. *Woman's Role in Economic Development.* New York: St. Martin's Press, 1970.

Bowers, J.K. "British Activity Rates: A Survey of Research." *Scottish Journal of Political Economy,* Vol. 22, No.1 (1975). pp. 57-90.

Bowles, S. "Aggregation of Labor Inputs in the Economics of Growth and Planning: Experiments with a Two-Level CES Function." *Journal of Political Economy,* Vol. 78 (1970). pp. 68-81.

Brown, C.V., E. Levin, and D.T. Ulph. "Estimation of Labour Hours Supplied by Married Male Workers in Great Britain." *Scottish Journal of Political Economy,* Vol. 23, No. 3 (1976). pp. 261-277.

Brown, R.S., M. Moon and B.S. Zoloth. "Incorporating Occupational Attainment in Studies of Male-Female Earnings Differentials". *Journal of Human Resources.* Vol. 15, No. 1 (1980a). pp. 3-28.

-----. "Occupational Attainment and Segregation by Sex." *Industrial and Labor Relations Review,* Vol. 33, No. 4 (1980b). pp. 506-517.

Bustillo, I. "Female Educational Attainment in Latin America: A Survey." Washington DC: The World Bank (PHREE/89/16), 1989.

Buvinic, M, M.A. Lycette and W.P. McGreevey (eds.). *Women and Poverty in the Third World.* Baltimore: Johns Hopkins University Press, 1983.

Cain, G.G. *Married Women in the Labor Force.* Chicago: University of Chicago Press, 1966.

-----. "The Economic Analysis of Labor Market Discrimination: A Survey" in O. Ashenfelter and R. Layard (eds.). *Handbook of Labor Economics.* Amsterdam: North Holland, 1986.

Cain, M., S.R. Khanam and S. Nahar. "Class, Patriarchy and Women's Work in Bangladesh." *Population and Development Review,* Vol. 5, No.3 (1979). pp. 405-438.

Carline, C.A. Pissarides, W.S. Siebert and P.J. Sloane. *Labour Economics.* London: Longman, 1985.

Chen, L., E. Hug and S. D'Souza. "Sex Bias in the Family Allocation of Food and Health Care in Rural Bangladesh." *Population and Development Review,* Vol. 7, No. 1 (1981). pp. 55-70.

Chiplin, B. and P.J. Sloane. *Sex Discrimination in the Labour Market.* 1976. London: Macmillan.

Chiswick, B.R. *Income Inequality: Regional Analyses within a Human Capital Framework.* New York: Colombia University Press, 1974.

Clark, C. *The Conditions of Economic Progress.* London: Macmillan, 1940.

Clark, K.B. and L.H. Summers. "Labor Force Participation: Timing and Persistence." *Review of Economic Studies,* Vol. 49, No. 5 (special issue) (1982). pp. 825-44.

Cochrane, S.H. *Fertility and Education: What Do We Really Know?* Baltimore: Johns Hopkins University Press, 1979.

Cogan, J. "Labor Supply with Costs of Labor Market Entry" in J.P. Smith (ed.). *Female Labor Supply: Theory and Estimation.* Princeton NJ: Princeton University Press, 1980a.pp. 327-364.

-----. "Married Women's Labor Supply: A Comparison of Alternative Estimates" in J.P. Smith (ed.). *Female Labor Supply: Theory and   Estimation.* Princeton NJ: Princeton University Press, 1980b. pp. 90-118.

Colclough, C. "The Impact of Primary Schooling on Economic Development: A Review of the Evidence." *World Development,* Vol 10, No. 3 (1982). pp. 167-185.

Coombs, P. H. *The World Educational Crisis: A System Analysis.* New York: Oxford University Press, 1968.

Cornia, G.A., R. Jolly and F. Stewart. *Adjustment with a Human Face.* Oxford: Clarendon Press. 1987.

Cross, R.B. and Allen in Cross (ed.). *Unemployment, Hysteresis and the Natural Rate Hypothesis.* Oxford: Basil Blackwell, 1988.

Da Silva, L. "Greater Opportunities for Women Related to Population Growth." Working Paper No. 11, Belo Horizonte, Brazil: Federal University of Minas Gerais, Center for Development and Regional Planning, 1982.

Da Vanzo, J. "Family Formation in Chile." Santa Monica: Rand Corporation, R830 AID, 1971.

De Tray, D.N. "Child Quality and Demand for Children." *Journal of Political Economy,* Vol. 81, no 2 (Part 2) (1973). pp. 70-95.

-----. "The Interaction Between Parents Investment in Children and Family Size: An Economic Analysis." Santa Monica: Rand Corporation, R1000RE, 1972.

Deere, C.D., J. Humphries and M. Leon de Leal. "Class and Historical Analysis for the Study of Women and Economic Change" in R. Anker, M. Buvinic and N. Youssef (eds.). *Women's Roles and Population Trends in the Third World. London: Croom Helm,* 1982. pp. 87-115.

Dex, S. and P. Sloane. "Detecting and Removing Discrimination at the Market Place." *Journal of Economic Surveys,* Vol. 2, No. 1 (1988). pp. 1-28.

Dolton, O.J. and G.H. Makepeace. "Interpreting Sample Selection Effects". *Economic Letters.* Vol. 24, No. 4 (1987). pp. 373-379.

Dooley, M. D. "Labor Supply and Fertility of Married Women: An Analysis with Grouped and Individual Data from the 1970 U.S. Census." *Journal of Human Resources,* Vol. 17, No. 4 (1982). pp. 499-532.

Dougherty, C.R. S. "Estimates of Labor Aggregation Functions." *Journal of Political Economy,* Vol. 80, No. 6 (1972). pp. 1101-1119.

Dougherty, C.R.S. and E. Jimenez. "The Specification of Earnings Functions: Tests and Implications". *Economics of Education Review.* Vol. 10, No. 2. (1991) pp.85-98.

Dougherty, C. R.S. and M. Selowsky. "Measuring the Effects of the Misallocation of Labor." *Review of Economics and Statistics,* Vol. 55, No. 3 (1973). pp. 386-390.

Duncan, G.J. *Years of Poverty, Years of Plenty.* Ann Arbor, Mich.: Institute for Social Research, 1984.

Duncan, G.M. and D.E. Leigh. "The Endogeneity of Union Status: An Empirical Test". *Journal of Labor Economics.* Vol. 3, No. 3 (1985). pp. 385-402.

Duncan, O. and B. Duncan. "A Methodological Analysis of Segregation Indices." *American Sociological Review,* Vol. 20, April (1955). pp. 210-217.

Easterlin, R.A. *Population, Labor Force and Long Swings in Economic Growth: The American Experience.* New York: National Bureau of Economic Growth, 1968.

-----. "Toward a Socio-Economic Theory of Fertility: A Survey of Recent Research on Economic Factors in American Fertility" in S.J. Behrman, L. Corsa Jr. and R.L. Freedman (eds.). *Fertility and Family Planning: A World View.* Ann Arbor: University of Michigan Press, 1969. pp. 127-156.

ECIEL. Determinantes de la Oferta de Trabajo en America Latina, Programa de Estudios Conjunctos sobre Integracion Economica Latinoamerica. Rio de Janeiro, Brazil, 1982.

ECLAC. (United Nations Economic Commission for Latin America and the Caribbean). *Los grandes cambios y las crisis. Impacto sobre la mujer en America Latina y el Caribe.* Santiago, Chile. December 1990

-----. *Women in Latin America and the Caribbean: The Challenge of Changing Production Patterns with Social Equity.* Fifth Regional Conference on the Integration of Women into the Economic and Social Development of Latin America and the Caribbean. Curacao, Netherlands Antilles. 16-19 September 1991.

Ehrenberg, R.G. and J.L. Schwarz. "Public-Sector Labor Markets" in O. Ashenfelter and R. Layard (eds.). *Handbook of Labor Economics.* Amsterdam: North Holland, 1986. pp. 1219-1259.

England, P. "Assessing the Trends in Occupational Sex Segregation, 1900-1976" in I. Berg (ed.). *Sociological Perspectives on Labor Markets.* New York: Academic Press, 1981. pp. 273-295.

-----. "The Failure of Human Capital Theory to Explain Occupational Segregation by Sex." *Journal of Human Resources,* Vol. 17, No. 3 (1982). pp. 358-370.

Ermisch, J.F. and R.E. Wright. "Entry to Lone Parenthood: Analysis of Marital Dissolution." Discussion Paper in Economics No. 9/90.   University of London: Birkbeck College, 1990.

Fallon, P. and D. Verry. *The Economics of Labour Markets.* Oxford: Philip Alan, 1988.

Finn, M. and C.L. Jusenius. "The Position of Women in the Ecuadorian Labor Force". Ohio State University: Center for Human Resources Research, 1975.

Frank, R.H. "Why Women Earn Less: The Theory and Estimation of Differential Overqualification." *American Economic Review,* Vol. 68, No. 3, (1978). pp. 360-373.

Fuchs, V.R. "Recent Trends and Long-Run Prospects for Female Earnings". *American Economic Review*, Vol. 64, (Proceedings) (1974). pp. 236-42.

Goldthorpe, J. and K. Hall. *The Social Grading of Occupations*. Oxford: Clarendon, 1974.

Goode, W.J. *After Divorce*. Glencoe, Ill.: Free Press, 1956.

-----. "Marital Satisfaction and Instability: A Cross-Cultural Class Analysis of Divorce Rates." *International Social Sciences Journal*, Vol. 14, No. 3 (1962). pp. 507-526.

-----. "Why Men Resist" in M. Yalom (ed.). *Rethinking the Family: Some Feminist Questions*. New York: Longman, 1982. pp. 131-150.

Grasso, J.T. and J.R. Shea. "Effects of Vocational Education Programs: Research Findings and Issues" in *Planning Papers for Vocational Study*, Vocational Education Study Publication No. 1. Washington D.C.: USGPO: National Institute for Education, 1979. pp. 101-194.

Greene, William. *Econometric Analysis*, McMillan, 1990.

Greenhalgh, C. "Male-Female Wage Differentials in Great Britain: Is Marriage an Equal Opportunity?" *Economic Journal*, Vol. 90, No. 360 (1980). pp. 651-675.

Gregory, R.G. and R.C. Duncan. "Segmented Labour Market Theories and the Australian Experience of Equal Pay for Women." *Journal of Post-Keynesian Economics*, Vol. 3, No. 3 (1981). pp. 403-428.

Griliches, Z. "Estimating the Returns to Schooling: Some Econometric Problems." *Econometrica*, Vol. 45, No. 1 (1977). pp. 1-22.

Gronau, R. "The Intrafamily Allocation of Time: The Value of the Housewives' Time." *American Economic Review*, Vol. 63, No.4 (1973). pp. 634-651.

-----. "Sex-Related Wage Differentials and Women's Interrupted Labor Careers: The Chicken and Egg Question." Cambridge, Mass: National Bureau of Economic Research, Working Paper No.1002, 1982.

-----. "Wage Comparisons - A Selectivity Bias." *Journal of Political Economy*, Vol. 82, No. 6 (1974). pp. 1119-43.

Gunderson, M. "Male-Female Wage Differentials and Policy Responses." *Journal of Economic Literature*, Vol. 27, No. 1 (1989). pp. 46-117.

Hall, M. and N. Tideman. "Measures of Concentration". *Journal of American Statistical Association*, Vol. 62 (1967). pp. 162-168.

Hamermesh, D.S. "The Demand for Labor in the Long Run" in O. Ashenfelter and R. Layard (eds.). *Handbook of Labor Economics*. Amsterdam: North Holland, 1986. pp. 429-471.

Haque, N. "Work Status Choice and the Distribution of Family Earnings." Santa Monica: Rand Corporation, 1984.

Harman, A. "Interrelationship Between Procreation and Other Family Decision-Making." Santa Monica: Rand Corporation, 1969.

Hashimoto, M. and L. Kochin. "A Bias in the Statistical Estimation of the Effects of Discrimination." *Economic Enquiry*, Vol. 18 No. 3 (1980). pp. 478-486.

Haveman, R. and B. Wolfe. "Education and Economic Well Being." in E. Dean (ed.) *Education and Economic Productivity*, Cambridge, Mass: Harper and Row, 1984. pp. 19-55.

Heckman, J.J. "Sample Selection as a Specification Error". *Econometrica*, Vol 47 No.1 (1979). pp. 153-161.

-----. "Shadow Prices, Market Wages and Labor Supply." *Econometrica*, Vol. 42, No. 4 (1974). pp. 679-94.

Heckman, J.J. and J. Hotz. "An Investigation of the Labor Market Earnings of Panamanian Males: Evaluating Sources of Inequality." *Journal of Human Resources*, Vol. 21, No. 4 (1986), pp. 507-542.

Heckman, J.J. and T. MaCurdy. "A Life Cycle Model of Female Labor Supply." *Review of Economic Studies*, Vol. 47, No. 1 (1980). pp. 47-74.

-----. "Corrigendum on a Life Cycle Model of Female Labor Supply." *Review of Economic Studies*, Vol. 49, No. 4 (1982). pp. 659-660.

Heckman, J.J. and R.J. Willis. "A Beta-Logistic Model for the Analysis of Sequential Labor Force Participation of Married Women." *Journal of Political Economy*, Vol. 85, No. 1 (1977). pp. 27-58.

Heer, D.M. and E. Turner. "A Real Difference in Latin American Fertility." *Population Studies*, Vol. 18, No. 3 (1965). pp. 279-292.

Hepple, B.A. *Equal Pay and the Industrial Tribunals.* Oxford: Martin Robinson, 1984.

Hill, A.M. "Female Labor Force Participation in Developed and Developing Countries: Consideration of the Informal Sector." *Review of Economics and Statistics*, Vol. 65 (1983). pp. 459-468.

Hofstede, G. *Culture's Consequences: International Differences in Work-Related Values.* London: Sage Publishers, 1980.

Horney, M.J. and M.B. McElroy. "The Household Allocation Problem: Empirical Results from a Bargaining Model" in T. Paul Schultz (ed.). *Research in Population Economics*, Vol. 6. Greenwich, CT.: JAI Press, 1988.

Hornstein, Z., J. Grice and A. Webb. (eds.). *The Economics of the Labour Market.* London: HMSO, 1982.

Humphries, J. "Women's Employment in Restructuring America: The Changing Experience of Women in Three Recessions" in J. Rubery (ed.). *Women and the Recession.* London: Routledge, 1988. pp. 15-45.

Iglesias, F.H. and M. Riboud. "Trends in Labor Force Participation of Spanish Women: An Interpretive Essay." *Journal of Labor Economics*, Vol. 3, No. 1 (Part 2) (1985). pp. S201-S217.

ILO. *World Labour Report.* Geneva: International Labour Office, 1987.

ILO. *Yearbook of Labour Statistics: Retrospective Edition on Population Censuses 1945-1989.* Geneva: International Labour Organization, 1990.

Jelin, E. "Women and the Urban Labor Market" in R. Anker, M. Buvinic and N. Youssef (eds.). *Women's Roles and Population Trends in the Third World.* London: Croom Helm, 1982. pp. 239-267.

Jones, F.L. "On Decomposing the Wage Gap: A Critical Comment on Blinder's Method". *Journal of Human Resources.* Vol. XVIII, No. I (1983). pp. 126-130.

Joseph, G. *Women at Work: The British Experience.* Oxford: Philip Alan, 1983.

Joshi, H. "Secondary Workers in the Employment Cycle: Great Britain, 1961-1974". *Economica,* Vol. 48, No. 189 (1981). pp. 29-44.

Joshi, H., R. Layard and S. Owen. "Why Are More Women Working in Britain?" *Journal of Labor Economics,* Special Issue (1985). pp. S147-S176.

Joshi, H. and S. Owen. "How Long is a Piece of Elastic? The Measurement of Female Activity Rates in British Censuses 1951-1981." London: Centre for Economic Policy Research, Discussion Paper No. 31., 1984.

----. "Does Elastic Retract? The Effect of Recession on Women's Labour Force Participation". London: Centre for Economic Policy Research, Discussion Paper No. 64., 1985.

Kanowitz, L. *Women and the Law: The Unfinished Revolution.* Albuquerque: University of New Mexico, 1969.

Keeley, M.C. *Labor Supply and Public Policy: A Critical Review.* New York: Academic Press, 1981.

Kelly, A. and L. Da Silva. "The Choice of Family and the Compatibility of Female Workforce Participation in the Low-Income Setting." *Review Economique,* Vol. 31, No. 6 (1980). pp. 1081-1104.

Khan, S. and M. Irfan. "Rates of Returns to Education and the Determinants of Earnings in Pakistan." *Pakistan Development Review,* Vol. 24, No. 3/4 (1985). pp. 671-680.

Khandker, S.R. "Determinants of Women's Time Allocation in Bangladesh." *Economic Development and Cultural Change,* Vol. 37, No. 1 (1988). pp. 111-126.

-----. "Women's Role in Household Productive Activities and Fertility in Bangladesh." *Journal of Economic Development,* Vol. 12, No. 1 (1987). pp. 87-115.

Kiernan, K. "Teenage Marriage and Marital Dissolution: A Longitudinal Study." *Population Studies,* Vol. 40, No. 1 (1986). pp. 35-54.

Killingsworth, M.R. *Labor Supply.* Cambridge: Cambridge University Press, 1983.

-----. *The Economics of Comparable Work.* Kalamazoo Michigan: W.E Upjohn Institute for Employment Research, 1990.

Killingsworth, M.R. and J.J. Heckman. "Female Labor Supply: A Survey" in O. Ashenfelter and R. Layard (eds.). *Handbook of Labor Economics.* Amsterdam: North Holland, 1986. pp. 103-204.

Knight, J.B. and R. Sabot. "Labor Market Discrimination in Tasmania". *Journal of Development Studies.* Vol. 19, No.1 (1982). pp. 67-87.

Kozel, V. and H. Alderman. "Factors Determining Work Participation and Labor Supply Decisions in Pakistan's Urban Areas." Paper presented at the 5th Annual General Meeting of the Pakistan Society for Development Economists, March 1988.

Kuznets, S. "Economic Growth and Income Inequality". *American Economic Review,* Vol. 45 (1955). pp. 1-28.

-----. *Economic Growth of Nations.* Cambridge, Mass.: Harvard University Press, 1971.

-----. "Quantitative Aspects of the Economic Growth of Nations: Industrial Distribution of National Product and Labor Force." *Economic Development and Cultural Change,* Vol. 5, No. 1 (Supplement) (1956), pp. 1-94.

La Belle, T.J. *Nonformal Education in Latin America and the Caribbean. Stability, Reform or Revolution?* New York: Praeger, 1986.

Layard, R. and J. Mincer (eds.). "Trends in Women's Work, Education, and Family Building." *Journal of Labor Economics,* Vol. 3, No. 1 (Part 2) (1985).

Lee, L.F. "Some Approaches to the Correction of Selectivity Bias". *Review of Economic Studies.* Vol. 49, No. 3 (1982). pp. 355-372.

-----. "Unionism and Wage Rates: A Simultaneous Equations Model with Qualitative and Limited Dependent Variables". *International Economic Review*. Vol. 19, No. 2 (1978). pp. 415-433.

Lehrer, E.L. and H. Stokes. "Determinants of the Female Occupational Distribution: A Log-Linear Probability Analysis." *Review of Economics and Statistics*, (1985). pp. 395-404.

Leibowitz, A. "Home Investment in Children." *Journal of Political Economy*, Vol. 82, No. 2 (Part 2) (1974). pp. S111-S131.

Levine, V. and P.R. Moock. "Labor Force Experience and Earnings: Women and Children". *Economics of Education Review*. Vol. 3, No. 3 (1984). pp. 183-194.

Levy, F. *Dollars and Dreams: The Changing American Income Distribution*. 1987. New York: Sage Foundation for the National Committee for Research on the 1980 Census.

Little, R.J.A. "A Note About Models for Selectivity Bias". *Econometrica*. Vol. 53, No. 6 (1985). pp. 1469-1474.

Lloyd, C.B. and B.T. Niemi. *The Economics of Sex Differentials*. New York: Columbia University Press, 1979.

Lockheed, M.E. and E. Hanushek. "Improving Educational Efficiency in Developing Countries." *Compare*, Vol. 18, No. 1 (1988) pp. 21-38.

Lucas, R.E. and L. Rapping. "Real Wages, Employment and Inflation". *Journal of Political Economy*, Vol. 77, No. 5 (1969). pp. 751-754.

Lundberg, S. "The Added Worker Effect". *Journal of Labor Economics*, Vol. 3, No. 1 (1985). pp. 11-37.

MaCurdy, T. "An Empirical Model of Labor Supply in a Life-Cycle Setting." *Journal of Political Economy*, Vol. 89, No. 6 (1981). pp. 1059-1085.

Main, B.G.M. and P. Elias. "Women Returning to Paid Employment." *International Review of Applied Economics*, Vol. 1, No. 1 (1987). pp. 86-108.

Malkiel, B.G. and J. A. Malkiel. "Male-Female Pay Differentials in Professional Employment." *American Economic Review,* Vol. 63, No. 4 (1973). pp. 693-705.

Martin, J. and C. Roberts. *Women and Employment: A Lifetime Perspective.* London: HMSO, 1984.

Martorell, R., J. Leslie and P. Moock. "Characteristics and Determinants of Child Nutritional Status in Nepal." *American Journal of Clinical Nutrition,* Vol. 39, No. 1 (1984). pp. 74-86.

Mason, K.O. "Strober's Theory of Occupational Sex Segregation" in B. F. Reskin (ed.). *Sex Segregation in the Workplace: Trends, Explanations, Remedies.* Washington DC: National Academy Press, 1984. pp.157-170.

Meyer, R.H. and D.A. Wise. "High School Preparation and Early Labor Force Experience" in R.B. Freeman and D.A. Wise (eds.). *The Youth Unemployment Problem: Its Nature, Causes and Consequences.* Chicago: National Bureau of Economic Research, 1982. pp. 277-339.

Michael, R.T. "Education and Derived Demand for Children." Journal of Political Economy in T.W. Schultz (ed.). *The Economics of the Family.* Chicago: University of Chicago Press, 1974. pp. 120-156.

-----. "Education in Nonmarket Production." *Journal of Political Economy,* Vol. 92, No. 2 (1984). pp. 306-327.

Miller, P.W. "The Wage Effect of Occupational Segregation of Women in Britain". *Economic Journal.* Vol. 97 , No. 388 (1987). pp. 885-896.

Mincer, J. "Labor Force Participation of Married Women: A Study of Labor Supply." *Aspects of Labor Economics,* National Bureau of Economic Research. Princeton NJ.: Princeton University Press, 1962. pp. 63-97.

Mincer, J. *Schooling, Experience and Earnings.* National Bureau of Economic Research. New York: Columbia University Press, 1974.

Mincer, J. and H. Ofek. "Family Investments in Human Capital: Earnings of Women." *Journal of Political Economy,* Vol. 82, No. 2 (Part 2) (1974). pp. S76-S108.

Mincer, J. and S.W. Polachek.   "Family Investments in Human Capital: Earnings of Married Women." *Journal of Political Economy*, Vol. 82, No. 2 (Part 2) (1974). pp. S76-S110.

Mingat, A. and J.P. Tan. *Analytical Tools for Sector Work in Education.* Baltimore: Johns Hopkins University Press, 1988.

Mohan, R. *Work, Wages and Welfare in a Developing Metropolis.* New York: Oxford University Press, 1986.

Mueller, E. "The Allocation of Women's Time and Its Relation to Fertility" in R. Anker, M. Buvinic and N. Youssef (eds.). *Women's Roles and Population Trends in the Third World.* London: Croom Helm, 1982. pp. 87-115.

Nakamura, A., N. Nakamura and D. Cullen. *Employment and Earnings of Married Females.* Ottawa: Ministry of Supplies and Services (1979a).

-----. "Job Opportunities, the Offered Wage, and the Labor Supply of Married Women." *American Economic Review*, Vol. 69, No. 5 (1979b). pp. 787-805.

Nelson, F. "Efficiency of the Two-Step Estimator for Models With Endogenous Sample Selection". *Journal of Econometrics.* Vol. 24, No. 1 (supplement) (1984). pp. 181-196.

Ngwira, N. "Effectiveness of Agricultural Extension Service in Reaching Rural Women with Timely and Appropriate Agricultural Information." University of Malawi: Center for Social Research, 1987.

Nickell, S.J. "Fixed Costs, Employment and Labour Demand Over the Cycle". *Economica.* Vol 45, No. 180 (1978) pp. 329-346.

----. "A Picture of Male Unemployment in Britain." *Economic Journal*, Vol. 90, No. 360 (1980). pp. 776-795.

Oaxaca, R. "Male-Female Wage Differentials in Urban Labor Markets." *International Economic Review*, Vol. 14, No. 1 (1973). pp. 693-709.

-----. "Sex Earnings Differentials" in G. Psacharopoulos (ed.). *Economics of Education: Research and Studies.* New York: Pergamon Press, 1987.

Oberoi, A.S. *Changes in the Structure of Employment with Economic Development.* Geneva: ILO. 1978

O'Farrell, B. "Women and Nontraditional Blue Collar Jobs in the 1980s: An Overview" in P. A. Wallace (ed.). *Women in the Workplace,* (1982). pp. 135-165.

Oi, W. "Labor as a Quasi-Fixed Factor". *Journal of Political Economy.* Vol. 70, No. 6 (1962). pp. 538-555

Olsen, R.J. "A Least Squares Correction for Selectivity Bias". *Econometrica.* Vol. 48, No. 7 (1980). pp.1815-1820.

Oppenheimer, V. *The Female Labor Force in the United States: Demographic and Economic Factors Governing its Growth and Changing Composition.* Berkeley, 1974.

Oswald, A.J. "The Economic Theory of Trade Unions: An Introductory Survey." *Scandinavian Journal of Economics,* Vol. 87, No. 2 (1985). pp. 160-193.

Pencavel, J. "Labor Supply of Men: A Survey" in O. Ashenfelter and R. Layard (eds.). *Handbook of Labor Economics.* Amsterdam: North Holland, 1986. pp. 3-101.

Peters, H.E. "Marriage and Divorce: Informational Constraints and Private Contracting." *American Economic Review,* Vol. 76, No. 3 (1986). pp. 437-454.

Phelps, E.S. "The Statistical Theory of Racism and Sexism". *American Economic Review.* Vol. 62, No. 4 (1972). pp. 659-661.

Pike, M. "Segregation by Sex, Earnings Differentials and Equal Pay: An Application of the Crowding Model." *Applied Economics,* Vol. 14, No. 5 (1982). pp. 503-514.

Polachek, S.W. "Potential Biases in Measuring Male-Female Discrimination". *Journal of Human Resources,* Vol. 10, No. 2 (1975). pp. 205-229.

Preston, S. "Health Programs and Population Growth." *Population and Development Review,* Vol. 20, No. 1 (1975). pp. 189-199.

Psacharopoulos, G. (ed). *Essays on Poverty, Equity and Growth*. New York: Pergamon Press, 1991.

-----. "The Perverse Effects of Public Subsidization of Education." *Comparative Education Review*, Vol. 21, No. 1 (1977). pp. 69-90.

-----. "Returns to Education: A Further International Update and Implications." *Journal of Human Resources*, Vol. 14, No. 4 (1985). pp. 584-604.

-----. "To Vocationalize or Not to Vocationalize? That is the Curriculum Question." *International Review of Education*, Vol. 33, No. 2 (1987). pp. 187-211.

Psacharopoulos, G. and M. Hinchliffe. "Further Evidence on the Elasticity of Substitution Between Different Types of Educated Labor." *Journal of Political Economy*, Vol. 80, No. 4 (1972). pp. 786-792.

Psacharopoulos, G. and R. Layard. "Human Capital and Earnings: British Evidence and a Critique." *Review of Economic Studies*, Vol. 46, No. 3 (1979). pp. 485-503.

Psacharopoulos, G. and Z. Tzannatos. "Education and Female Labor Force Participation".   Paper presented at the Sixth World Congress of Comparative Education, Rio de Janeiro, July 6-10. 1987.

----. "Female Labor Force Participation: An International Perspective". *The World Bank Research Observer*. Vol. 4, No. 2 (1989). pp. 187-202.

-----. "Female Labor Force Participation and Education" in G. Psacharopoulos (ed.) *Essays on Poverty, Equity and Growth*, Pergamon Press for the World Bank, (1991).

Reskin, B. F. (ed.). *Sex Segregation in the Workplace: Trends, Explanations, Remedies*. Washington D.C.: National Academy Press, 1984.

Ribich, T. *Education and Poverty*. Washington D.C.: Brookings Institute, 1968.

Roberts, H.V. "Statistical Biases in the Measurement of Employment Discrimination" in E. R. Livernash (ed.). *Comparable Worth: Issues and Alternatives*. Washington DC.: Equal Employment Advisory Service, 1980. pp. 173-196.

Rosen, H.S. "On Interindustry Wage and Hours Structure." *Journal of Political Economy,* Vol. 77, No. 2 (1969). pp. 249-73.

----. "Taxes in a Labor Supply Model with Joint Wage-Hours Determination." *Econometrica,* Vol. 44, No. 3 (1976). pp. 485-507.

Rosenhouse, S. "Identifying the Poor: Is Headship a Useful Concept?" New York: Population Council, 1988.

Rosenzweig, M.R. and K.I. Wolpin. "Government Interventions and Household Behaviour in a Developing Country." *Journal of Development Economics,* Vol. 10, No. 2 (1982). pp. 209-225.

Rubery, J. (ed.). *Women and the Recession.* London: Routledge, 1988.

Safilios-Rothschild, C. "Female Power, Autonomy and Demographic Change in the Third World" in R. Anker, M. Buvinic and N. Youssef (eds.). *Women's Roles and Population Trends in the Third World.* London: Croom Helm, 1982. pp. 239-267.

Sahn, D. and H. Alderman. "The Effects of Human Capital on Wages and the Determinants of Labor Supply in a Developing Country." *Journal of Development Economics,* Vol. 28, No. 2 (1988). pp. 157-173.

Sapsford, D. and Z. Tzannatos (eds.). *Current Issues in Labour Economics.* Houndmills: Macmillan, 1990.

Schultz, T.P. "An Economic Model of Family Planning and Fertility." *Journal of Political Economy,* Vol. 77, No. 2 (1969a). pp. 153-180.

-----. "Returns to Women's Education." Washington DC: The World Bank (PHRWD/89/001), 1989b.

-----. "School Expenditures and Enrollments, 1960-1980" in D.G. Johnson and R. Lee (eds.). *Population Growth and Economic Development.* Madison, WI.: University of Wisconsin Press, 1987.

-----. "Secular Trends and Cyclical Behaviour of Income Distribution in the U.S." in L. Soltow (ed.). *Six Papers on the Size Distribution of Wealth and Income.* New York: Columbia University Press, 1969b.

-----. "Women's Changing Participation in the Labor Force: A World Perspective". *Economic Development and Cultural Change,* Vol. 38, No. 3 (1990). pp. 457-488.

-----. "Women and Development: Objectives, Frameworks, and Policy Interventions." Washington D.C.: The World Bank, 1989a.

-----. "Women's Work and Their Status: Rural Indian Evidence of the Labor Market and Environment Effects on Sex Differences in Childhood Mortality" in R. Anker, M. Buvinic and N. Youssef (eds.). *Women's Roles and Population Trends in the Third World.* London: Croom Helm, 1982. pp. 202-238.

Selowsky, M. *Who Benefits From Government Expenditure: A Case Study of Colombia.* Oxford: Oxford University Press, 1979.

Shapiro, D.M. and M. Stelcner. "Public-Private Sector Earnings Differentials in Canada, 1970-1980". Concordia University. Department of Economics: Working Paper No 1986-3. 1986, Montreal.

Siebert, W.S. "Comparable Worth: An Evaluation." University of Birmingham: Institute of Economic and Business Studies. Mimeograph, 1989.

-----. "Developments in the Economics of Human Capital" in D. Carline, C. A. Pissarides, W. S. Siebert and P.J. Sloane (eds.). *Labour Economics.* London: Longman, 1985. pp. 5-77.

Sivard, R.L. *Women: A World Survey.* Washington DC.: World Priorities, 1985.

Sloane, P.J. "Discrimination in the Labour Market" in D. Carline, C. A. Pissarides, W. S. Siebert and P.J. Sloane *Labour Economics.* London: Longman, 1985. pp. 78-157.

Smith, S.P. *Equal Pay in the Public Sector: Fact or Fantasy?* Princeton NJ: Princeton University Press, 1977.

Standing, G. *Labor Force Participation and Development.* Geneva: International Labour Organization, 1981 (2nd edition).

Stelcner, M., and J. Breslaw. "Income Taxes and Labor Supply of Married Women in Quebec." *Southern Economic Journal,* Vol. 51, No. 4 (1985). pp. 1053-1072.

Stromquist, N.P. "Empowering Women Through Knowledge: Policies and Practices in International Cooperation in Basic Education." Stanford University: SIDEC School of Education, 1986.

Thomas, D. "Intra Household Resource Allocation: An Informational Approach." University of Yale Economic Growth Centre, 1989.

Thurow, L.C. *Generating Inequality.* 1975. New York: Basic Books.

Thurow, L. *Poverty and Discrimination.* Washington DC: Brookings Institution, 1969.

Tilak, J.B.G. *The Economics of Inequality in Education.* New Delhi: Sage, 1987.

Tokman, V. "Policies for the Heterogenous Informal Sector in Latin America:. *World Development.* Vol. 17, No. 7 (1989). pp. 1067-1076.

Treiman, D.J. and Hartmann, H. I. (eds.). *Women, Work and Wages: Equal Pay for Jobs of Equal Value.* Washington DC.: National Academy Press, 1981.

Tzannatos, Z. "The Economics of Discrimination: "Theory and British Evidence" in D. Sapsford and Z. Tzannatos (ed.). *Current Issues in Labour Economics.* Houndmills: Macmillan, 1990a. pp. 177-207.

-----. "Employment Segregation: Can We Measure It and What Does the Measure Mean?" *British Journal of Industrial Relations,* Vol. 28, No. 1 (1990b). pp. 105-111.

-----. "Equal Pay in Greece and Britain". *Industrial Relations Journal,* Vol. 18, No. 4 (1984). pp. 275-283.

-----. "A General Equilibrium Model of Discrimination and Its Effects on Incomes." *Scottish Journal of Political Economy,* Vol. 34, No. 1 (1987a). pp. 19-36.

-----. "The Greek Labour Market: Current Perspectives and Future Prospects." *Greek Economic Review,* Vol. 9, No. 2 (1987b). pp. 224-238.

-----. "The Long Run Effects of the Sex Integration of the British Labour Market." *Journal of Economic Studies,* Vol. 15, No. 1 (1988). pp. 5-18.

-----. "Reverse Discrimination in Higher Education: Does It Reduce Inequality and at What Cost to the Poor?" *International Journal of Educational Development*, Vol. 11, No. 3 (1991). pp. 177-192.

Tzannatos, Z. and J. Symons. "An Economic Approach to Fertility in Britain Since 1860." *Journal of Population Economics*, Vol. 2, No. 2 (1989). pp. 121-138.

Tzannatos, Z. and A. Zabalza. "The Anatomy of the Rise of the British Female Relative Wages in the 1970s: Evidence from the New Earnings Survey." *British Journal of Industrial Relations*, Vol. 22, No. 2 (1984). pp. 177-194.

UNESCO (United Nations Educational, Scientific and Cultural Organization). *Compedio de estadisticas relativas al analfabetismo*, 1990 Edition No. 31. Prepared for the International Education Conference. Geneva. September 3-8, 1990.

UNICEF (United Nations Children's Fund). *The Invisible Adjustment: Poor Women and the Economic Crisis*. Bogota: The Americas and the Caribbean Office. April 1987.

Visaria, P.M. *The Sex Ratio of the Population of India, 1961*. Census of India Vol. 1, Monograph No. 10. New Delhi: Office of the Registrar General of India, 1971.

Wales, T. and A.D. Woodland. "Sample Selectivity and the Estimation of Labor Supply Functions." *International Economic Review*, Vol. 21, No. 2 (1980). pp. 437-468.

Weinger, O. *Sex and Character*. (1906) London: Heinemann.

Weiss, Y. and R. Gronau. "Expected Interruptions in Labor Force Participation and Sex-related Differences in Earnings Growth." *Review of Economic Studies*, Vol. 58 (1981). pp. 607-619.

Welch, F. "Measurement of the Quality of Schooling". *American Economic Review*, Vol. 56, No. 2 (1966). pp. 311-327.

Westoff, C.F. "Fertility Control in the U.S.A." in Proceedings of the World Population Conference, Vol. II, pp. 245-247. New York: United Nations, 1967.

Williams, J.E. and D.L. Best. *Measuring Sex Stereotypes: A Thirty-Nation Study.* Beverly Hills, Calif.: Sage Publications, 1982.

Willis, R.J. "Wage Determinants: A Survey and Reinterpretation of Human Capital Earnings" in O. Ashenfelter and R. Layard (eds.). *Handbook of Labor Economics.* Amsterdam: North Holland, 1986. pp. 525-601.

Willis, R.J. and S. Rosen. "Education and Self-Selection." *Journal of Political Economy*, Vol. 87, No. 5 (Part 2) (1979). pp. S7-S36.

World Bank. *World Development Report,* 1990. Washington D.C.: The World Bank, 1990.

----. *World Development Report 1991,* Washington DC: The World Bank. 1991

----. *World Tables.* Johns Hopkins, Baltimore: University Press, 1983 (3rd edition).

Wright, R.E. and J.F. Ermisch. "Gender Discrimination in the British Labour Market: A Reassessment". *Economic Journal.* Vol. 101, No. 406 (1991). pp. 508-522.

Zabalza, A. and J.L. Arrufat. "The Extent of Sex Discrimination in Britain" in A. Zabalza and Z. Tzannatos. *Women and Equal Pay: The Effects of Legislation on Female Employment and Wages in Britain.* Cambridge: Cambridge University Press, 1985. pp. 70-96.

Zabalza, A. and Z. Tzannatos. *Women and Equal Pay: The Effects of Legislation on Female Employment and Wages in Britain.* Cambridge: Cambridge University Press, 1985.

INDEX

abscissa 170
added worker effect 18-19
Africa 6, 20, 49, 56
age
  and earnings 160, 162
  and participation *see* participation
agriculture 19, 20, 53, 74-75, 79, 83, 84
Argentina 6, 22*fn*, 26, 29, 81, 99, 106, 164, 188
Asia 6, 7, 20, 53, 56, 57
Atkin Report 146
Australia 31, 145
Austria 103

Bangladesh 163
Belgium 105
Bolivia 6, 11, 13, 19, 31, 44, 60, 81, 88, 102, 104
Brazil 13, 17, 19, 20, 48, 81, 106, 177, 183
Britain 11, 18, 31, 105, 102*fn*, 145, 146, 166, 198
Buenos Aires 22*fn*

Canada 18, 103, 174
capital markets 196, 197
censorship, in data 174*fn*
characteristics, comparable (in wage decomposition analysis) 180
childbearing (*see* also fertility) 6, 16, 22, 25-27, 49, 61
child care 25, 26
child mortality 32
children, and economic adjustment 2*fn*
Chile 6, 13, 43, 93, 177, 183
China 163

Colombia 13, 17, 43, 48, 81, 88, 93, 99, 104, 164, 184
comparable characteristics (in wage decomposition analysis) 180
comparative findings
    decomposition of the wage differential by country 203
    efficiency gains and employment differentials 142, 148, 149
    employment dissimilarity by occupation 90-91
    employment dissimilarity in EEC and Latin America 105
    hours of work by country 204
    lambda, sign, value and significance 211
    potential experience by country 208
    of earnings functions 204-210
    of participation functions 185
    of the constant term (and the male pay advantage) 210
    simulated female wages 144
    years of schooling by country 206
comparative statistics
    annual rates of output growth 8
    employees in the labor force 58-59
    employment in agriculture 75
    employment in industry 77
    employment in services 78
    female overrepresentation by employment status 82, 84
    female overrepresentation by industry 83, 84
    female participation 5, 45, 54
    female participation by income 54
    female participation by religion 54
    fertility 8
    illiteracy 8
    industrial classification 107-111
    labor force 39
    life expectancy 6, 8
    male participation 45
    minimum age and the labor force 107-111
    occupational classification 107-111
    participation and teenage fertility 28
    participation by age by world region 62-71
    per capita income 8
    regional per capita incomes 6fn
    relative (female to male) labor force 42
    relative (female to male) participation rates 45
    relative (female to male) wages 5
    sectoral distribution of the labor force 79

comparative statistics (continued)
  wages in the public and private sectors 201
compensating differentials 159
constant term
  and decomposition of wage differentials 191, 192*fn*, 193
  in earnings functions 153, 154, 156-158, 161
  and male pay advantage 210
consumer preferences, and discrimination 146, 152
contraception 25, 27
Costa Rica 22, 23, 29, 43, 89
Cyprus 56
decomposition, of employment changes 19, 92-96
decomposition, of wage differentials
  and discrimination against men 191
  and education 191, 206-207
  and experience 191, 208-209
  and hours of work 191, 204-205
  and the constant term 191, 210
  aggregate findings 30-32, 187, 188, 189
  effect of specific variables 153, 184, 190-191
  as an index problem 156
  shift and slope effects 153-157
Denmark 105
discouraged worker effect 18
discrimination
  and customer preferences 152
  and efficiency gains 4*fn*, 21, 135-149
  and employers 152
  and fixed costs 152
  and legislation 20, 26, 31, 32-33, 104, 152
  and training 152
  as a slope effect in the earnings functions 153, 156
  as a shift effect in the earnings functions 153, 156-157
  demand factors 151, 152, 177, 178, 179
  distributional effects 138
  indirect 178
  "justified" 155, 184
  positive *see* quotas
  statistical 152
  supply factors 151-152, 178
  upper bound of 22-24, 187, 194, 198

dissimilarity,
   by employment status 82, 84, 89, 90-91, 93-95, 99-102
   by occupation 88-97, 102-104
   decomposition of changes in 92-96
   horizontal 96
   in employment distributions 72-107
   index *see* Duncan index
   industrial 83, 84, 103, 104
   relation to misallocation 98
   sex ratio and structure effects 92-93, 94-95, 103, 104, 105
   vertical 96
distribution, assumption about (*see* also truncation) 171-172
domestic servants 26, 184, 187
Dominica 41
Duncan index 86-88, 144
Dutch Equal Pay Act, 1975 180

earnings functions
   and compensating differentials 159
   and employment status 181
   and hours of work 179, 183, 204
   and on the job training 161
   and potential experience 10-11, 162, 208
   and selectivity 12-13, 167, 172, 211
   evaluation of 10, 163-168
   returns to education 29, 30, 161, 206
   standardization before decomposition 180
   theoretical basis 158-163
earnings
   permanent 179
   see also wages
Eastern Europe 56
Ecuador 81, 99, 106, 141, 192
education
   and decomposition of wage differentials 191, 206-207
   and employment in the public sector 192
   and fertility 27
   and participation 23, 25-27, 184-187
   and wages (*see* also earnings functions) 26, 28
   distributional effects 29, 30
   enrollment in 40
   formal 163

education (continued)
  nonformal 164
  policy for women 29, 30
  type of 10, 163-164
  vocational 164
EEC *see* European Economic Communities
efficiency gains 21, 61, 135-149
elasticity
  of female labor supply 145, 167
  of male labor supply 166
  of substitution 141*fn*, 148-149
El Salvador 56
employment dissimilarity *see* dissimilarity
endogeneity 163, 166, 167, 178*fn*
England *see* Britain
error term
  in earnings functions 154, 155, 172
  in structural models 176
errors
  and optimization 178
  and preferences 178
  from omitted variables 163, 173
  in budget constraints 178
  of measurement 163, 165
  of specification 163
European Economic Communities 31, 102, 104
experience in earnings functions
  actual 165, 167
  and decomposition of wage differentials 10-11, 164-165, 191
  and industrialized countries 11
  imputed 11
  in earnings functions for men 164
  in earnings functions for women 165
  potential 10, 11, 165, 190
  potential, definition of 162

family
  effects on participation 48, 175, 176
  income/production 27
  work 12, 19, 38, 55, 73, 92, 93*fn*, 103, 106, 184, 199
female overrepresentation in economic sectors) 81*fn*
fertility 6*fn*, 25, 32

fertility rate, total 6, 8
female headed households 26, 27, 61, 186
formal sector 60, 86, 96, 192, 199
France 105, 145
fridge benefits, of employment 33, 179

general equilibrium, and discrimination 137
Germany 105, 145
Greece 56, 105
Grenada 41
Guatemala 6, 41, 43, 99, 141, 164, 177, 192, 200
Guyana 56

habit formation, and participation 176
Haiti 41
health, and labor force participation 186, 187
heteroscedasticity 175*fn*
home production 27, 74, 194
Honduras 6, 13, 41, 43, 44, 93, 99, 164, 177
horizontal dissimilarity *see* dissimilarity
hours of work 57, 183, 204, 179, 191
human capital
    informal 164
    unobserved characteristics 166
    see also education

illiteracy 164
immunization 25
index of dissimilarity
    and misallocation 97
    definition 86
    estimates of 90-91, 94-95, 103, 105
    interpretation 87
    relation to employment reallocations 97-99
    see also Duncan index
India 163
industrialized countries 10, 20, 26, 31, 48, 49, 53, 102, 145, 165, 196, 199
intertemporal substitution (labor supply) 176
Ireland 105
Israel 56
Italy 105, 145

Jamaica 6, 14, 17, 43, 44, 60, 10
Japan 102, 103, 145

Kingston, Jamaica 22*fn*, 26

labor force 38-55
  by industrial sector 80
  growth of 40
  relative (female to male) 40-41, 42
  size 37-38, 39
lambda
  definition of 170
  empirical estimates 189*fn*, 190, 211
  sign of 174, 175, 211
  significance of 175, 211
  see also selectivity
legislation 33, 56, 57, 60, 61, 92, 104, 198
life expectancy 40
Luxembourg 104, 105

marital stability 26
measurement errors *see* errors of measurement
Mexico 11, 13, 18, 48, 81, 89, 99, 102, 106, 183
Middle East 7, 16, 38, 49, 53, 55
migration 104
Mill's ratio *see* lambda
minimum wage 56
misallocation 97-102
  and relation to dissimilarity 98

Nepal 56, 163
Netherlands 105, 145
Netherlands Antilles 9
New Zealand 31
Nicaragua 163, 175
nonworkers, effects on earnings functions *see* selectivity
Norway 103
nutrition 6, 25, 32

occupational
  choice 27, 180
  mobility 49
older workers 40, 48, 53
  see also labor force, and participation
omitted variables *see* errors from omitted variables

Panama 13, 93, 164, 177, 200
Paraguay 41
participation
  and age 15, 16, 22, 25, 44, 53, 62, 175, 177
  and childbearing 6, 16, 22, 25-27
  and education 22-23, 26, 44, 184-187
  and effects of children 186
  and family characteristics/formation 175, 176, 186
  and female headed households 186
  and habit formation 176
  and ill health 186, 187
  and income 22
  and racial groups 186
  and residence 187
  cyclical effects 8, 18
  differences between married and single women 186
  effect of older children 186
  effect of young children 186
  female by age 46-48
  female by world region 52
  findings of participation functions 184
  functions 22, 174
  male 44, 53, 55
  rate, definition 37
  relative (female to male) 17, 44, 49, 50-51, 60
  trends in 13, 37, 60
  urban/rural 7, 22, 187
pay *see* wages
pensioners 18*fn*
pensions 16, 40, 44, 48
Peru 6, 11, 43, 56, 81, 88, 93, 99, 102, 106, 177
Portugal 105
positive discrimination *see* quotas
public sector 7, 12, 15, 16, 20, 30, 60, 61, 192
  and wage premium 193, 200, 201

quotas, in employment 144

rate of interest (and human capital formation) 159, 161
reallocations, in employment 93-102, 104-106
religion 54, 55

sample selection rule 173
second generation models of labor supply 168
segregation (*see* also dissimilarity) 49, 137
selectivity 10, 12, 23, 163, 167
   and estimates of discrimination 177, 188, 203
   and male participation 177
socialist countries 55
South Africa 138
South Europe 53
South Korea 57
Spain 105, 145
Sri Lanka 56
statistical discrimination *see* discrimination
substitution, elasticity of 141*fn*, 143, 147*fn*, 148-149
Sweden 103, 145

Tanzania 192*fn*
taxation 26, 61
Thailand 57
trade unions 92, 146, 152
training 152, 161, 162, 166
truncated, distribution (*see* also selectivity; lambda) 169, 170-171, 174

U-hypothesis of participation and economic development 53
unemployment 86, 165
   benefits 33
United Kingdom *see* Britain
United States 6, 17, 18, 102, 103, 145, 175, 198
unobserved variables 175
Uruguay 6, 43, 48, 141, 164

Venezuela 6, 13, 26, 29, 31, 81, 106, 164, 184
vertical dissimilarity, *see* dissimilarity

wage offers 12, 23, 168, 176, 177, 189, 190

wages
    choice of, for decomposition analysis 179
    if women had men's employment distribution 144
    if women had men's wage distribution 144
    in the public sector 192
    permanent earnings 179
    relative (female to male) 5
welfare gains *see* efficiency gains
welfare implications of employment interruptions 48

younger workers 18*fn*, 40, 48, 53